THE
WORLD
OF MUSIC
ACCORDING
TO STARKER

THE

WORLD

OF MUSIC

ACCORDING

TO STARKER

Janos Starker

INDIANA UNIVERSITY PRESS

BLOOMINGTON AND INDIANAPOLIS

This book is a publication of

Indiana University Press
601 North Morton Street
Bloomington, Indiana 47404-3797 USA

http://iupress.indiana.edu

Telephone orders	800-842-6796
Fax orders	812-855-7931
Orders by e-mail	iuporder@indiana.edu

The paper used in this publication meets the minimum
requirements of American National Standard for Information
Sciences—Permanence of Paper for Printed Library Materials,
ANSI Z39.48-1984.

Manufactured in the United States of America

Library of Congress Cataloging-in-Publication Data

Starker, Janos.
  The world of music according to Starker / Janos Starker.
     p.   cm.
  "List of recordings, 1947–1999": p.
  "List of music publications": p.
  Includes index.
  ISBN 0-253-34452-2 (cloth : alk. paper)
  1. Starker, Janos.   2. Violoncellists—United States—
Biography.   I. Title.
  ML418.S734A3 2004
  787.4'092—dc22   2004004353
  2 3 4 5 09 08 07 06 05

TO THOSE IN

musical life's trenches, in

orchestras, theater pits, bands,

ensembles, and schools, those

who serve unstintingly the

highest of ideals and guarantee

the future while preserving

the past.

Contents

ACKNOWLEDGMENTS

I would like to acknowledge the invaluable help of Gayle Sherwood of Indiana University Press, and Professor Emilio Colón of the Indiana University School of Music, in the final preparation of this book.

THE
WORLD
OF MUSIC
ACCORDING
TO STARKER

PRELUDE: SCOTCH AND SODA

It requires a strong ego to believe that one's own life, the life of a professional musician, is worthy of the attention of the reader. My belief is, however, based on some facts. In seventy years I have performed in front of some millions. My LPs and CDs—which number a hundred or more—are in homes and libraries on five continents. I have assisted thousands in finding rewarding lives in the world of music. I have also written about music and published music. The life of an internationally famous concert artist involves glamour and limelight. Musicians whose manifold activities put them in the public eye have access to glory and all its trimmings, but we are in the trenches as well: in orchestras, recording studios, and teaching studios. These are where we spend most of our waking hours when not on the road. My story focuses more on the trench life than on the glamour, and is dedicated to those toiling for the cause of music.

The ultimate origin of this book was a dinner conversation I had with Joseph Papp, the famed theatrical director and producer, in New York in the 1970s. We had met years before, at the start of our careers, when our incomes were modest though our dreams for the future were big. But by then he had power and fame, and controlled four theaters in downtown New York. Out of the blue he turned to me and said, "Janos, why don't you do something in one of the theaters. From time to time they are idle between productions." I stared at him. "Joe, remember I am a cellist, not an actor." "Sure," he said, "but you could play, teach, or whatever." I told him I would think about it, but I had things on my mind other than the theater. A few weeks later I received a letter from an experimental theater in Chicago. They wanted to know if I would like to try out some new material that summer, when no regular productions would be under way, as the great comedienne Lily Tomlin had recently done. I burst out laughing and wrote back the same answer I had given Papp. A while later an apologetic note came back, saying that they were thinking of a cello master class.

Soon afterward I was on my way to Europe. As usual on an airplane, I couldn't sleep. A best-selling book came to mind, *Everything You Always Wanted to Know about Sex but Were Afraid to Ask.* I thought, what about concert audiences? What do they want to know? Autograph seekers try to ask some questions in the greenrooms, but there is never time to answer. Only the handful of people who share the after-concert suppers can have a chance to ask the artist about music, family, or whatever. So I wrote up a proposal for what became my *Scotch and Soda Bit,* and Papp and the Chicagoans both bought it. The format was a stage with a table and two chairs: one for me, one for the cello. On the table were a bottle of scotch, a glass with some ice, an ashtray, cigarettes, and a lighter. It is fairly well known that I have never in my life taken a drink before a performance, and the drink on the stage was a prop to make everyone feel comfortable in the presence of an artist they presumably admired. I began by explaining my purpose, which was to answer all the questions audiences would like to ask, but have no opportunity to. I sat down, and to give form to the happenings, I played a Bach prelude. Then I announced that in case I did not cover some area of interest in my talk, the evening would end with an open discussion. Then I had a token sip of scotch and lit a cigarette—those were the days before the Nicotine Gestapo—and began with the first group of frequently asked questions.

1. When and where were you born?
2. When did you start playing the cello, and why?

3. Who were your teachers?
4. Were your family musicians?
5. When did you first play in public?
6. Who is your favorite composer?
7. Why do you teach?
8. Who picks the programs?
9. How much do you practice?

When I grew tired of my own voice I reenacted my first public appearance at age six, then played an etude as if practicing, then again as an encore. Then came the family questions.

10. Are you married? Do you have children?
11. Where did you play last, and where will you next?
12. Who were the influences in your life, musical or otherwise?
13. What are your hobbies?
14. Who are your favorite musicians?
15. What is your reaction to reviews and critics?

Then another musical interlude and a short break. Then the professional questions began.

16. What instrument do you play and what strings do you use?
17. How do you practice?
18. How do you rehearse with piano and orchestra?
19. How do you make recordings?
20. How do you select students?
21. What is your teaching philosophy?

Next the open conversation began. By then the atmosphere was relaxed, as though the audience had been invited into my home rather than to a concert. They asked about playing in orchestras and teaching, about different kinds of music, about playing an instrument; parents asked for advice about their musical children. Last was the musical coda.

Over the years I have done this *Scotch and Soda Bit* in Chicago, Canada, and Holland, where English is almost a second language. On occasion a pianist sat by so as to help demonstrate some points. I can't help feeling that this book, this entire attempt at autobiographical remembrances, is an extended version of the *Scotch and Soda Bit*, without music. In writing it, I suffer from a single great frustration: not having kept a diary. I did so only once, when I was touring Portuguese Africa, and was able to write two articles that were published in a music magazine to much acclaim. (The story of that tour appears here as chapter 9.) Now, however, I must try to gather stray threads of memory. This effort was recently helped when an Ecuadorian journalist sent me forty-five questions for an Internet interview. It felt as if the scotch and soda sessions still continued.

In a lifetime of face-to-face, radio, telephone, and TV interviews, I must have covered all the topics that a musician's life involves. The dozens of stories I have penned, both nonfiction and fiction, express my views and philosophies. My task here is to select what is of interest in an autobiography. I have always been rather allergic to autobiography as a genre, so it is no wonder that at one point I indulged in writing the *Autobiography of a Stomach*, which dealt with data pertinent to the first group of questions above, though it is certainly not complete.

ANACRUSIS: THE AUTOBIOGRAPHY OF A STOMACH

I was born on a hot July night in a hospital named Saint Janos. When the young lady whom I would later address as Mother saw that the body of a boy encapsulated me, she grew furious. Two boys had already graced her labors and she wanted a girl.

"What shall we call him?" the doctor asked.

She sulked. "I don't care."

The doctor, whose name was the same as the hospital's, suggested, "Janos."

"O.K."

I was disappointed. Why should I be trapped in a Janos? A stomach such as I ought to be in a . . . what? To hell with it! However, to make certain that I wasn't taken for granted, I made both my presence and my displeasure known. Nurses had to work overtime cleaning that little fellow. You may, of course, call my reaction nasty. Intellectually I might even agree. But I considered myself an exceptional stomach from the very beginning. I knew that whoever had me as an integral part of his body was a lucky person, one fated for success in the family of humans.

Remember, I could have chosen to be the stomach of a four-legged creature, a race horse, show dog, or prize tiger. But I felt my creative potential could best express itself in a two-legged creature, and so I allowed myself to be the component of a boy. Now if, from the very beginning, I had not asserted myself, assuredly I would have been taken for granted. A stomach *is* a stomach, you know, even though all those dumb, damned medical men, who think they know everything, suppose that once they've seen any stomach they know all stomachs.

I was determined to show them how wrong they were and decided right away to mold a unique creature; and, further, to make sure he knew who I was and never took me for granted. You may think it tedious that I keep saying "taken for granted," but it is a disgusting fact that stomachs are taken for granted. Think! For years nothing but milk, baby food, applesauce and the like are dumped into us; then soup, vegetables, a little meat or fish. No one ever asks what we would like to have. True, I eventually got my caviar and scotch, but that took so many years. For decades I suffered onions, brandy, cheap wine, schnapps, and, by God, all those fatty Hungarian dishes—though some of it wasn't bad, like an occasional Wiener schnitzel.

Now my fellow knows better. Still, whenever he forgets I have to remind him right away. Except then the silly fool pops some guck into me. I think he calls it Di-Gel. Stupid! As long as he behaves, I let him get away with just about everything. It's only when he becomes neglectful that no pill can pacify my fury. With age, I must say, he has become increasingly respectful, but I am way ahead of my story. I must try to be faithful to chronology.

It was 1928 when I first started hearing funny noises, and none too happily, you may be sure! They came from a four-stringed instrument called a fiddle. The little fellow sat on the floor and held the thing against me. He kept plucking the strings until his mother came in. She laughed, but just the same took it away from him. It belonged to his older brother. I hated those noises so much that I gave him a pain to remember. He couldn't eat for two days. How was I to suspect then that he'd make me endure such noises for the rest of my life?

For the next two years I tried to forget the incident of the fiddle. During that time he mumbled, whistled, obsessively organized and hid empty boxes, papers, and toys, and fought for possession of his treasures. He gave me little real trouble, except for spinach. I hate the stuff!

To be fair, I never learned whether he or his mother was responsible for trying to force that loathsome green substance into me. But I protested so much that even the doctor put a stop to its ingestion. He said something about an allergy. If you think, though, that I am going to tell the life story of the fellow I live within, think again. If he chooses, he can do that himself. I am only interested in relating my actions and reactions, my likes and dislikes during a long life, and correcting at least some of the misrepresentations about people's achievements. You don't know the role my friends and I play in making our landlords, so to speak, successful and famous. To tell the whole truth, we've also ruined many . . . but I keep digressing.

One day later on, something like a fiddle again was pressed against me, but this time it was much larger, and the little fellow sat on a chair holding it. I had mixed feelings. And on a Sunday soon after, I found myself in a hall with lots of children whose parents sat around. He pressed that thing against me again, but quite a nice tune came out of it. By then I knew it was called a cello. The people applauded and my little fellow was pronounced a child prodigy. Ah, perplexity! I rather liked the tune, but after mulling over the idea of hearing it and other such tunes for the rest of my life, I wasn't sure if I should permit this. A week later the same thing happened; the same tune, and people applauding. This time, though, the music wasn't so nice. I heard scratchy, impure sounds, and even wrong notes, as I later learned to call them. I became furious. If I had to live with that bulk pressed against me, then I had better make certain it was well used. I vowed right then and there that if he ever played less than well, I would stop him.

I gave him fierce pains whenever he wasn't prepared for his lesson, so fierce that his mother had to take him to the doctor. The medicine man looked and looked, but finally shook his head in bafflement. He couldn't find anything wrong. He thought the problem must be a nervous stomach. I laughed to myself. If only he knew! But why should I tell him? He was the doctor.

Years passed and the tunes improved. I was impressed. The little fellow wasn't all that bad! I began to like the whole idea. As he became more and more proficient we were invited to rich homes where I enjoyed some marvelous food. Most of my friends had to subsist on potatoes, soup, and vegetables, while I was served ambrosia cooked by famous chefs. But then I began to worry. What if he doesn't improve? Will my luck hold? What if he stops and gets lazy? After all, the cello does have to be practiced. So I worked out a little deal with myself. When he played well I made him feel good—so good that he forgot all the pain I created when I felt he hadn't practiced enough. When he really didn't play well, I doubled him over in agony. I was a bastard!

The strategy worked. Things went smoothly for quite some time; indeed, until the day when a gun was shoved against me. I hotly resented this and got really upset, but I couldn't do much to improve things. This was war and survival became the only thing that mattered. I couldn't afford to be picky. There were days when nothing got into me. During all that time I behaved like an angel. Then the war, like all wars, ended and our old routine resumed.

Before concerts, after concerts, I pushed my fellow until he learned his business. From time to time, of course, there were inescapable changes, such as a stretch when nothing came my way but French food. It took a while to adjust, and just about the time I had, he started feeding me fried shrimp, steak, and hamburgers! Steadily! That's when I knew we had become Americans.

For a period after, I heard horrendous noises day and night, including singing. That was the time my silly fellow didn't want to play alone except on recordings. So I was made to listen to opera and more opera until I couldn't suffer another cadenza, and I let him know it with a vengeance. Did he resign from opera in a hurry! I thought we would return to old times and routines then, but no, he went to the Chicago Symphony Orchestra. I agree, it was less noisy than the opera, but I had to put up with that Reiner character all the time. I tell you, there were days when I and a hundred of my friends threatened to mess up that clean stage in Orchestra Hall. But I have to confess, during concerts almost all of us purred with pleasure. So much so that I decided my fellow must be a little like that Reiner person; no fooling around, no compromising with music, no chumminess with musicians unless they were really good, and no show biz.

I kept the faith. If he ever got ideas about lowering our standards I kicked him so hard that he stopped in his tracks. Sure, he got all the credit for high principles, taste, style, impeccable intonation, and seamless sound. You've read it all, he hopes. But my presence edited out scratchy sounds, slimy sentimentality, unnecessary and unmusical gestures, and out-of-tune playing. I monitored him constantly and stopped any compromises cold, every time.

There's another confession to make. Way back when he was making his first recordings, I was my usual finicky self. I refused to let him get away with the tiniest lapse. The poor guy couldn't take it, and hurried to a famous doctor. That s.o.b. really did know his business! He almost figured me out. He gave him some pills and told him to take one if his stomach gave him trouble. I didn't like this at first, but nowadays there are times when I don't mind at all. I'm not getting any younger either, and so I decided that if he doesn't know, by now, all I've taught him, the hell with him. Some mornings I just go on sleeping and let him be. But if he tries to pop a second pill into me on the same day, I send it right back up. I'm not that old yet!

So life goes on. He respects me, and I'll admit that I respect him more and more as the years pass. I'm even willing to state, in retrospect, that if one must be the stomach of a cellist, I would rather be Starker's than anyone else's, until the end. Now you know.

BLOOMINGTON, INDIANA, 1977, 2001

ANACRUSIS

1   HUNGARY

I was born on July 5, 1924, in Budapest, but whether that was a good day or a bad one is up for interpretation. As I indicated earlier, I was named after the hospital I was born in and the doctor who delivered me. My father, a hardworking tailor, scraped together the means to support his wife, my brothers (who were eight and four when I was born), and me in a two-room walk-up apartment that shared a communal toilet. He hailed from a part of Poland that had been tossed around between Russia and the Austro-Hungarian monarchy, which explains why he bore a German surname. My mother had come to Hungary from the Ukraine to join her brother, who had fled there to escape conscription in the Russo-Japanese War of 1904–1905. They met in Budapest and were married in 1915. Father never made enough money to buy Hungarian citizenship, and so the whole family remained aliens, having to renew a permit every year in order to stay. I never met any of my grandparents.

Neither of my parents had a musical background, but Mother, coming from poverty and with little education, had dreams of educated, musical children. She saved pennies to afford violin lessons for my brothers. My brothers' fiddles, which I played with while they were in

At age 10

school, were my earliest toys and my first exposure to music, of sorts. My second exposure came at age four in the form of radio. I listened to music through earphones. At age six I was given a cello. By then our living standards had improved; we had moved to a fourth-floor walk-up, with three rooms, a bathroom, and even a peasant girl as a maid.

My cello teacher was Fritz Teller. Six weeks after I began, I was put on stage in a children's theater. Some sang and danced, and I played two little tunes and learned to take a bow. The show went on for six Sundays and got worse and worse. My parents decided to take me to Teller's teacher, Adolf Schiffer, who had been David Popper's student and succeeded him at the Franz Liszt Academy of Music. For a year and a half a graduate student of his worked with me weekly, and Schiffer saw me every other week. In 1931 Mother took me to my first concert. Pablo Casals played. Schiffer introduced me to him, saying something about my being talented. Casals planted a kiss on my cheek, and I'm told I didn't wash my face for a week. My fate was sealed. Two years later, when I was already in the preparatory class of the Academy, I attended a recital in which Béla Bartók played with Emmanuel Feuermann. It was a revelation. I felt sure that was how a cello should sound. (A recently published biography of Feuermann quotes me as saying that if he had lived longer he would have surpassed Casals. I said, or meant, that he would have done so as a cellist, not as a musician. Quotes are dangerous. I was attacked in the '60s when a quote from me appeared in an interview: "Casals does harm to cello playing." What I said was that at his age (he was around ninety), when electronically reproduced through radio, records, and TV, he gave a wrong picture of contemporary cello playing. My remark was edited. When in the '70s I said, "At this moment there are three cellists equally active on all continents: Fournier, Rostropovich, and myself," the headline read "There are but three cellists, says Starker." It was easy to imagine the reaction in the cello community.)

The years went by: elementary school in the morning, and in the afternoon Mother lugging my cello to lessons, and eventually some classes at the Academy. School was easy; with the help of my older brothers I learned to count, read, and write at age five. I could add and multiply three-digit numbers in my head, a feat that earned me acco-

Age 12, with Adolf Schiffer (1936)

lades and chocolates. At age eight my teaching career started. I was told to practice weekly with a six-year-old girl named Eva Czako (who became a renowned cellist and married the violinist Georges Janzer), and I was paid. I became a money-earning professional, practicing two to three hours a day.

In 1933 the Great Depression reached Hungary and Father's business went belly-up. It took him and his partner a year to crawl out of bankruptcy. That year our lives were darker than I had ever known. We lived in two windowless rooms in a slum area. I landed in a hospital with a mouth infection. They kept me there to fatten me a bit. I practiced there and entertained the nurses and doctors. By '34 we again had three rooms and life was rosy. It took us another six years to acquire an old beat-up piano, however, which explains why I never learned to play the piano.

Besides my counting prowess, which has never improved since I was five, I cannot recall any special talent like those that often mark exceptional musicians. I had no absolute pitch, nor a photographic memory. I did have a good ear, which made me twinge at the slightest deviation from centered pitch. After playing a piece three or four times, I knew it; some of them I remember to this day. But since my days at the Metropolitan Opera my memory for music has gradually weakened. I have played Wagner's *Ring* and the rest of the operatic literature innumerable times, and now when I listen to the radio I cannot tell which opera I am hearing, though I can recognize the composer. Of the three aspects of memory—aural, visual, and digital—it is probably the last one that I could call my strength from childhood on. When one speaks of digital talent, one assumes a person has special hands. Not me. I have standard-size hands, not big, not small. I have no real stretch such as a tenth on the piano, and on top of that, around the age of ten I twisted my left little finger, which in turn forced me to develop my thumb. This may be partly responsible for the admiration I received for the deftness of my left hand.

At ten I entered the gymnasium, or secondary school. Eight years there led to the equivalent of a high school degree, which I never earned. When I was fourteen Adolf Schiffer, my cello teacher, suggested that to concentrate on music I should quit school. I did. A year later he had to

THE WORLD OF MUSIC ACCORDING TO STARKER

retire and suggested that I continue studying with him privately. I did, and quit the Academy. After another year I stopped going to him regularly. From age twelve I had been allowed to join the classes of two extraordinary teachers. Imre Waldbauer taught string quartets. The leader of the then most prominent quartet, he was a man of extraordinary knowledge and musicianship. In a two-hour session one could learn more from him than in six months of cello lessons. Leo Weiner, who taught piano chamber music, is a legend about whom volumes have been written. From the 1920s to the '60s all Hungarian musicians of any future consequence attended his classes; conductors, pianists, string players without fail name him as the most important influence in their lives. I am no exception. I was lucky to play for him in quartets, and drink in the principles he preached.

My name became known in musical circles in 1936, when I performed the Locatelli Sonata in an Academy student recital. Then in '38, on six hours' notice, I substituted in a performance of the Dvořák Concerto: my first time playing it with an orchestra. In 1939, the first performance in many years of the Kodály Solo Sonata marked me as an up-and-coming cellist. But there was a hitch, the biggest obstacle of my life until the end of World War II. In spite of their religious Jewish upbringing, my parents led lives minimally influenced by religion; nonetheless my origin stigmatized me. I was not only a Jew, but also an alien in the country of my birth.

In spite of rampant anti-Semitism, Jews were generally tolerated in Hungary until the rise of Hitler. From then on the screws were tightened, step by step. New laws forbade my brothers to enter university. Teachers were fired to satisfy quota restrictions. The budding Nazi Party drafted more and more laws preventing Jews from owning or even leasing property. Incidents of harassment increased. In 1941 the government decided to repatriate resident aliens. The police gathered several thousand Russian and Polish Jews, including my uncle, his entire family, and several more distant relatives, and herded them to the Ukraine, where nearly all were slaughtered. The atrocities stopped after some mild international uproar, and a relative of ours, a woman whose family had been killed and who had herself survived being shot, walked back to Budapest and lived with us until the Final Solution descended.

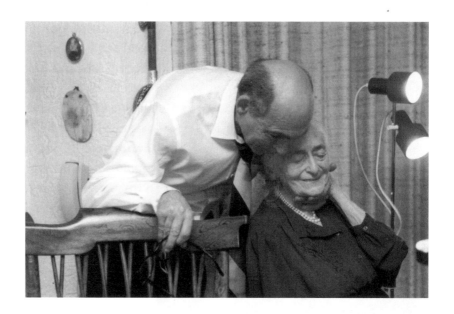

With Amalka Baracs in London

With Edith Lorincz, Elizabeth Horvay, and Francis Akos, Budapest (1942)

group had sessions with Leo Weiner and played in private homes. Once or twice a week I joined some doctors and lawyers for marathon quartet evenings. They weren't very good, but I learned the repertory and the food was better than at home; in addition, they revered me. I played some shared recitals, of the kind that were common in the nineteenth century, with the singer Vera Rozsa. I also shared the stage with her actress sister, Maria, who read poetry interspersed with my cello solos. I fell madly in love with Maria, but unfortunately she was married. My friendship with both of them has lasted until today; Vera is now a famed vocal teacher in England.

The National Hungarian Jewish Cultural Association (Omike) founded a concert series and formed an orchestra and even an opera company, which performed in halls it owned. Outside of these specifically Jewish performances the law allowed only one Jewish performer in four, and then only one in eight, in any public event. That led to one of my great triumphs. In 1942 or thereabouts I hired the most prominent hall in Budapest, the Vigado, and engaged eight Aryan musicians and a pianist. They played the Mendelssohn Octet, and then I proceeded to play my recital. The hall was sold out. The prominent booking agency that had sold the tickets grabbed the idea, and scheduled Schubert's Octet as cover for a recital by a great Hungarian Jewish pianist, Imre Ungar, who had been silenced by then. But the police caught on to the ruse and put an end to the practice.

Around that time came my big break, which determined my life from then on. A colleague of mine, a woman violinist, introduced me to a friend of hers. The friend's nickname was Macko, which means "teddy bear." She was fortyish, a college professor, a friend of the best writers in Hungary, and one of the homeliest ladies I've ever seen. Her husband, employed in a business, was similarly lacking in looks. She had heard me in concerts and become curious as to what kind of mind someone like me would have. She invited me for coffee (over which we both smoked like chimneys) and began to ask me questions: Why had I stopped going to school? Didn't I miss studying? What were my interests outside of music? Eventually she offered me a schnapps and my tongue loosened up and gave vent to my frustration. I had been leading the life of a professional musician, performing and teaching, since I was fifteen, but at what price? My education was full of holes, as was my musical training. My studies of harmony were at best cursory, and not until I was eighteen and nineteen did I take some composition lessons. I had first-class teachers, but I spent far too little time with them to learn what I needed.

By the time our meeting ended, we had agreed to meet once a week for a few hours of talk, and these meetings continued for two years. I worked on expressing myself on whatever topic was at hand: what I had done during the week and what I was reading. She gave me books: history, art, and literature. The only outside help I received was in math, from a cellist friend: not a particularly good cellist, but a very bright young man. In 1943, at Macko's urging, I spent two months studying hard for the school exams and earned a qualification equivalent to the first two years of high school.

Macko gave me the works of Shakespeare and Shaw in English, which I did not speak. My brothers and I had had about ten lessons in English a couple of years before, from a woman tutor who pretended to be English to impress us. I also had a few months of Berlitz French behind me, primarily due to an attractive young girl. The attraction was moribund and so was the learning. But eventually the experience served me well, when I lived for a time in France. In 1936 I had picked up Italian when I spent a summer in Cortina d'Ampezzo with my teacher, Adolf Schiffer, and his wife who vacationed there every year. I had also studied German for four years in the gymnasium. In my haphazard schooling and language learning I was much like my father. His minimal education was conducted in Hebrew and Yiddish, but when he died at eighty-six he spoke Russian, Polish, Hungarian, German, and English, in addition to his childhood tongues: none of them well, but enough to communicate with those who spoke nothing else.

But life was becoming more and more troubled. Racial laws were tightened, so that I was not allowed to take the final high school exams. The concert series my friends established under the aegis of the Jewish community in Szeged, then the second largest city in Hungary, came to a screeching halt. The Budapest concert organization was faced with ever-increasing interference and eventually closed. My brothers were called up for the infamous labor service and marched first to eastern

THE WORLD OF MUSIC ACCORDING TO STARKER

Three brothers: Ede, age 24; Tibor, age 28; Janos, age 20 (1944)

Hungary and later, when the war with the Soviet Union intensified, to Yugoslavia, where they were killed at a place called Bor in the fall of 1944. My age group had not yet been called up. Because I was an alien, unemployed, and not in school, I was at risk of arrest. Through some former schoolmates, with whom I remained in close touch through the years, I learned that it was possible to be hired for menial jobs, such as cleaning up in a sulfur plant, carrying loads, or moving heavy machinery. We lined up in front of the factories at 7 A.M., hoping the foremen would choose us, in which case we would work until 5 or 6 P.M. and receive enough money to buy food. Usually the work lasted only two or three days at a time, and eventually the police stopped the practice, as they had the concerts.

Germany occupied Hungary in March 1944, and in April Jews were required to wear the yellow Star of David. Most of the populace immediately began treating us like lepers—thankfully, there were some exceptions. Shortly after that, the police announced that foreigners had to present themselves at immigration offices. I told my parents that I would go; they should sit tight and wait to see what happened to me. On the streetcar ride I was accompanied by Eva Uranyi, whom I had known for just over a year, and who was to become my wife. She was a piano student at the Academy, very young, brazen and fearless, with flaming red hair. Her father, a businessman, had been a first lieutenant in the army reserve since World War I. He had long ago hidden his Jewish origins by converting to Catholicism, and was married to an Aryan woman. That meant that Eva was safe. She would come to our house almost daily, smoke a pack of cigarettes while listening to me practice, and then leave again.

Eva was a unique woman. She had a keen intellect and a limitless willingness to help not just me but anyone in need, even animals, often at great risk to herself. Musicians and others who had escaped from the labor brigades came to her. She made false documents for them, found places to hide them, and gave them money, clothes, and whatever else they needed. On this day she watched two policemen at the immigration center take me away, and she immediately went to my parents. They left our apartment and disappeared, going into hiding in a rented room on the other side of the city. For the next three months my only communication with them was through Eva.

I was taken to a school which was being used as a holding center for hundreds of men and women of all ages. I had nothing with me but a pack of cigarettes and the clothes I wore. The facilities were minimal; we were given a blanket and a towel, and washrooms were about one to a hundred people. Some little food was distributed daily by the Jewish help organizations, as the inmates were primarily aliens mixed with some Aryans who were accused of helping Jews or of anti-state actions. We were guarded by policemen. There was a daily roll call, when we were lined up in the courtyard and asked to volunteer for work. Being one of the youngest there, and wanting to get out of that filthy place, I volunteered immediately. To my surprise, I was always turned down, while about fifty people were led away to waiting trucks. Where to? No one knew, although there were rumors: some transports were said to leave the country. Day after day, the same thing. I was turned down while others were told to join the group that was taken away.

I spent six days at the school, and during this time I was able to form some friendships and even arrange some clandestine meetings, primarily when the air-raid sirens sounded. The guards would lock the outside gates and run to the basement, and the prisoners were left alone. Since Budapest was not yet actually being bombed, we could enjoy a semblance of freedom for a couple of hours. Occasionally a guard, bribed by Eva, came to me and handed over a pack of cigarettes and even some food. But her efforts began to endanger her life. Officers of the secret police saw her too often around the school and became suspicious. From then on she stopped sleeping at home and moved daily from place to place.

After six days I asked the policeman who did the selecting to please let me go. "You are sure?" he said. I answered yes. So I was put on a truck with others and, to our surprise, we were unloaded on Csepel-sziget, an island in the Danube. Life here was very different than in the school. The guards were soldiers, not police, and women and men were separated. Men were taken to a row of huts that had been partly destroyed by U.S. carpet-bombing. The only furnishings were some straw sacks to sleep on. We dug open-air latrines, and after passing the soldier guards, we could attend to our needs by daylight or moonlight. We did not know, in Budapest, that this island was the home of one of the largest industrial complexes in Hungary, owned by the Weiss family. They were Jews, but had been given the rank of baron by Emperor Franz Josef. Goering had made a deal with the family at the beginning of the war. He flew them to Switzerland, paid an unfair but still hefty sum into a Swiss bank, then took personal possession of the plant and converted it to build Messerschmitt fighter planes. Eighteen thousand workers labored there. Shortly before we arrived, the factories were carpet-bombed. There were shelters for only six thousand people, and many were killed or injured. Much of the plant was also damaged, and output reportedly dwindled to one plane a day.

The other men and I were assigned first to repair the damaged roofs of our huts, then to form squads to find and neutralize unexploded bombs. The mess hall had been destroyed in the raids, and though its structure had been rebuilt, work was still in progress to restore the interior and provide electricity. For the first week we were given one thin slice of bread with a slice of goat cheese in the morning, a slice of bread with a fruit jelly at noon, and in the evening a third slice of bread with goat cheese. The next day the routine would be repeated, with the places of the jelly and cheese reversed. On the fifth day they gave us some watery soup with a few spinach leaves floating around in it. Groans of hunger were audible everywhere, especially at night when the fleas in the straw sacks were swarming over our bodies.

The morning roll call was followed by the formation of work brigades. No matter what trade they asked for, I put my hand up. So for the first week I worked with the roof repair gang, then on the bomb squad, then digging air-raid trenches, hauling bricks, or whatever was needed to clean up the aftermath of the raid. By the second week our conditions had improved. Field kitchens were set up and a semblance of a meal was served at least once a day, and we settled into a routine. I even received some short notes assuring me that my parents were all right. The notes were in cigarette packages and occasionally came with a can of food.

Most of my fellow inmates were middle-aged lawyers and businessmen. As they were collected from their homes, they had had time to snatch some clothes and food, and put gold coins in their money belts. All I had was two packs of cigarettes and some matches I had collected in the school. The wealthier ones bribed soldiers to smuggle messages out and food in. News of the war filtered in now and again, but we had no access to newspapers. In any case, the government-controlled press had only praise for Axis victories. D-Day was a faint, distant event of scant significance.

I had little contact with my fellow prisoners. I was still a foreigner, and the Jews were blaming people like me for their misfortunes. If not for us, they claimed, they would still be living comfortably in their posh homes. Some of the soldiers displayed more sympathy for me than my fellow prisoners did. This was not a concentration camp, but an internment camp meant to protect the populace from unsavory characters. That I was a musician, born in Hungary, made no difference. My resentment of the misuse of power, influence peddling, and discrimination among people in the same boat got a lifelong boost from my experiences on Csepel Island.

Most of the soldiers were decent peasant boys and did not bother us. The lieutenant in charge of them, however, was a sadist. When he learned of the smuggling he ordered some men into his barrack and used them as punching bags. One day, when I was luckily working in the plant, he ordered all those who were in the camp to run. When I got back I was told that two people had died of heart attacks. His atrocities were stopped by the military commander of the island and the plant, a reserve colonel who, as I later learned, was responsible for the fact that I did not land in Mauthausen, the infamous concentration camp in Germany. When Eva found out that I was on Csepel Island, she used her contacts to have two policemen sent to the commander asking him to transfer me to the labor service, which she thought would be safer. Supposedly he said that I was already working on Csepel and refused to let me go. The labor brigade included several of my early schoolmates. They all ended up in Mauthausen, and only two survived.

My luck held, though. One morning I was put to work in the kitchen, which had not been destroyed. It cooked for six thousand people. We had to haul boxes, pots, sacks of flour, garbage, whatever, all day. From time to time cooks and aides would toss us bread, rolls, and other food, and so I gradually regained the weight I had lost.

One morning the call went out for an electrician. As always, I put up my hand, although I knew no more than how to plug in a radio and change a light bulb, and I was chosen. I was sent to the mess hall, where two electricians were working on the newly installed wall fans. There were a few others whose job was to troubleshoot all over the plant. They all stayed in a cubicle marked *High Voltage, Dangerous, Do Not Enter.* Inside they played cards, ate, and drank. My guess is that in their eight-hour work day they may have worked one hour. (In later years I was often reminded of them when driving past road construction crews.) One of the capers they pulled a few times was to throw the master switch for the kitchen and the meat freezer. Darkness fell, and soon someone came banging on the cubicle door. Two guys went looking for the trouble—in the freezer. One took a big chunk of meat and hid it under his jacket, then they both returned, turned the switch back on, and received accolades for their prowess. Then on their hot plates they roasted the meat and shared it with me. That group of electricians, to this day, represent the best of mankind I ever encountered. Not one ever made a disparaging remark, though they all knew that I was a prisoner and they found out quickly that I was no electrician. But I did manage a small triumph one day. For the most part I carried things, as an assistant, but when the time came to install the switches for the two wall fans I was told to do one of them. I managed some screws, but then the wires had to be connected. I tried to be a little slower than my partner, my chief, and kept lighting cigarettes and wandering over to see what he was doing. The job could have been done in a couple of hours. It took two days, during which I imitated what he did as best I could. The dreaded moment arrived. He flipped his switch on—nothing happened. He tried again; again nothing. I was shaking, as if coming on stage for a performance. Then he flipped mine. The fan started. My chief shook his head, then my hand. In fifteen minutes he fixed his and the day's work was finished.

Some days later three hundred American planes carpet-bombed the plant again, and again hit the mess hall. Unfortunately they started to drop the bombs a bit early; many struck the huts a few hundred meters

THE WORLD OF MUSIC ACCORDING TO STARKER

before the mess hall where I and my fellow inmates lived. The V-shaped trenches we had dug saved my life, but did not save twenty-two people next to me. The huts were reduced to rubble. We dug out the victims with shovels and bare hands and gave them what help we could. Eventually some rescue squads showed up, not particularly concerned about the dead. A few of the injured men were taken away. Frantic women prisoners defied the guards and ran to our camp looking for husbands; some found their bodies.

In the middle of the commotion policemen arrived and called for me by name. They took me back to the city, to the school that was still the clearing-house for transports. I was rather afraid of what might happen next, but after a day I was simply told to leave; I was freed. I went to Eva's parents' home and had my first bath in three months, putting on clean underwear and removing the Star of David. Two days later the fog of mystery that had shrouded the past three months was finally lifted. A Swedish couple was living in Budapest: Waldemar Langlet was a professor at the university, and his wife was an amateur pianist and a friend of my teacher Adolf Schiffer. He and I sometimes played music together. About a year before, the Swedish government had asked Langlet to head the Swedish Red Cross in Hungary. When I was arrested he procured for me an invitation to become the principal cellist in the Goteborg Symphony, and in order to get me out of Hungary he arranged a Swedish passport for me. That was why I had never been selected for the transports out of Budapest and Hungary. The Hungarian officials were unsure what status I had. When the raid was over they did not want to antagonize the Swedish representatives, so they let me go.

Raoul Wallenberg had arrived in Hungary in July 1944, and his heroism in distributing Swedish protective passes and setting up safe houses flying the Swedish flag is well known. The Langlets also saved many people by such tactics. What they did for me, however, was independent of these larger efforts. The risk, of course, was that someone might recognize me and question the validity of my Swedish passport, knowing I was not a Swedish citizen. Fortunately, Eva's father, a reserve officer, was named commander of a civil defense battalion and put in charge of a district of Budapest. He took me into the battalion and issued me papers, and I served in civilian clothes until the end of the siege of Budapest. My primary responsibility was to shepherd people down to the public shelters during air raids. I moved around quite freely. Battalion members were quartered in a public school but, for a change, I was in charge. We were fed, and we led an almost human existence. I had a few scares in restaurants and on the streets, when policemen recognized me. But they were either bored or unsure, and my papers were not challenged.

One morning in November, my parents asked me for advice. A Lutheran priest, one of my father's customers, had asked them whether they were willing to be baptized, since having written proof that they were not Jews might help them to survive. I told them, for God's sake why not, if it could help? That same evening Eva's parents, understandably worried about their daughter, asked me what my plans were. Plans? I was just scrambling to stay alive. I told them that if I survived the war, I would marry Eva when I had established my career and could support her. They were silent for a moment, and then asked why they should believe me. "What do you expect me to do?" I asked, and they answered, "Change your religion." I told them sure, if that was what they wanted. Two days later my parents and I went to a church, where we were sprinkled with holy water and received papers certifying that we were Lutherans. My father's conversion haunted him until he died, although he knew of Maimonides' admonition to do anything necessary to survive.

A few days later Laszlo Szulner, an acquaintance of mine, sent me a message by Eva. Szulner worked in Wallenberg's office, as did Eva occasionally, and Wallenberg had managed to get the authorities to agree to allow a trainload of Jews to go to Sweden. At the top of the list for evacuation were an official of a Swedish company and I, because our papers had been issued in Sweden rather than Hungary. Szulner was worried that Eva's situation was becoming hazardous. He suggested that if I married her, she could flee with me.

Eva and I discussed the situation and agreed that we should get married. But a problem arose: Eva was Catholic and I was now Lutheran. One of Eva's relatives found a Catholic priest in Buda who took it upon himself to secure a papal permit for a Catholic to marry a

Lutheran! The marriage was sanctified in the back of the church, with the cousin as a witness. When the rite was over I returned to my post at the school, and Eva went home.

The air raids intensified, and Budapest was gradually surrounded by Russian troops. The full siege began on Christmas Eve, with constant street fighting and bombardment. Streets going east and west were impassable, as Germans from one side and Russians from the other machine-gunned anything that moved. Luckily the school, being on a corner, had multiple entrances.

The Germans killed horses and used them as barricades, but the Russians quickly overran them, and soon people were swarming over the carcasses, cutting them up for food. One day the fighting neared the school and most of my brigade ran away to their families, leaving sixty or seventy people in the school basement who had no shelters in their homes. Each shelter was supposed to have one person trained in first aid, but our medic was among those who fled. In the midst of this, someone came banging on the door begging for help; across the street a man who had ventured out to try to find some food for his family had been injured by a Russian bomb. No one wanted to leave the shelter. The messenger pleaded, and I saw that the medic had left his kit behind. I picked it up, and he and I counted one, two, three and sprinted. Gunfire rang out, but we made it. We went into the basement, and a crying woman came to me and said, "Please, Doctor, save my husband." He was lying down, bloody from his abdomen to his knees; he had been struck by shrapnel. My medical knowledge was based on films I'd seen and my one stay in a hospital at age nine, but I did the best I could. I asked for warm water, washed my hands, and looked into the kit. I found scissors to cut off his clothes, disinfectants to clean him, and gauze to bandage him, and, to my surprise, the bleeding stopped. By then it was dark, so I was able to get back to the school.

The next day, my friend Harry Breuer came to the shelter. We had met when he showed up one day wearing a Red Cross armband, and it turned out that we had friends in common. He had escaped from Yugoslavia and with false papers got a job in a hospital; his dream was to become a doctor. He was from an area that had been Hungarian territory before the First World War and spoke Hungarian as well as Serbian, Croatian, and German. Now he roamed the city and offered first aid to whoever was in need. I urged him to look at my patient, and we counted one, two, three, and ran for it as I had done before. The man was doing all right, and Harry congratulated me profusely and suggested that we work together. I was bored to tears in the shelter, and joined him.

Three days later the school was overrun by Russian troops. They stole watches and raped some women, but did no other harm. They used the school as a base from time to time, where they could rest up between attacks. Harry's shelter was also occupied as the Russians advanced street by street, and he and I began sleeping in a house we called our "medical center." The two of us, with our Red Cross armbands, continued our work, roaming the safer streets to dispense medicine and first aid to the injured. I had a greyish blue overcoat, which looked to the soldiers like a German outfit, and on occasion Russian guns were pushed against my chest. We would gesture frantically, pointing to our armbands and saying "doctor"; Harry's ability to speak Slavic languages also helped keep us safe. Eventually, since we also helped Russian soldiers, a major who was a district commander gave us some Russian papers and several times invited us to join him for dinner when the fighting slackened in the evening. We had no idea what was going on elsewhere in the city. No telephones were working, no streetcars were running. Still, most people had returned to their homes.

Harry came up with a great idea. Many of the soldiers were infected with some venereal disease. At the time the only cure available was sulfa drugs. With the help of some soldiers we broke into abandoned pharmacies and collected whatever sulfa pills we could find, and started dispensing them among the soldiers. Within a day we became famous and received food, chocolates, cigarettes, and gratitude in return. Unfortunately, our supply was limited; fortunately, we realized that the sulfa pills looked much like antacids. So we started to mix them together. Aside from the thefts from pharmacies, which were not for my direct benefit, I have to confess I did steal once. I found clean shirts in a chest in an abandoned house and I took one, leaving my soiled one in its place.

Harry and I heard that the Russians were near the apartment house

THE WORLD OF MUSIC ACCORDING TO STARKER

where Eva lived, which was about an hour's walk from the school, and we set out to try to reach her. We came to within about three blocks of Eva's house, and encountered a large group of drunken soldiers in a restaurant. They were drinking anything they could find and stuffing everything else into suitcases, and they pressed us to join them. After sharing drinks with them we were reckless enough to try to get the last three blocks, but shots were coming from everywhere and we had to turn back. We spent a little longer with the soldiers, and then Harry casually picked up a suitcase of booze and canned food and we walked an hour back to our "medical center." Why the soldiers didn't shoot us in the back as we walked away with their suitcase is one of life's many unsolved mysteries.

Two days later, joined by my father-in-law in civilian clothes, we reached Eva and found her and her family relatively well. Pest fell to the Russians on January 14, 1945, and Buda a month later. The city was in ruins, but I found my parents. We had survived and were, for all practical purposes, free.

2   I HAVE A DREAM

I am not a writer. I am a professional musician and teacher who has lived through historic times. I have traveled on five continents and set foot in all fifty of the United States, sitting endless hours in planes, trains, and cars, and so writing became a therapeutic exercise to reduce tension and get rid of aggravation.

When my subject was music-related, I was often asked to publish my work. But when I had discussed issues touching the lives of many, I hesitated. I have frequently questioned the validity of opinions expressed by movie stars and sports and rock idols: not their right as citizens to say whatever they like, but the significance that others attach to their utterances.

My views of the world are rather unconventional and troublesome, born of my past and tempered by advanced age, grandchildren, and the well-documented achievements of a working life, a life of which more than half (forty-three years) has been spent living in Bloomington, Indiana, a city I chose to be my home.

Fifty-two years ago I left the country of my birth, because I couldn't stomach the changes from Fascism to Socialism and then Communism, with the same people in charge after every transition. Today I am watching the same spectacle in a number of countries pretending to build democracies.

Fifty-two years ago I received a letter in Paris, where I struggled as an upcoming artist, inviting me to become an instructor at Indiana University. It was signed by two men: Herman B Wells, then chancellor of the university, and Wilfred C. Bain, dean of the School of Music. These two men built our school to greatness. The document allowed me to enter the U.S., and after ten years of professional activities—in Dallas, New York, Chicago—I ended up as a professor of music in Bloomington.

At that time, forty-two years ago, milk was delivered to my door, which was not locked. Thirty-five years ago cows were grazing next to my house. To have a nice dinner out, we had to drive to Indianapolis.

Meanwhile I was roaming the world, visiting London, Paris, Berlin, Rio, Tokyo, Sydney, and hundreds of other places. When not in concert halls I saw splendor, abundance, and utter misery. In the halls wherever I was, a spirit of unity prevailed—the love of music brought together individuals of totally different backgrounds, regardless of their color, religion, and nationality. But outside of the halls, under the guise of religion or nationality, the same people went on killing their fellow human beings, as if God commanded them.

Reading history tells us that it has always been this way, but unfortunately we are living it now, with all the blessings of our so-called civilization. So the former pastures are filled with hundreds of lovely homes, with security systems, cable TV, sewer systems, and a mall down the road. The material benefits are unquestionable, but human behavior has not changed, and here lies the quandary for someone like me.

Yes, we Americans are blessed with the visions of the founding fathers. Do we really need commandments to remind us not to steal, kill, rape, and so on? Do we need to discuss the pros and cons of capital punishment, when we are keeping murderers—bestial criminals whose guilt is proven beyond the shadow of a doubt—in prison for life, which is far more cruel? We give sick animals injections to terminate their suffering.

Do we have to be Republicans or Democrats to decide when to terminate unwanted pregnancies and condemn people to life imprisonment? Which church do we have to belong to to decide whether life or afterlife is more precious?

I have watched the end of colonialism and seen more people starved and killed by neighboring tribes than died under the hated oppressors. I have watched the newly independent nations raising their flags, sending out their ambassadors, and building palaces for their new home-grown dictators, who overthrew the previous ones. I have seen stone-throwing youths sent to their bomb-laden deaths, and followed by grieving parents. At the end, as in the halls, all I see everywhere is the desire to have a home, raise children, and educate them to better themselves: all people wish to be left alone to seek happiness, and to fulfill the responsibilities to their community that their happiness brings.

I cannot belong to any party, nor does a Sunday sermon give me solace or answer these questions. I pray to my God that the day will dawn when not only cures for cancer and AIDS will be found, but also a common chord will be sounded to eradicate the exploitative nationalism that serves only the few.

When no religion will claim supremacy over others.

When no white, brown, black, or yellow pigmentation will determine human worth.

When the interpretation of laws will not be used to free criminals and offensively enrich its practitioners.

Then maybe more and more members of society will sit in concert halls around the world and praise the beauty given to them by the likes of Bach, Mozart, Beethoven, and their contemporary counterparts.

We will not be around to see it, but wouldn't it be nice if our great-grandchildren could live in such a world?

Of course, it could be worse. What if I were living in New York, Chicago, or Los Angeles?

And now tell me that I am not a chauvinist.

BLOOMINGTON, INDIANA, FEBRUARY 2001

3 ROMANIA, AUSTRIA, AND SWITZERLAND

ROMANIA

Doing justice to the next part of my memoirs will require me to dredge up long-lost memories of what this phase of my life was like. But all I really remember is that I wanted to get out of that hellhole. True, I no longer had to fear the Fascists and the Nazis, and I was no longer at constant risk of deportation. But the Hungarians who were named by the Russians to run the city were those who managed to change their colors: Nazis supposedly not guilty of murders, Communists who had fought alongside Tito or lived in Russia. Such people are commonly called "hustlers" today. I could still see the dead bodies floating in the Danube River, people murdered up to the very minute of the Russian takeover. Nazi butchers were running for positions in the newly formed, so-called democratic parties. Since I had a job offer from Sweden, I hoped to get there somehow and start a new life as a professional musician. Although tens of thousands of people had disappeared or been killed, some of my friends had survived, and as soon as the city was liberated they began organizing concerts and other activities for the future. I wanted no part of this.

My father succeeded in reclaiming his shop and apartment and resumed his work as a tailor, helped by his ability to speak Russian with the occupying forces. I was daily caught by Russians rounding up work brigades, some of which ended up in the Soviet Union for years. Only my Swedish passport and the Russian papers the district commander had given me, stating my services to the Soviet forces, saved me. In the midst of this I caught a bad cold that laid me low for a while, and during that time I rediscovered my cello, which I hadn't touched for almost a year. When my fever was gone, Eva and I went to the railroad station. We had heard that freight trains were leaving for Romania, and we managed to get on one. Our parents stood by with tears in their eyes, saying goodbye. I began my new life and career with a cello, one suitcase (and one for Eva), a small gold chain, some Hungarian and foreign money gathered by our parents, and the address of Gabriel Banat, a violinist colleague and good friend of Eva's who had studied in Budapest and now lived in the Romanian city of Timisoara—Temesvar, in Hungarian. (He recently retired from the New York Philharmonic.)

The train rolled slowly south. It was February, and bitter cold. The wagon we shared with twenty others had a huge hole in the roof. It moved slowly enough that a few people jumped off the train to quickly gather whatever dry wood they could, and we lit a fire in the middle of the wagon. The smoke caught the attention of a group of Russian soldiers. With machine guns on their shoulders they jumped in and joined us around the fire, warming their hands as we were; then at a signal they systematically robbed us of whatever they could find, said goodbye with smiles, and left.

The next day we reached the border, where our train finished its run. Romanian border guards and Russian soldiers asked for papers. Nobody had any that were acceptable to them. When I stupidly displayed my minimal Russian, picked up during the siege, and even mentioned that I had a Russian mother, one soldier wanted to arrest me as an AWOL Russian. Luckily the Romanians all spoke Hungarian and saved me from disaster. As darkness fell, the Russian commander noticed that I was carrying a cello. He asked if I was a musician, and when I said yes, he invited me to come and play for the soldiers. My musical background hardly prepared me for such an occasion. They took Eva and me to a

THE WORLD OF MUSIC ACCORDING TO STARKER

guardhouse, gave us vodka and food, and began to sing. I tried my best to remember every tune I had heard in my childhood and accompanied them as well as I could. The rest, because of vodka and fatigue, is a blur. All I remember is that the guardhouse had one small bedroom. The commander took us there, closed the door, and went back to his comrades. The next morning one of his soldiers walked us to the other side of the railroad yard and put us on a Romanian train. I still consider that performance the most successful of my life.

Romania had escaped destruction and life there was close to normal, which was very strange for those of us coming from years of hell. The train took us to the border town, Arad, which had previously been Hungarian; everyone there spoke Hungarian, German, and Romanian. No one asked to see our tickets or identification. Soviet soldiers were everywhere, resting up from battle duties. War refugees and survivors of the camps were making their way home, as were soldiers, although the war was still going on. The Allies were closing in on Austria and Berlin, but we neither knew nor cared much about it. All we wanted to do was to get to Sweden, where I had a job waiting.

We arrived in Arad with nothing but our one suitcase each, plus the cello, but I luckily found that a Hungarian paper bill and the gold chain had fallen through a hole in my jacket pocket into the lining, and the soldiers who robbed us on the train had missed them. The money had been printed by the Nazi regime and was already worthless, but in Arad they didn't know it yet, and we changed it into enough Romanian currency to buy dinner, a room for the night, and tickets to Temesvar.

Once in Temesvar we went to Banat's address and found the apartment locked, so we asked around and found the house of the owners, who rented the apartment to the Banats. What happened next was worthy of a comic opera. We knocked, and a young woman opened the door and saw my cello. When we asked about our friends, she yelled for her mother to come. Banat had often spoken of us, so they knew who we were. They ushered us into their living room and bombarded us with questions about the war. Our friends were in Bucharest, but they assured us we could stay in the apartment as long as we wanted—but before anything else we must have a bath! This was a luxury we had almost forgotten. We changed into clean clothes from our suitcases' meager

ROMANIA, AUSTRIA, AND SWITZERLAND

contents, the father and son arrived, and they served us food. In a daze we ate, were led to the apartment, accepted the keys, and promised to return to see them the next day.

This family, the Naschitzes, virtually adopted us, and the bond has lasted up to the present day. The father, a lawyer, and the mother, a doctor who was not then practicing, have since passed away. Their daughter became a successful doctor in Germany and has recently retired. George, their son, who was about our age, became a lawyer in New York. He was a nearly fanatic music buff, and throughout the years gave the loudest cheers at my New York performances.

We spent the night as if in a dream, wondering what would happen next. The following day, well rested, we asked around and sold the little gold chain. Now we had money in our pockets, we had been given food, we had no rent to pay: suddenly we were rich, at least for a while. The Naschitzes had belonged to a chamber music society and knew many musicians and music lovers. Now they phoned their friends all over town to tell them that the great cellist, Starker, had arrived. They all wanted to know how they could hear me. They had escaped the brunt of the war, the butchery and bombs, and were just beginning to normalize their lives; they were hungry for anything to do with music. "How about having a soirée in a week?" the Naschitzes asked me. "We have a piano, and people want to come. They are willing to pay for it. You can certainly use some money." The last sentence hit home. The Naschitzes were willing to simply give me some money, but I was not willing to accept it. On the other hand, I had not practiced in almost an entire year, and my only "performance" in a year and a half had been for the border guards. Eva had been scheduled a year before to play Beethoven's First Piano Concerto, but the performance had been canceled and she had not touched a piano since.

I told them I would think it over. Fortunately I had stashed four or five pieces of music in my suitcase, almost as an afterthought. We went back to the apartment and I took out my cello and began practicing. After three hours of work, I felt I could make it. My self-assurance was mainly due to my age: I was not quite twenty-one. Poor Eva was shaking. I asked her to practice every day, so as to be able to play one piece, not too demanding. She did so, and the rest of the program was me alone, playing Bach and Kodály. The soirée was a roaring success and was repeated in other homes, resurrecting my professional life and putting money in my pocket.

After about two months, however, Gabriel Banat's father returned to Temesvar and needed the apartment. We decided that it was time to go to Bucharest, and the Naschitzes called their friends and other music lovers there to tell them we were coming. By the time I arrived several concerts had been arranged, and eventually I had a recital in the Atheneul, a well-known concert hall, with one of the most renowned accompanists of the country, named Buchholz. Soon after I was invited to play with an orchestra, but I cannot remember if it was the Radio Symphony Orchestra or the Bucharest Philharmonic.

In my one suitcase, at my father's insistence, I had packed a dinner jacket made by him, so I was able to appear on stage in the proper regalia. Two incidents stand out in my memories of this time. Once, after a very successful recital, we came home to find the toilet plugged up. I took off my jacket, reached in, and fixed the problem by hand; the event has ever since symbolized for me the highs and lows of a musician's life. Another time, we decided to cook, although neither of us had any idea how. I felt that, having watched my mother, I should be able to make a Wiener schnitzel. We bought the ingredients, but trouble arose when I remembered that the veal had to be pounded thin. We had no tool to do this with, but we did have a little traveling iron, and that's what I used. When the last phase of the operation came, I put the meat into the hot butter in the pan, and immediately each piece curled up into a ball. Oops! I had forgotten to cut slits in the skin. Well, it tasted good, and we were fed.

The idea of getting to Sweden gradually faded into a dream. We rented an apartment and lived day to day. I was a young artist on the rise, and was invited to become principal cellist of the Bucharest Philharmonic in the fall. On May 8 the war in Europe ended. I listened to a celebratory concert broadcast from London, featuring Pablo Casals. I believe he played the Elgar Concerto.

Through all of this, I was trying to find out what had happened to my brothers. I met and questioned dozens of returning labor camp survivors. Some said they had seen them in Yugoslavia; others in Ger-

CELLOS

A slight digression is in order, to discuss my cellos. I did not own an instrument until May 1946. I started with a rented quarter-size cello. When I was about nine I was loaned a half-size Gigli cello, and three years later a three-quarter-size instrument, but the maker's name eludes me. When I was fourteen I had a student named Anton Toszeghi, who dabbled in the cello while studying medicine. His mother, a kind woman who used to accompany me, felt that her family's cello was too good for her son and loaned it to me unconditionally. It was made by Piatellini. That was the instrument I used before and after the war, until in 1946 I purchased a Martin Stoss Viennese cello in Vienna. I paid for it in flour, sugar, and fat smuggled out of Hungary, where, by then, food was more plentiful than in Austria. That instrument carried me to France, where my first Kodály recording earned me the Grand Prix du Disque in 1948, and then to the United States. I returned the Piatellini to Hungary with profuse thanks. Some thirty-five years later, a Swiss student entered my studio with a cello that looked familiar. It was the Piatellini. He had bought it from Andreas von Toszeghi, Anton's son and the grandson of the woman who had lent it to me years before. With the proceeds Andreas bought a fine viola. His father had gone on to become a prominent doctor in London, where he helped to save thousands of lives, including that of my father. He was truly a great man.

In 1950 Emil Herrmann, the famed instrument dealer, loaned me the Lord Aylesford Stradivarius, which had been owned for a short time by Gregor Piatigorsky. I played it for fifteen years, although on occasion, when a potential buyer appeared at Herrmann's, I returned it and borrowed another Strad or a Guarnerius.

The story of my parting with the Lord Aylesford is worth telling. Some time around 1960 Herrmann, who had become a good friend, called me and said that he had sold the cello. The buyer did not take possession of it, donating it instead to Ivan Galamian's Society for Strings, and I continued to use it. He also promised that if I ever wanted to buy the cello, I could do so at a very advantageous price. In 1965, however, I received a letter notifying me that the cello had to be sold and offering me the option to buy it at a price almost double that which Herrmann had promised me five years earlier. At a dinner in New York in the company of Mr. Herrmann and my friend George Lang, Galamian reduced the price increase to 50 percent. We shook hands and the agreement was sealed. A week later a letter from the Society's lawyer insisted on an extra 10 percent. In utter disgust at the breach of agreement, I returned the cello to the Society. Years later, I visited Henry Werro in Bern, the luthier who had eventually purchased it. As he was unable to find a buyer for it, he had decided to reduce its size. When I looked at my partner of fifteen years, I felt sick. I ran away from Werro's shop and never saw him or it again. Lord Aylesford was recently acquired by the Nippon Music Foundation.

The same day I returned the Lord Aylesford to the Society for Strings, a note reached me from Philadelphia's William Moennig & Son, offering for sale a Goffriller cello. I asked them to send it. Forty-eight hours later I bought the cello, and it has been my companion ever since. All this happened while I was recording the Bach suites for Mercury Records; I did the first recordings with the Strad and the rest with the Goffriller.

Until then I also had the use of a copy of the Lord Aylesford, made by Eugene Knapik in Chicago. I needed a special large case for it, and since I was in London, I stopped in at W. E. Hill & Sons, on Bond Street. They brought up an old case, and in it they found an 1848 Hill cello, untouched; the case had never been opened. I bought both the case and the cello. The Hill eventually went to Lawrence Block, and the proceeds helped me acquire a Testore. And the Testore ended up in Seattle, after it helped toward the purchase of a filius Andreas Guarnerius of 1707. The Strad copy eventually found its way to John Cloer.

Sometime in the 1980s a friend attending a Sotheby auction called and told me that a French cello was up for bid. I had her buy it on my behalf, and she brought it to me. It looked horrendous, but had a beautiful sound. When Kenneth Warren Sr. looked at it, he said that it was an authentic Claude Pierray of 1709. But the original varnish was mostly destroyed and painted over badly. Warren's chief restorer, Mr. Pethes, painstakingly removed all the varnish and applied his own. The cello, a small ladylike model, looks lovely and has a warm chamber-music sound.

On a visit to Cremona, Italy, I met Mr. Morassi, the head of the school of violin-making there. He measured my Goffriller and set out to make a copy of it. The cello reached me in Chicago a year later, and it took six months to make it playable. In Oporto, Portugal, I met Antonio Capella and his son, another Antonio, who also made a copy of the Goffriller: the father began it, and the son finished the work after his father's death. I use it in my school studio to this day. I also have two other copies, one by Lawrence Wilke and the other by Tom Sparks. These copies are used by students, as needed.

In 1986, in the middle of the Third American Cello Congress in Bloomington, Indiana, an itinerant Hungarian fiddle dealer showed up. From the trunk of his beat-up Cadillac he dragged out two cellos that looked to be in the same shape as his car. But both had Stradivarius labels inside. I tried one, and it sounded phenomenal. The other was in need of major repair, but had a good sound. On a lark I bought both. Shortly after the Congress, I had a date with the Cleveland Symphony, and I played my new supposed Strad. Many people inquired enviously about it, and I used it on many occasions, in New York, Paris, and elsewhere. In an effort to discover its provenance I had it tested, and was finally told it was a composite instrument, mostly French. When Jacques Francais looked at it, he said it was German. But it has French varnish, I pointed out, and he replied that the Germans often used French varnish. René Morel declared it to be Czech and said to repair it would cost more than it was worth. Whatever the truth, it still sounds better than most instruments in the stratospheric price range.

ROMANIA, AUSTRIA, AND SWITZERLAND

I received a letter from a couple in Erie, Pennsylvania, who were in charge of selling off part of the estate of a woman who needed money, offering the Pope Benedict Strad for sale. Included in the envelope were newspaper clippings from the twenties, testimonials, certificates, and pictures, all attesting to the instrument's authenticity. I had two days free between performances in Canada and with the Cleveland Orchestra, so I stopped in Erie. The couple met me and led me to an ancient mansion. On the living-room table was a case. I took out the cello, which was beautiful. I tried it. It sounded heavenly; fittingly, it had angels painted on its back.

The lady of the house, an old woman in a wheelchair, was on the second floor and wanted to meet me. She told me that she had studied cello at a college in Boston more than fifty years before. Her father, who was one of the Pennsylvania oil millionaires, gave her the cello as a Christmas present. Now she had to sell her paintings and the cello as well. I was excited at the prospect of acquiring a Strad no one knew about, and at a price lower than other Strads were selling for at that time. I told her I had to try it in a hall, but she was reluctant to let me, because it wasn't insured. So I got on the phone, and within an hour I had insurance underwritten by Lloyd's of London.

I got in my car with the Pope Benedict and my Goffriller. I was having a hard time concentrating, not just because of the chance that I had another Strad in my hands, but because of the publicity that would erupt when news of my find broke. As soon as I had checked into my hotel in Cleveland, I called Kenneth Warren in Chicago, only to be told that he was in Cleveland for my concert. I finally reached him, and he jumped in a car and came to my hotel. We said a quick hello, and I brought the Strad from the bedroom to the living room. From twenty feet away Ken said he thought it was a Ruggieri, but he wasn't sure, because the ribs seemed wrong. He would have to open it to be certain. He also said that it was worth only a quarter of the asking price, although its sound was very good. I offered to buy it at a reduced price, but was refused. So after the next day's rehearsal I drove back to Erie, canceled the insurance, and left the cello with its owner. Herbert Goodkind's *Violin Iconography of Antonio Stradivari* lists the Pope Benedict cello, but gives no details whatsoever. Years later a student told me about a friend who acquired a beautiful Ruggieri for a price slightly higher that what I had offered for it. That was the end of the Pope Benedict saga.

My second wife Rae named four of my cellos. When I acquired the Goffriller she named it Star, for "Star-ker," and when I purchased the Guarnerius she continued the theme by naming it Nova. The two Strad-labeled composites she named Nebula 1 and 2. Nebula 2 has been repaired and now belongs to Indiana University's instrument collection.

Through all the years, however, I never craved ownership of an expensive instrument, though I did learn that they can be good investments. I also learned that the public often rates a performer higher if he or she owns a great instrument. Such ownership stamps musicians with success, often beyond their artistic merit; reviewers wax eloquent about their Strads, Del Gesus, and so on. I recall colleagues feeling as I did, and I performed on superb copies of their instruments. I am not the only one who feels this way, but it is among the things that have made me an outsider.

As far as bows are concerned, from 1939 until 1954 I played with one French bow, a Hoyer that my mother had bought for me. Then, in Chicago, I bought a La Fleur bow from Kenneth Warren. Now I had two! I felt rich. When, years later, the tip of the La Fleur broke on the day of a concert, I shivered in dread. What if that had happened when I had only one bow?

Today I have around twenty-two bows, French, German, Canadian, and American, but three have special meaning to me. One is a Tubbs bow that belonged to my teacher, Adolf Schiffer, and has Schiffer's name on the silver of the frog. The Hungarian cellist Janos Scholz, who had also studied with Schiffer, bought it after Schiffer's death and gave it to me. Another is a Henryk Kaston bow, made for my old friend John Mundy of the Met Opera. Engraved in the frog's screw are tunes from the musical he composed for Broadway. When I last saw John, in a London pub, he said that he wanted me to have his bow when he was gone. I joked about it. Sadly, he died shortly afterward, and his wife sent me the bow, saying it was in John's will that she should do so. The third is a Vigneron bow that was owned by Pierre Fournier. His widow, Junko, my dear friend, wanted me to have it. I insisted on having Pierre's name engraved on it, and when I go my name will be added and someone else will carry it on.

I also have some exotic instruments from Africa, Asia, and South America, which I display on the walls of my studio. Once when I was playing in Prague, my friend Milos Sádlo, who on occasion taught in my studio at Indiana University, told me that a five-stringed Brescian cello was on sale in a nearby shop. The luthier was in bad financial straits, and I bought the instrument. Sádlo managed to get it to Munich despite the laws restricting the exportation of artwork. A Dutch former student of mine, Marijke Verberne, a member of a group called the Five Century Ensemble, used the cello for years. It now belongs to the Early Music Institute at Indiana University's School of Music, along with its antique bow.

many; others in Russia. After years, the most reliable report was that they had been shot and buried in Bor, Yugoslavia.

Around June, probably because I had done so much heavy labor the year before, a hernia in my left side began bothering me. I had concerts scheduled for the fall, and the job offer was good, but the prospect of a summer in Bucharest with no musical activities was unappetizing. So Eva and I decided to go back to Budapest; I could have a hernia operation there, and we could see our parents. On the way we stopped in

Temesvar, where I left the cello, since it was risky to travel with it. We planned to return to Romania at the end of the summer, but fate decided otherwise.

Train travel had improved by that time, though the trains were packed with people. Eva and I were not the only ones who climbed through the windows of the cars to get on. In any case, we arrived in Budapest to a happy reunion. The ruins of the city were partially cleared, elections were being held, and the worst inflation in history was beginning.

I had my hernia operation, but while recuperating I caught pneumonia. Penicillin was not yet available, and I nearly died. While I was on the mend, an emissary came to see me from the reemerging opera house, poised to open in September. Leaning on a cane, I went to the opera house and met with the triumvirate that was in charge: two singers, Mihaly Szekely and Pal Komaromi, and the conductor Ferenc Fricsay. I knew the singers superficially; Szekely had sung opera in the Omike. I found myself in a most peculiar situation. They appealed to me to help save the culture of Hungary, the culture of our country. My country? I had lived my life in Hungary as a stateless nobody. They assured me that that was in the past, that it was a new world. And they offered me the sun and the moon: the position of first solo cellist of the opera and the Budapest Philharmonic. (As in Vienna, the one orchestra served both functions.) My salary would equal that of the music director, my wife would have free box seats, and I would not have to play every performance. I told them that I didn't have my instrument, as it was in Romania, and they told me I could go and get it, and they would pay for the trip. But I couldn't travel yet, I pointed out, and anyway by then the border control officers were asking for Hungarian documents, which I didn't have because I wasn't a citizen. (I had expected to have to bluff my way back, with the help of my Swedish papers.) There was a silence, and then they said they would take care of the problem. Four days later I was presented with a Hungarian passport. At the age of twenty-one I became a citizen of the country I was born in.

I accepted the job, but I still resented—and still do resent—the way Hungary had treated me and my family. I had been let in, but I was still an outsider. I could not feel pride in being the youngest person ever to take the post of first solo cellist, and I could not see myself living in a country that had caused us so much suffering. But I decided to do the best I could there for a while.

I trekked down to Temesvar to fetch my cello, partly by Russian trucks and partly by train. The trip took so much longer than expected that I missed rehearsals for the opening weeks of operas and ballets. I arrived only in time for opening night, and had to sight-read an obscure opera by a Hungarian composer, Ferenc Erkel. *Tosca, Rigoletto,* and *Bluebeard's Castle* followed. My sight-reading ability carried me through them all. At the fourth stand of the cello section sat the man who had been Adolf Schiffer's assistant and had taught me for the first two years of my studies. He never spoke a word to me; he may have been jealous that I had surpassed him. My assistant was a man whom I had met ten years before, whom I called Uncle George. He tried to pull some gags on me, like telling me that because of where I sat, I had to turn pages. I did so for a week, and then called his bluff. I said, Uncle George, you turn, and he smiled and turned the page.

My agreement with the Philharmonic stipulated that I could meet my commitments in Romania, and in November I left for a month of recitals and orchestral appearances there. The Romanians understood my change of heart in accepting the orchestra position.

While in Bucharest I received an invitation to visit the composer and musician George Enescu. I knew little about him, but I had heard Romanian musicians speaking about him with awe. Why he asked me to visit him, I never found out. He may have heard about my performances from others. In any case, as a result of his invitation I had what was probably the greatest musical week of my life.

He had a palatial home in the city. I was ushered into his studio, where I saw a man with a bent spine, soft-spoken and kind. He asked about me and my life, and suggested that we play some Brahms. He brought out the score of the E Minor Sonata and sat down at the piano—until then I had heard only that he was a violinist. We played through the sonata. When we finished, he said, "I still remember hearing Brahms playing it," paused for a moment, and added, "you cannot play it this way anymore." Then, without music, he began playing the F Major Sonata. I joined in, and we played it through. He said, "I played it with Casals twenty years ago. His playing was stunning. Are you free tomorrow?" he asked. "Come, I am playing three Beethoven sonatas for some friends. I have little time to practice and my wife invited some friends so I can rehearse for a concert."

When I arrived the next day, there were perhaps a dozen people in the room: ladies with velvet ribbons around their necks, solemn-looking gentlemen in elegant outfits. On the wall was a huge picture of Enescu dedicated to "My Beloved Princess." A chair like a throne bore the sign "Reserved." The group chatted, then sat down, and Enescu went to the piano, on which his violin lay in its case. His pianist sat at the keyboard. Enescu took out his fiddle, tuned it, and began the *Spring Sonata*—and I went into shock. He scratched and played out of tune, and there was no way for me to escape. I gritted my teeth and tried to concentrate on anything else. But suddenly, ten minutes into the sonata, Enescu began playing like another person. The sounds were glorious, his phrasing was incredible, and he was perfectly in tune. It was probably the only time in my life that listening to music has brought tears to my eyes. I have never heard such music made since, with the exceptions of Wilhelm Bachhaus, who played the Brahms D Minor Piano Concerto four times in a week, in Chicago ten years later, and when Jascha Heifetz recorded the Brahms Violin Concerto with Reiner, also in Chicago the same year.

Enescu finished the piece and went on to the other sonatas. Suddenly the door opened and a stunningly beautiful woman entered the room. I wish I were a talented enough writer to describe Mrs. Enescu, the Princess Cantacuzino; the best I can do is to say that many years later, when I saw Gloria Swanson in *Sunset Boulevard*, I was reminded of her. Enescu kept playing. The princess proceeded to the chair reserved for her, saluting her gathered friends. Once seated, she took some slips of paper from her purse, wrote on them, and nudged her neighbors to pass the notes on to their recipients. When the sonata was finished she grandly declared, "Why do we need anybody else while he is alive?" The concert came to an end, and some tea and biscuits were served. I left.

The next day a snowstorm struck Bucharest and most of Romania. Enescu was to conduct a symphony that night, but the piano soloist was stuck in Cluj, so the manager of the Philharmonic called to ask whether my friend Gyorgy Sebok, who was staying in the same Bucharest hotel I was, could possibly jump in. Sebok agreed, of course, and played Mozart's D Minor Concerto. Getting to the hall was difficult in the knee-deep snow, but I will always be glad I did; the second half of the concert, which included Brahms's First Symphony, still rings in my ears. That night the Bucharest Philharmonic sounded like the foremost orchestra of the world. (Sadly, on other occasions they were no better than fourth-rate orchestras in any other corner of the globe.)

The storm was capped by an earthquake, with its epicenter only about thirty miles away in the oil fields of Ploesti. We spent the next day stuck in our hotel. The following day I was to give a recital with my Romanian pianist. At noon I was told by phone that he had slipped on ice and couldn't walk. Sebok was ready to jump in again, but by concert time the pianist had arrived and the concert went on as scheduled. The following day Enescu was again on stage, this time as a pianist accompanying our mutual friend Gabriel Banat, the violinist. They played three sonatas, including one of Enescu's. Their performance of the opening of the Brahms A Major Sonata still rings in my mind as one of the greatest musical joys I have ever had. All in all, Enescu performed four times in eight days, as a pianist, violinist, conductor, and composer. No wonder that I consider him the greatest musician I ever encountered. I heard him in Vienna and Paris later, but never contacted him. The "outsider" in me prevented it.

With my concerts over, I returned to Hungary. I played three or four operas a week and occasional Philharmonic concerts, as well as a few solo appearances such as at a concert put on by the newly founded Hungarian-American Society, where I played Bloch's *Schelomo*. I learned it in two weeks. I also played Beethoven's Triple Concerto with two women, conducted by Sergio Failoni, an Italian who made Budapest his home. We called him our Toscanini. He conducted everything by memory and had an explosive temper, but was a very good musician. At the end of that performance a scene took place that I will never forget. The impresario of the event, Imre Kun, who before the war had been the Hungarian equivalent of Sol Hurok, ceremoniously handed me my fee: an American one-dollar bill. Life in Hungary at that time pretty much revolved around money. Because of the inflation my salary was immense, but it was the equivalent of three dollars a month; one dollar was enough to live on for a week. Hungarian currency lost value by the hour. When salaries were paid they had to be immediately spent, or by the next day the money would be worth half what it had been. Shopping was done with gold or foreign currency, or by trading a shirt for a chicken, porcelain for eggs, and so on. Peasants from the country brought in food and collected clothes and other valuables in return.

A memorable event took place on a Saturday in January 1946. The next morning I was to play the Dvořák Concerto, with Ferenc Fricsay conducting, but we had no opera duties on that Saturday night. By that time phone service was slowly being restored, and around 2 P.M. the phone rang. A singer had fallen ill and the Saturday program had to be changed to *Tosca*. That was Fricsay's repertoire and my contract stated that I had to play when important solos were involved. There was no way out; we had to be there. In the first act a gruesome pain hit my lower back. My arms were functioning, but the rest of me couldn't move. Fricsay looked at me. My face must have been chalk-white. "What is it?" he whispered. I said I couldn't move. It may have crossed his mind that I wanted out because of the concert the next morning. He told me I couldn't leave before my solo in the third act, but once that was over I could go. I sat there like a zombie and couldn't leave the pit between acts.

The solo was over and Cavaradossi began his aria. Somehow I staggered out of the pit and walked home with my cello, a ten-minute walk that took almost an hour, over streets covered in ice and snow. When my family saw me they called a doctor. In those days doctors made house calls. One came, gave me a painkiller shot, and said that it looked like lumbago, an annoying ailment that has plagued me once or twice a year ever since, and these days, constantly. Next day I found out that it did not affect my playing, so long as I moved carefully and tolerated the pain. I used the cello as a cane, walked slowly onto the stage, and played. That was my last performance in Budapest for twenty-five years, until I returned in 1971 and, among other things, played Dvořák again.

Around that time I got an invitation to travel to Vienna. It was a weird proposal. The violinist Victor Aitay, my childhood friend, was now concertmaster of the opera and had a string quartet. He and I had a mutual friend, a doctor in whose house we had often played chamber music before the war. The doctor was an amateur violist who went back and forth between Vienna and Budapest for reasons I don't remember. Now he offered us a written contract from an American woman major whereby the Aitay Quartet and I were engaged by the American special services to perform concerts for them in Vienna. Vienna was under four-power occupation at the time, governed by the United States, Britain, France, and the Soviet Union.

No money was mentioned in the contract, but we didn't care. Victor's wife's relatives in the U.S. were trying to get them out of Hungary to somewhere where they could get a visa for America, and getting to Austria was a step toward that. For me it was a chance to get out of Hungary. I had a passport. I asked for a leave of absence and obtained it. (Thirty years later, when on tour in Japan with the Philharmonic, I responded to their welcoming me by saying that I was still a member, as I had never resigned or been fired.) So did Victor and the other members of his quartet. We all—Victor and I, our wives, and his quartet—boarded the train in Budapest. However, the Soviets controlled the part of Austria bordering Hungary, and at the border they asked for our papers and travel permits, which we did not have. Whether they were stunned by seeing so many instruments, or they were drunk, I'll never know, but they let us pass into Austria. I was finally in the West, away from Hungary.

AUSTRIA

My travels to that point had carried me to various towns in Hungary, three cities in Romania, one town in Czechoslovakia (Košice, when it was for a short time returned to Hungarian rule by the Germans), and Cortina d'Ampezzo and Venice in Italy, on a summer trip with my teacher in 1936. I got sick at our first dinner in Venice, and instead of enjoying the beauty of that glorious city, I stayed in bed and lamented the fact that we had taken a vaporetto boat instead of a gondola. So arriving in Vienna meant a lot to me, with its grand history and all the great musicians who lived there. My knowledge of the city was based on the brief account my second brother had given of his boat trip there from Budapest, a graduation gift from Father in '38. Unfortunately, I found it a dreary sight, with snow and dirt everywhere. Only eleven years later did I discover what a beautiful place it really was.

It was dark by the time we reached the Vienna Hungarian Institute, where we were to be housed, and they gave us rooms without charge. The next day we went to see the major who had sent us the contract. She was nowhere to be found. Instead we were told by a captain to get lost; the major had been dishonorably discharged for hiding a Nazi. We were told to forget the contract. That is how our Western tour started. We didn't know what would come next. The three other members of Victor's quartet were afraid to live in such insecure conditions. Their families were back home, so they decided to return. Eva and I stayed in Vienna with the Aitays.

The conditions were certainly bad. The four powers were in charge of the food supply, each acting as provider for a month at a time. The Russians gave salt herring; the French, salad; the Americans, Canadian bacon; and I can't remember what the British distributed. Bread was in minimal supply. Restaurants served watery soup, chicory coffee, and on occasion some potatoes. In the Russian months Vienna smelled of salt herring, and wherever one went salt herring was served, perhaps with tea and a tiny slice of bread or a cracker. Our main difficulty was finding food. Fortunately, we had brought some with us, as well as lots of cigarettes, not just to smoke but to trade. Since the black market flourished, as it did everywhere, we were often saved by trading our cigarettes. Our colleagues who had returned to Budapest reported the troubles we were having, and our parents got to work. My father found some Russian soldiers to bring a suitcase full of goodies to Vienna, and we held a party in the Institute and shared our bounty. The Aitays started receiving letters from America with banknotes in them.

Somebody here and somebody there told somebody else that Hungarian musicians were staying at the Institute, and that they were good. One day we were invited to visit and play for the family who owned the Bösendorfer piano factories. Among others there was a teenaged pianist, and we played a trio with him. His name was Friedrich Gulda. Also among the guests was the head of the Universal Publishing Company. He told us that Universal would be bringing the French composer Oliv-

THE WORLD OF MUSIC ACCORDING TO STARKER

ier Messiaen to Vienna. Yvonne Loriod would play his *Visions de l'Amen* at a house concert, and a public concert was planned where his *Quartet for the End of Time* was to be played. He asked whether we were interested in participating. We were, but the event itself is a blur in my memory; only recently, when Victor sent me the program, did I remember that Messiaen himself was the pianist. The fourth performer was Professor Wildgans, a clarinetist, musicologist, and critic. Thirty years later I played the Quartet again, but again I have little memory of the performance. I never adored Messiaen as everyone else did; his music does not speak to me. The only other time I have met him was in 1972, when Antal Doráti and the National Symphony Orchestra performed and recorded his *Transfiguration of Our Lord Jesus Christ.* Loriod was the pianist and I played the minuscule cello part.

My performance in that Vienna concert must have been noted, as I was asked soon afterward to play a recital in the same hall. In fact, Victor and I became so well liked that, to our surprise, the Americans invited us to play for them. What I remember best about that performance is the language problem. I was, with my minimal English, the translator between the American officers and us. We had a morning engagement and then were to play in the afternoon for the Americans, and that day we ran out of food. After our performance the officers served us some coffee and drinks, but heard our stomachs gurgling. After we confessed the problem, they hustled up something edible. We went back to the Institute with lots of cigarettes, chocolates, and some canned food. It was a highly profitable Sunday.

My recital was scheduled, and an American lieutenant volunteered to play piano for me. Schubert's Arpeggione Sonata was on the program. The only version of it I knew then was Cassado's concerto transcription, with the piano reduction. The concert went well, and I was applauded and paid. But the next day a review appeared that was among the most memorable of my life, and which greatly affected my future. The gist of it was highly complimentary, but one sentence stated that I played as if sleepwalking. I realized that there was truth in it. A few days later I attended a concert where Yehudi Menuhin played, and I was shocked. I had heard him in Budapest when he was about fourteen or fifteen and been awed, like everyone else. Now his sound was cramped, and his breathing was audible at the back of the hall. He was struggling. I couldn't sleep for days. How could this happen to a miraculous child prodigy? And if it could, then it could happen to me as well. Was I a sleepwalker? Did I really know what I was doing? I began a lifelong effort to learn everything I could about every aspect of instrumental playing and music making. As a boy I had had some lessons from Imre Waldbauer and Dezso Rados, who had a scientific approach to playing and teaching, applying physical, mental, and acoustical principles. One of my brothers studied with Rados before the war started. On occasion he invited me and talked a blue streak about the mechanics of playing. What he said made little sense to me then, but when I began my search in '46 some of the subjects those two violinists had touched upon became vital to my thinking.

A communication reached us from George Lang, Eva Aitay's cousin. George was a student of Rados's, but lived in the Hungarian city of Székesfehérvár. He knew me from concerts, but I only vaguely recollected having seen him. Now he told us that he had managed to cross into Austria and was in Badgastein, in the American zone. He, Eva, and Victor were awaited in America, but they had to be in the American zone to send their visas to the Salzburg consul. He urged us to join him there; his hotel in Badgastein was inexpensive and the city was beautiful. But this would mean giving up the free summer lodging in Vienna.

The Aitays were hoping to get their visas in Salzburg soon, so for them there was no choice. For me a plan presented itself. We heard of an international musical competition, including cello, which was to be held in Geneva in October. By that time Sandor Vegh had arrived in Vienna with his quartet and with Eva Czako, who had been my six-year-old pupil when I was eight, and who would later marry Georges Janzer, the quartet's violist. Vegh was already a fairly established member of the European musical community, and he was busy organizing activities for his quartet. They entered the Geneva Competition and suggested I apply as well. If accepted, I could get a tourist visa and get away from the Russian zone. All I had to do was find ten Swiss francs for the application. I managed to find them and was accepted. Soon we were on our way to Badgastein to spend four months there, until we could travel to Geneva.

We met George Lang, and my lifelong friendship with him began. Soon Francis Akos, my former trio partner, also joined us, and a few weeks after he arrived he married the daughter of the owner of the Hotel Hindenburg, where we were staying. (He became assistant concertmaster of the Chicago Symphony Orchestra in 1955, and retired in October 2003.) The group of us were like a family. We talked long into the nights, and took daily walks in the mountains trying to solve the problems of the world. Everyone diligently practiced and eventually even performed in small venues. I played one concert with a former Liszt Academy piano professor, Joseph Csiby, who felt about Hungary much as I did and also got out. He eventually died in Montreal. Ernst von Dohnányi also played a recital in Badgastein, when the U.S. command allowed him to interrupt his detention. He was falsely accused of being a collaborator, and it took years to clear his name.

Badgastein was, at that time, the center for U.S. refugee relief efforts. The little town was overrun by hundreds of survivors of concentration camps. The United Nations Relief and Rehabilitation Administration (UNRRA) arranged to bring them there, and generously supplied them while they waited for the various permits needed to go to America, Mexico, Canada, South America, or wherever. Our group were legitimate applicants for UNRRA's help, and several of us availed themselves of it and received food and a small amount of money. I didn't feel that I qualified and never received anything. My father lovingly made me silk underwear, which I hated, so Eva and I traded it for cigarettes, canned food, and occasionally money. Our parents were doing fairly well, and would send us enough money to pay the hotel bill when they found someone traveling to Austria. It wasn't an easy time, but we survived and had lots of laughs, trying to foresee the future.

In July Lang and the Aitays received their visas and after teary goodbyes they left for the U.S. Eva and I stayed in Badgastein, with occasional short visits to Salzburg, until October, when we left for the Geneva Competition.

When the Austrian train arrived at the border, we had to get off. Polite officers examined our documents and found them in order. They stamped them for a three-week stay and guided us to a Swiss train. We were overwhelmed by the change, like Dorothy waking up in the land of Oz. After years of drab, war-torn cities, we sat in a clean railroad car. Food carts were rolled along the aisles. Looking out the windows we saw majestic mountains, stunning lakes with pleasure boats sailing across them. Every garden plot was planted with fruit trees, every meadow held placidly chomping cows, and every vineyard was loaded with grapes. It was paradise. After a few hours we arrived in Geneva and walked to a little hotel, the cheapest we could find, suggested by the competition brochure. It was one week before the start of the competition, and my frame of mind was less than felicitous. All I could think of was where to go after the competition was over. Not back, that was for sure, not to Austria or to Hungary. Ever since the shock of hearing Menuhin in Vienna, my self-confidence had been at its lowest. In Badgastein I had spent 3 1/2 months practicing more, and more analytically, than ever in my life before or since. My fingers were in great shape, but my mind was miles away. I wasn't expecting to pass the first round, but to my great surprise I reached the finals, one among ten.

The Vegh Quartet arrived a couple of days after we did. Like me, they had applied to enter the competition for the sake of the visa. Eva Czako told me she couldn't play, as she hadn't touched the cello in four months. I told her to start practicing; she had five days. She also reached the finals. We all played. If in Vienna I was a sleepwalker, in Geneva I played as if in a coma. All I remember is that I played Bach's C Minor Prelude and Fugue with a speed that could break the Olympic record for the hundred-meter dash. Then I played the Haydn D Major Concerto, first movement, with piano. As I later learned, it was broadcast and our Temesvar friends heard it and even loved it.

When the results were announced, I received a bronze medal for sixth place. Eva placed third and received a few hundred Swiss francs. Two more Hungarians were also finalists. Ede Banda, the cellist of the Tatrai Quartet, came fifth, and Paul Szabo, the fourth member of the Vegh

Quartet, came ninth. Antonio Janigro, who before the war had already won the Vienna Competition and others, ended up second. Everyone had taken it for granted that Janigro would win. He was among the handful of cellists who impressed me in my youth, and his life only increased my early appreciation.

The winner of the competition turned out to be a French lady, Raymonde Verrandeau. A few months later, in Paris, my wife and I met Charles Bruck, a budding conductor who became a dear friend. Bruck left for London to conduct Verrandeau in a performance of the Schumann Concerto to be recorded by Decca, but returned two days later saying the lady could not record even one side. She returned to Marseille, and for all I know she died eventually in obscurity. I may be wrong.

Although the competition was over, our visas had a few more days. Another Hungarian cellist friend showed up, George Bekefi. He had been so abused in the labor camps that he could not play. He had a cousin, a U.S. soldier stationed in Paris, who came to Geneva to arrange for Bekefi to go there. Thanks to the cousin we had a few lovely days in Geneva: boat rides on the lake, good meals, ice cream, and other pleasures. We learned from another Hungarian colleague that it was possible to get Belgian visas, if the French government would issue transit visas to allow us to cross France. The transit visas were "nonstop" visas; they did not allow us to stay in the country. Nonetheless we obtained the stamps, got on a train to Belgium, and got off in Paris.

Almost fifty years later I was again in Geneva, giving a radio interview. In the course of our talk, the interviewer stopped and said that they had a surprise for me. They played a fragment, about four minutes long, of my performance of the Haydn concerto in 1946. I recognized my own playing, but the cadenza and Gevaert arrangement used in those days now sounded totally alien to me. I was pleased, though. My playing in a comatose state was far better than I thought.

ROMANIA, AUSTRIA, AND SWITZERLAND

4 "MOZART METER" — A STORY

After a long and strenuous concert season, covering no fewer than four continents, I not only needed a vacation, but wanted to relax in my own country for a change. I loved mountains and therefore decided to explore the Rockies, those peculiar and awesome prodigies of Earth. That, at least, is what I always felt them to be from the elevated perspective of an airplane. Reflecting now on my experiences, I am inclined to revise that impression. Perhaps the world itself is an awesome prodigy, with unexpected beauty to be found everywhere.

I had maps prepared and the car serviced. I supplied myself with traveler's checks, credit cards, bottles of water, a flashlight, a blanket, and whiskey (just in case, you understand)—everything said to be necessary for a lengthy vacation alone, far away from everything familiar. And I departed, in search of peace and quiet.

Hundreds of miles sped by while I rejoiced in the risky freedom of having no advance reservations in hotels or motels. I drove on or stopped as the mood struck me, until on the third day I caught my first exciting glimpse of distant mountains. The pressure of the past months began to ebb. It was a glorious day, with white clouds fluffed above the mountains. Only the passing buzz and blare of auto horns created any disturbance; everyone seemed to be in such a hurry. Even those with a honeymoon gleam in their eyes pressed down on accelerator pedals as if their very lives depended on reaching their destination as quickly as possible.

Not me, I said to myself, and pulled off the road to consult the map. A black line ran parallel to the superhighway, and so at the next exit I liberated myself from the race. The deepening afternoon gave way to a splendid twilight. The road was well marked, and I turned left, then right, as I passed through small towns and villages. At a roadside restaurant I ate and had the car filled with gas, and then drove on. Why cut short a perfect day? I decided to drive for another hour before stopping for the night; I felt good, at peace with the world and with myself.

The road turned, and I followed the white stripe along its right edge. As night fell, I suddenly realized that I was nowhere—I was lost, but not shocked. I'm accustomed to losing my way. The better the instructions, the likelier I am to stop at the homes of strangers and ask directions. I pulled over to study the map, but couldn't make heads or tails of it. Side roads were marked, but I didn't recall turning off the main road. I drove on, but saw no signs, no houses, nothing, and so I reversed my direction.

I came to a fork, where there was a choice of roads, but no signs. I must have lost the main road somewhere earlier. But how to proceed? My options were to go straight ahead or to the right; straight ahead seemed as good as any. My watch showed almost ten o'clock. Glancing at the sky, filled with a myriad of stars, I estimated that I was heading north, in keeping with my general plan. I had plenty of fuel, so I wasn't worried on that account, and since there were no signs of life, I was determined to go on until I found something. I couldn't be that far out of the way; I'd been on the highway at dinnertime.

The road looked well maintained and my headlights shone on trees ahead; I was passing through forests. I turned on the radio. A distant station was transmitting rock-'n'-roll, another rattled off the latest international crisis, but I wanted neither. At the same moment I reached for the knob, the car began to jerk and pull. With both hands, I clutched the wheel to stay on the pavement, but to no avail. The right rear wheel

"MOZART METER"—A STORY

skidded off the road into a small depression; of course, that was the tire that was flat.

A flat tire is exasperating, no matter how carefree you are otherwise. I told myself to take it easy, that it wasn't a big problem. At least changing it would be a start on physical exercise, which I'd already planned as part of this vacation. I raised the trunk lid, pushed aside a few suitcases, undid the retaining screws, and freed the spare tire. I assumed I'd be on my way in a few moments as I placed the jack under the car, cranked it up, and began to loosen the lug nuts. Or rather, tried to loosen them. I tried and tried again, but they wouldn't give way. I told myself that I couldn't possibly be in such decrepit physical condition, and tried once more. Unsuccessfully. Drops of perspiration beaded my forehead. What now? I lit a cigarette. One last try. Then I remembered that the last time the tires had been rotated, the mechanic had used an electric gadget to tighten the nuts. Bully for me and my memory—but what on earth was I to do?

I returned the spare to the trunk and took out the flashlight, locked the car, and started to walk. Since the flashlight was large enough to be a weapon, I felt fairly secure—though at the same time I was assuring myself that no one was anywhere near me in the first place. I walked on in unbroken silence for a few minutes and then was startled by the sudden barking of a dog, quite close. I controlled my breathing and flashed the light around. Left of the road, the forest opened onto some sort of path. There was a mailbox with no name on it, only the number 5553, suggesting there was at least one house nearby. Yet, looking down the path, I saw only trees. I decided to follow it anyway, whereupon the barking grew louder. After some fifty yards, I came to a gate, and about a hundred feet beyond I could see a garden and house.

Suddenly two powerful beams of light hit me from the roof of the house. The door opened and an odd-looking man stepped out. At a distance he seemed late-middle-aged and rather hunched.

"Yes, what is it?" The accent was heavily German, with a "v" in "what" and hissing "s"s. The voice had a faint tremor. To a magnificent German Shepherd, now visible in the light, he said, "Quiet, Ludwig. Stop!"

I spoke slowly. "Forgive me, sir, for coming at this time of night. But not only have I lost my way, I've also had a flat tire, about half a mile away."

"Can't you fix it?"

"I tried, but I can't loosen the lug nuts."

"I don't think in this case I can help you."

"Oh, I didn't mean that. But might I call a garage, or a service station, from here?"

The man came forward, the dog beside him. For a while he stared at me with a strange expression; then, hesitantly, he said, "There is no phone here."

"Do any of your neighbors have one?"

"There are no neighbors."

I looked past him to the house; music was playing within, on a radio or hi-fi system. "Excuse me, but that's the Brahms B-flat Piano Concerto. Who's playing?"

The old man was startled. With suspicion in his voice, he asked, "Are you a musician?"

"Sort of," I mumbled. "But . . . I don't want to disturb you any longer. I have to find help somewhere. Sorry for the intrusion. Good night." I turned and began to walk toward the road.

"Wait! You!" the man called. "For twenty-five miles around here you can't find help. You wish to walk all that?"

I stopped in my tracks. Twenty-five miles? "But sir, you have electricity here. And what about the mailbox with those numbers?"

He opened the gate and led me up the path to the house. It was a large, simple ranch-style building, and it was filled by the sound of the concerto. I had sunk into a comfortable armchair, tired from the unaccustomed hike.

"What kind of sound system do you have?"

Rather than answer my question, the old man left the room, saying curtly, "Just a moment."

I glanced around, thinking, so far so good; at least I am under a roof. But where the hell was I? The room was tastefully appointed, in the style of a conventional middle-class German parlor. Books lined the walls on shelves up to the ceiling. I saw at least five languages repre-

"MOZART METER"—A STORY

sented, yet, oddly, all the volumes were on musical or electronic subjects. The music stopped abruptly and the old man reappeared.

"I am sorry, but I must ask you questions."

I was flabbergasted. "I beg your pardon?"

"I say, do you know my name?"

"But how could I? We've never met."

"I am Professor Trumpfl," he declared, staring intently at me.

I introduced myself in turn. "Should I really know you, sir?"

The professor's expression relaxed, and in a calmer voice he offered me a drink.

"Gladly! May I have some whiskey?"

"I only have beer or schnapps."

I studied him as he poured out a schnapps. He seemed younger than he had at first glance. Late fifties, I guessed, of medium height, a bit paunchy, with a sunken chest and the hunched, narrow shoulders of an unathletic man. He wore shapeless pants, a pink shirt, a short flannel bathrobe, and (bizarrely, considering the place and the hour) a striped bow tie. His nose was prominent, but, as if God had suddenly changed his mind, it turned inward near the tip. His thick lower lip almost completely obscured the upper one, nearly brushing the base of his nose; it gave his face the appearance of a vase. He was partially bald, yet thick black hair grew from the middle of his skull rearward, and was carefully combed.

He brought two glasses, and in walking the few steps to me, he pushed his right leg forward with his whole body while he dragged the left. Both his feet turned inward. Handing me a glass, he sat down and seemed to drift off, his expression hazy and wandering. We sat in silence until he returned to reality. Watching me from the corner of his eye, he asked, "Who are you, tell me, and what are you doing in this place? And how do you happen to know the Brahms piano concerto?"

"Believe me, sir, I am just as surprised to find myself here as you seem to be by my unscheduled visit."

"Visit?" He came suddenly alert.

"I meant that jokingly! I *am* rather well known in my field, and had planned a more or less incognito vacation in the mountains. I got off the main road, and . . . here I am."

"What field?"

"I am a jazz pianist."

The professor began to laugh—at least I think that was what he was doing. He kept his mouth closed, but short intervals of crackling, coughing noises escaped (or tried to, anyway) from his esophagus. I was both taken aback and annoyed.

"You find my profession funny?"

"Oh no, not at all. Forgive me. It is just that . . . I might as well explain. But are you not hungry?"

"No, thanks, I had dinner on the road."

"Does anyone know where you are?"

"I hardly think so. That is, I told no one where I might be going."

The professor took a few sips of schnapps before he spoke, softly, slowly. "The electricity does not come from anywhere. I have my own generators."

"But isn't it difficult, to live so far from others? What about food, supplies?"

"To live by others, is it so good? I get the post once each week. I receive fuel once a month. If I wish, I can reach the town by car in an hour." My eyes must have lit up at this, for he went on, "I know. Tomorrow I will assist you. But at this time of night, I am not, as I believe you say, up to driving you there and then back again home. You are welcome to sleep here . . . if you like."

I hardly had any choice. The schnapps was cozily warming the inner me, and the tension engendered by my strange reception was subsiding.

"Professor, I don't wish to disturb your evening further. But I would enjoy hearing the Brahms myself. It was my graduation piece."

"What?! From where did you graduate?"

"Curtis."

"You said, I thought, that you were a jazz pianist!"

"Correct, but I have my diploma from the Curtis Institute."

"Why, then, did you turn to jazz?"

"I didn't. Contemporary music did, and I took the road to specialization." This question was asked of me often, and I had my stock answer.

"You never regretted this? Not to play the classics? Bach, Beethoven, Mozart?"

"Oh, I play them for myself, but not in public any more." This was, in fact, a painful subject for me; reflexively my brows had knotted.

The professor regarded me with a smile. "Frustrated? Had no success?"

I bristled. "No, sir! If I am frustrated, it is with music and musicians, not myself. I had success, but I got sick and tired of the nonsense in classical music."

The professor leaned back, took a large gulp from his glass, and asked, "What do you mean by 'nonsense'?"

"I don't want to bore you with professional talk. When I meet music lovers, I feel they shouldn't be bothered by knowing too much about music. They should just enjoy it—have likes and dislikes—have favorites, and not be influenced by the so-called experts."

The professor was shaking; the croaking noises I had heard previously now pressed against his lips from within. "Well, my boy, this is good! Professor Trumpfl a music lover! Krk-krk-krk."

"I'm sorry, have I said anything out of line?"

"Come!" He stood and led me into an adjoining room.

I stopped at the doorway and gaped; the sight was incredible! The room was at least four times the size of the living room. Electronic machinery, including dozens of tape recorders and turntables, lined three of the walls. One of them was entirely occupied by a mechanism that resembled a computer but was filled with needles, tapes, and other assorted gadgets, the likes of which I'd never before seen. Elsewhere, metal filing cabinets reached the ceiling. The place looked like a combination of a recording studio, IBM headquarters, and an atomic energy laboratory.

The professor moved through the room, sidestepping steel ladders on wheels that ran in tracks in the ceiling. A door at the far end of the room opened onto a few stairs that led us downward to yet another huge room. This one resembled a public library! Row after row of metal shelves held records, tapes, and printed scores, thousands upon thousands of them. Some music lover!

The professor grinned and said, "So, look!" I reached up, at random.

THE WORLD OF MUSIC ACCORDING TO STARKER

Next to a sign—*Mozart: Köchel 491/Concerto for Piano and Orchestra, Nr. 20, in C Minor*—were a huge number of recordings, all by different artists and orchestras. The scores filed with them included a variety of editions from several countries. I looked at the signs along the row: Mozart concertos for piano, violin, flute, oboe, horn; operas, symphonies, chamber music; they seemed to go on forever. I went to other rows. Bartók, Stravinsky, Prokofiev . . . I was dazed.

"Ja, my boy, I am not just a 'music lover.'"

When we'd returned to the living room, I couldn't contain myself. I burst out, "Please, Professor Trumpfl, will you explain all of this? Forgive me, but I've never seen anything to compare with it in my whole life. You . . . here . . . why?"

"Slowly, slowly," he answered, smiling. "I will tell you. I wondered to myself why I allowed you to enter, but I felt in some way that I trusted you. And I could not help but be amused when you thought of me as just another music lover. I almost saw myself again as a young man, when you spoke about the 'nonsense' going on in the field of music." He refilled our glasses.

"May I smoke?"

"Of course, please. You may have observed tonight that I was not born in this country?"

I nodded, careful to avoid any word that might hurt the familiar pride anyone foreign-born may feel about his language skill.

"I am a native of Germany—you would call it East Germany today? I, too, graduated as a pianist. I have my Artist's Diploma from the Leipzig Konservatorium. My father was an architect who loved music, but he was a practical man. He insisted that I pursue studies other than music, but his persuasion was very subtle. Instead of declaring that music was not a good profession, he only stated that the true artist must know the world around him. 'Do not shut yourself into an ivory tower,' he instructed me. 'You are in the twentieth century; be a twentieth-century artist. Through music of the past, express your world. All the great musicians have used individual techniques in different eras to communicate their messages. Arrive at your own conclusions by observing, studying, and understanding your world.'"

I must have betrayed some impatience in the way I put out my cigarette, since the professor, after taking another sip of his schnapps, said, "I know already what you think. The point that my father made to me, that great music from different eras was the road to individual expression, is doubtless debatable. But I only tell you his words, and how he persuaded me to go beyond music for music's sake—or so I thought then. I finished gymnasium, or your high school, where my best subjects were mathematics and physics. My music studies proceeded in parallel, and two years later I graduated as a pianist. Composition and conducting, these I studied also. I was thought to be a future musical artist, and played in concerts—with quite some success, might I say. I appeared with singers and instrumentalists as coaches and accompanists. But this did not satisfy me.

"To myself I said, perhaps I was not born for the stage. But why not? I had the technique, the training; I worked hard, I loved music, and no one doubted my talent. So? That is why I smiled when you made your comment about 'nonsense.' I became furious after every concert, my own or another artist's. I played music that I had studied for years with fine teachers and had also heard performed by fine artists. I had developed a concept of that work which I was able to call my own, and of which audiences showed me their approval. But then, on the next day, I would read the newspapers. In one I found that 'a talented pianist played with excessive romanticism, understandable at his age.' In another I read, 'what a pity that the young generation of today turns to cold logic instead of permitting true human sentiment to flow from the great masterpieces.' For me, at that time, such contradictions were still acceptable, and I settled a dilemma for myself by saying that I had not established a contact, a rapport, with these writers. *Aber,* when one writer said that the second movement was deliberately slow, and another criticized the relationship of tempi and dynamics, I became furious!

"To myself today, I call this the wounded pride of youth. Yet the same thing happened to great artists when I heard them; everything was criticized in a way that presumed the writers knew more about the music than any performer. Often, when a less-known musician played the same works, I would find praise heaped upon him, making him appear to be superior to the masters. I nagged my friends with questions: 'How

THE WORLD OF MUSIC ACCORDING TO STARKER

do you know who is great?' We had endless and inconclusive arguments that would only stop if someone said, with cynicism, 'Charisma? Bah!'

"Naturally, such arguments were based on many factors—authority of presentation, technical prowess, ability to color, and a grasp of musical structures—important-sounding words! But when the name of an artist was spoken, this created a chaos, a total chaos! No matter *who* it was, furious controversy would always follow. Some would say that X was not even a decent technician, others that X could not even play in tune. Still others would say, 'beautiful tone but no rhythm.' *Und so weiter.*

"I will never forget, to the day I die, the time when a friend, a fine musician himself, mentioned a recording he had heard. 'Fantastic,' he said. 'What is the artist's name?' I asked. It was someone I had hardly even heard of. We were in the home of a wealthy music patron—in Europe then, such people were delighted to entertain us, the young promising ones, in their homes. We would play for hours and hours, all types of music. After we were served food and drinks, which were their form of remuneration, we would launch into our verbal fights. The hosts felt themselves insiders, as well as listeners."

The professor had made me chuckle. "Do you think those 'earlier days' took place only in Europe?" I asked. "We had the same thing in Philadelphia and New York when I was a student. I'm certain it still goes on there today, and everywhere else for that matter."

"So then you know what I mean. But I don't wish to sound condescending. Those people and their homes provided opportunities for us not only to make music, to try out compositions on severe critics, but to articulate our youthful opinions, so strong at that age. As I was saying, this friend was raving on about a recording. Our host interrupted with a gleam in his eyes; he had just purchased that same recording! After so much praise I was anxious to hear it and asked if he would play it. What I heard was a fairly good, clean, but undistinguished performance, with the most obvious choices of expression. My friend insisted that it was by far the best Beethoven concerto ever recorded, and there was no use arguing. In succession he dismissed records by several leading artists. The party fell into groups, pitted violently against one another. Comparisons were flung about; careers were built or ruined; attempts to clarify why one performance was superior to others were laughed away. We hurled insults at one another, and smiled in a way meant to suggest that opposing views were incompetent or simply ignorant.

"When I finally left, I could not help shaking my head in disbelief. Could it be possible that there was no objective way to determine what is good or not good in the performance of a musical composition? After all, as music is created it is written down on paper. Notation shows us what a composer wishes. He adds symbols for dynamics, and tempo markings. Why is it, then, that we play the same notes differently, and during the same performance hear different things? Are there no principles for music, *principles* that one can follow and learn, that anyone can hear and know?"

The professor fell silent. For a while he seemed thousands of miles away, and then he sighed deeply. "No. And that was more than forty years ago."

I was spellbound. And my ego was bruised. Forty years ago! I had hashed over the same questions and arguments myself. Where is there an answer? Could the same questions have been posed and debated heatedly hundreds of years ago? Will they be asked forever? A hundred, a thousand questions were on my tongue, but Professor Trumpfl rose.

"My friend, it is very late. I must go to sleep now."

"But—"

"You bring back some of the things from your car. I will arrange a bed for you. If you are still interested in my tales tomorrow, you don't have to run away."

Without even trying to hesitate politely, I accepted. "I'll be glad to stay. Thank you!"

In a daze I went back to the car. The professor had quieted Ludwig, who obviously wasn't used to strangers entering or leaving the house. I brought back a small overnight bag. When the professor led me to a little guest room, I was astonished to see a morose old woman in a worn housecoat preparing the bed. She was obviously half asleep and didn't notice us enter.

"Don't mind her, she's deaf as a doorknob, but takes good care of me. See you in the morning. *Schlaf wohl.*"

THE WORLD OF MUSIC ACCORDING TO STARKER

I had a difficult time falling asleep. Where was I? I still didn't know. Who was he, and what was he doing with so much equipment and so much music? I had to find out. Thousands of questions!

When I awoke, the sun was almost above the house. I opened the shutters to see trees all around, and a small kitchen garden that had rows of green peppers, potatoes, lettuce, onions, and tomatoes. It struck me as ludicrous. Professor Trumpfl and those thousands of records, tapes, and scores—all the equipment somehow didn't fit with home-grown green peppers. The window of the bathroom, which was adjacent to my sleeping quarters, faced in a different direction. I was startled to see several houses some distance away in the forest. I couldn't see a soul, but the professor must have been lying when he said there was no one else for twenty-five miles. But why?

After shaving, I stepped out of the bath to see the old woman standing at my bedroom door, knocking. She carried a tray with coffee, bread, and marmalade. I could hear that the Brahms concerto was playing again, somewhere in the house, but this time by a different artist. The smell of coffee made me realize how hungry I was and so, taking first things first, I breakfasted. It was good coffee!

As I ate, thoughts about this strange house filled my mind, mixed with the dreams I had had. I had been back in music school; my teacher was pacing up and down the studio while I played; he was beating tempo with his hands, next with a pencil on the piano, then on his desk. "Discipline, Bob, discipline, for God's sake! Don't rush, don't slow down here, keep the beat!" A huge metronome had hung from the ceiling, almost the full height of the room. Every time I departed from synchronization, lights flashed and I was hit on the head.

I was recalled from these images when the professor greeted me with "Good morning. Feeling better?"

"Thank you, yes. I had a good rest. But I'm more confused than ever. Why did you say there was no one around here for twenty-five miles?"

"Ah, you saw the houses. No one lives in them. Come, let us have a short walk. Then if you decide to depart, we fix your car."

"Fix the car? You said—"

"Come, come. Did I not tell you I am an engineer? But you couldn't expect an old man like me, even though I have tools, to go out in the night and fix a flat tire for a stranger. If you choose to leave, tell me and we shall fix your car."

"How about that walk, Professor?"

"Ja, ja. But what should I call you?"

"Bob, if you don't mind."

Flowers were in bloom outside the house, which was a rustic structure. It looked as if, from time to time, new parts had been added on. It was quite large—and no wonder, considering that those recording—or whatever—rooms were gargantuan. Except for the path, tall trees grew everywhere, and though it was midday I couldn't see the road. As we circled the house I observed a huge generator, a high antenna, a water tank, and, nearer now, the houses out among the trees. Wires ran from the generator to each house.

"Did you build all of these?"

"No. This was an Army camp during the war—World War II, of course. I mean, not what you would consider to be a camp. There were many in the area, but this one was a planning center, of sorts. Quite secret work—coding and decoding. I was a lieutenant assigned here."

"When did you come to America?"

"As I told you last night, I studied more than the piano. When I grew sick of the stupidity of my musical contemporaries, I turned to electrical engineering. Then Hitler came into power, and my father sent me over here to finish my studies. When the war began, I volunteered for military service and spent two years right here. When the war was over, I had no inclination to take a job. So much killing, including my family in Germany . . . I just moved from place to place, and even gave piano lessons. I went again to concerts, but the old frustrations flamed up. My fingers, however, had passed their prime. As a player I could do nothing important any longer. Yet I felt I had to do *something;* music really is my life. A lack of music was my greatest suffering during the war. You know how it is in America when you are far from any big cities: nothing but country music and bebop in those days, now rock and Nashville. I hope that is not what you play?"

"Oh no, sir. Progressive jazz. I've written some."

"Ah! But you did say that you studied at Curtis? You must be different."

THE WORLD OF MUSIC ACCORDING TO STARKER

"Professor." I was breathing a bit more heavily. "Jazz is a far more disciplined form of musical expression than most people think."

"You must tell me about it. I have to admit my knowledge is vague."

"I'll be glad to. But will you tell me first why you are here now?"

" 'Now,' Bob, means almost twenty-five years." It was funny to hear him speak my name; it sounded more like the German *Bub,* boy, than Bob. "My father, to my surprise, had managed to transfer a substantial amount of money into Switzerland during the war, and this I inherited. I found myself without the need to work for a living. I invested the money with the help of a friend and am better than comfortable. In 1948 long-playing records and tape recorders appeared. I began to collect them furiously, but the more I acquired the more sick I became. Never had I heard so much junk—yes, *junk* is the word—played so badly, by people who bought tape recorders and taped their performances in their basements. All this they dumped on the public!"

"But why did you buy them? In any field, the goal of most people is a fast buck. In those days, I imagine, there were so few records that anything seemed attractive to those who didn't know quality. They just wanted to collect a novelty."

"Of course I knew! But I wanted to find out what made them so bad. I collected so many records that my apartment became too small to hold them. At the same time, some Army comrades held a reunion, and one of them said, 'When everybody gets fed up with living in the city, they all want to go to the South Seas. But not me. If I had the money, I'd buy our old camp and retire there to write my big war novel.'

" 'Are you crazy?' I asked him. 'How can someone buy an Army camp?'

" 'Surplus,' he replied. 'Look, the place is abandoned, right? You could get it for peanuts. *If* you had the money to fix it up. And if you had the guts to live alone in a forest. Remember, the nearest town had only three hundred people. Movies were shown only on Fridays in the church basement.'

"A week later, I arrived here and bought the camp. Everyone thought me to be crazy—they do still, but this is their problem. Today, many people think differently of what I did, but that is another story."

"What do you mean, Professor?"

"Some other time," he replied in a manner that seemed to take for granted my staying on as a houseguest. And frankly, the more he spoke, the less I thought about the car or my vague vacation plans. I kept asking myself, what's the difference? I'm away from everything mundane and disturbing. Why not stay, if he lets me?

"Professor Trumpfl, I'm not sure how to say this . . ."

"You want to stay! My boy, let us have lunch. I have not talked so much for a very long time. I am hungry!"

"Lunch" was only its name; it was more like dinner. Professor Trumpfl still lived more like a German than an American, obviously. We had a potato soup—heavy, but tasty—then roast meat with more potatoes, and for dessert, noodles with poppy seeds and sugar. My season of hard work, just over, had cost me ten pounds, so that I could overlook a temporary surfeit of starch. The old woman served, seeming only a degree less morose than previously. Erika was her name, and she had worked for the professor's family when he attended high school in Germany. Through her, he found out about his father's bequest, and when he decided to settle in this place, he arranged for her emigration to the U.S. Although he communicated with her in a kind of sign language, she wasn't totally deaf. In one bombing raid, a detonation nearby had damaged some auditory nerves, and these were further deteriorating with age. Lucky for her, the professor said, since she couldn't abide classical music. The hearing loss kept her from being annoyed by his constant playing of records. This last comment gave me an opening for a question I'd almost choked on during lunch. "Tell me, please, Professor, why do you need several record players, tape machines, and all the other equipment? To listen to and enjoy music, aren't one phonograph and tape player enough?"

He signaled Erika for coffee before answering. "I've told you already that I am not just a music lover. What you saw in those two rooms last night is a complex electronic system for measuring *everything* in music. Including style and emotion."

I spilled my coffee. "Sorry for my clumsiness, sir. But what you just said astounded me, to put it politely."

"Why?"

"Well . . . for one thing, you said how fed up you got with everyone's totally different responses to any piece of music. Total disagreement, you said. About tempi, expression, technique, intonation . . . How could *anyone* suppose that such a thing as style might be definitively measured? On many things we may agree, you and I. But taste? All of the arts are subject to taste—likes and dislikes. My God, I would sound idiotic if I tried to quote all the wrong-headed judgments of music in the last century alone. I'm sure you know all of them; I saw some of the books on your shelves—collections of articles that called Brahms an amateur, Wagner a nonentity, Beethoven an uninspired piano teacher!"

Trumpfl went "krk-krk-krk" in his nose. "Hold up, my boy. That's it exactly! That is how it was, and still is. But tomorrow? That will be another story. Today, man can go to the moon. Today we have machines. Come along and see what tomorrow may establish!"

I worked hard to stifle a cynical smile, saying to myself, so what if he's a nut? Laughter is relaxing, and he appears harmless. As we entered the larger studio, I noticed that a tape player was running, but we heard no sound.

"Professor, you left the tape running."

"On purpose. Look!"

In a corner, another machine was recording what looked like a seismograph or a cardiogram.

"What is that for?"

"One of the important tests. Time and coincidence." I must have looked stupid because the professor continued, "Let me explain. These machines evaluate intonation, volume, and dynamics. They separate sound from notes through a multichannel desynthesizer and slow down, as well as speed up, tempo."

I stayed with Professor Trumpfl for ten days, though they seemed only a few hours. I resented the nights; sleep wasted precious time and senselessly interrupted Professor Trumpfl's monologues. I seldom spoke, other than to ask occasional questions. There was no point in arguing; apart from the fact that almost everything he said was what I wanted to hear, he posed questions to himself and pointed out contradictions among many diverse views. He was at the same time teacher and student. He had pored over hundreds of books on subjects only remotely related to music and instruments. He explained in such detail the playing of strings and wind instruments that I felt I could almost play them with ease.

His rooms of electronic equipment eventually came to seem logical, not even dramatically inventive or novel. Often I had to remind myself that Professor Trumpfl had designed and built these machines himself, twenty-five years earlier, when few or none even imagined them. Today they are almost commonplace, and could surely be improved upon.

I confess that I'm not describing Professor Trumpfl's work in the same sequence he revealed it, sometimes rambling, always lecturing. I was so fascinated in the beginning that I quite forgot to take any notes, and when I finally realized that I should, I was afraid of antagonizing him. As I write these words, I feel myself obsessed with the professor's ideas. He was, beyond any doubt, a fanatical man. Perhaps my reason for trying to record all that he told me—not me, actually, but anyone who would listen—is a hope that I am now better able to evaluate his words than before, when I was under his actual spell—a spell so strong that only on rare occasions, while listening to one of the few truly great artists of our time, have I felt similarly mesmerized.

"Remember," he said, "that there are magnificent performers, who can charm and delight us in live performances. Yet when we hear these same performances on recordings or later on the radio, we are perplexed that they could have affected us so. We take notice of wrong notes, faulty intonation, imprecise rhythm, haphazard tempi, exaggerated dynamics, or wrong choices based on the composer's text. There is nothing inherently objectionable about the application of individual ideas to any composition, so long as these do not destroy the music's structure. Live performances affect us mainly because of an artist's communicative powers, but that never should happen at the expense of a musical composition as a work of art. The event versus the concert. This, however, is one of the most debatable areas in the aesthetics of music.

"We *can* agree on the main elements of music: melody, which is horizontal; harmony, which is vertical; and meter and rhythm. What seems to cause subjective dispute—the expressive content of music—I like to call the diagonal element. There is little need to tell you now that I was searching for a truth, in respect to music, which incorporates these

THE WORLD OF MUSIC ACCORDING TO STARKER

elements. I am not concerned with the music of today that clearly disregards these elements, although it fascinates me to hear a sophisticated mixture of percussive sounds, or sounds arrived at by electronic manipulations. I made such sounds with great pleasure in my childhood, using those old crystal-radio buttons. The Ondes Martenot was a precursor of today's electronic instruments, forty years ago. I am also fascinated by sound clusters based on mathematical formulas. Yet I must confess my pleasure here to be purely intellectual, in the sense that it makes me happy when a work reminds me of something I know already—a harmony learned as a variant of one of the tonal systems—or simply when I can be proud of knowing what someone else is attempting to do. I am, in other words, interested in studying only music that has traditional dimensions in art.

"My first obsessions focused on the recognizable and measurable elements in a particular performance. Not 'concept' or 'message,' but the very tiniest measurable details: intonation, obviously, correct notes, correct note-lengths, coincidences of notes, and therefore beats, rhythms, consistencies of tempo. I thought at first that measuring such things would be easy, only to encounter unbelievable difficulties. With intonation, for example, I found the problem of variable pitch in solo instruments as well as in orchestras. With note length I fell into the quicksand of evaluating dotted notes, the most complex of music-making problems. Coincidences of notes? Romantic pianists drove me to despair with their habit of playing chords ahead of melody lines, and then with their attempts to justify this mannerism on the ground of stylistic 'correctness.' With rhythm, I came up against theories beyond counting, such as the *gallant* style of the past—the disregard of bar-lines, the various idiosyncrasies regarding triplets and quintuplets . . . and on and on!

"At first I set modest goals; I checked only for intonation and correct notes. I transferred all of my records to tape, first the 78s and subsequently all the LPs. Then I listened to the music an octave lower. This was a revelation! I heard hundreds, literally hundreds, of wrong notes I had missed before. Faulty intonation, badly vibrated tone, such inexactness that it made me sick—sick at myself! *How* was it possible that I had heard none of this before? I returned to the correct speed and began

"MOZART METER"—A STORY

then to hear more distortions than before, but not as many as at the lower speed and lower pitch. I argued with myself that this system was ridiculous—what did it matter if I could not hear the mistakes at the proper speed? Nobody else could hear them either. All the same, I continued with my listening, both ways.

"After a few weeks, I found myself hearing all the dirt in performances, just as if they had been slowed down! I had developed my ear to an acuteness missing before. Maybe ten years later, I visited some recording studios, to observe the process itself. To my joy, I found there several good engineers in the control booth with hearing similarly developed. People who operate tape machines day and night can recognize discrepancies not heard by famous artists performing in front of the microphones. But I had to *prove* this!

"*That* is when I built my sound-note separator machine, which remains the most important basic testing tool I have today. The machine is connected to an oscillator-printer—you see it in the corner there. With this, I had a printed text documenting my findings, or rather, the machine's findings. In the early years, I made a tape of every individual sound made by every instrument. Every chord I constructed separately, from the sounds existing on those tapes. When I built my computer, I fed all of this data into it; then the process of testing became routine. Mind you, this I don't need myself; I can detect the very finest differences. But I insisted on checking my own accuracy, should there be any doubt, and still do so.

"You yourself must realize, of course, that the question of intonation is far more complex than any single-note accuracy. Tremendous amounts have been written about harmonic, or lyric or tendency, intonation, the varying pitches required in different harmonic structures. My own measurements incorporate the overtone series as well—in that box beside the separator—and with this I have established *qualitative* intonation as a criterion of sound production for different styles and types of music!"

At this point, I could not stifle the impulse to interrupt. "Professor, when you speak of an 'established criterion,' you imply that you have discovered such a thing."

"Oh no, my boy, not at all. I have discovered nothing. I have only

THE WORLD OF MUSIC ACCORDING TO STARKER

measured performances of the same music by great artists and found startling similarities, in spite of superficially different attitudes and details. Actually, this is the basis of all my experiments. You saw the machine on the left wall of the room? The largest one of them all? It is able to play five tapes of the same music simultaneously and print all five on the oscillator tape so that one can easily observe coincidences as well as differences. The version that represents, so to speak, a median is the one I feed into the computer, where it serves as a reference. By now, that computer must contain nearly the entire literature of music. This machine I call—jokingly, of course—*Musicus Maximus!*"

Here I asked the question that had bothered me throughout. Namely, that if such a library existed, why could not musicians be taught correctness and truth from the start, thus doing away with all the dirt?

There was a long silence before he answered.

"Do you remember how suspicious I was when you first came? Back in 1951, my place was under surveillance for weeks. When I finally realized this, I invited all the watchers in and showed them everything. Imagine, it was the CIA! They had suspected me of electronic spying for the Russians, but apologized and then left me alone. Some time later, the same thing occurred, but this time it was Russian undercover agents, trying to obtain what they believed was equipment for space research.

"Strangest of all, however, was just recently. First three Russians, and later on five Japanese, all came and offered me a fortune for *Musicus Maximus.* How they found out about it I can only guess—probably through CIA files. I tried explaining to them that the machine could not mass-produce Heifetzes, Bachhauses, or Reiners by the dozen. But they still will not believe me, and from time to time someone arrives either with big offers or with tiny cameras. I am certain that right now in Moscow and Tokyo there are groups working to duplicate my experiments. I wish them luck! I thought at first you were one of them. Mind you, most of my machines are everywhere in use today. My work is far easier now since the development of multichannel recording consoles. In the beginning, I myself had to rerecord everything with the separator in order to measure bass and treble registers. Today, it takes only one-fourth the time to get the same measurements. It also helps me hear

"MOZART METER"—A STORY

how stupidly some sound engineers destroy balances by monkeying with the multichannel controls. Some are obsessed by the idea of soloists, so they push up the levels on them beyond all reason. Think, it's as if Mozart meant decorative runs of sixteenth notes to be heard at the expense of a melody written maybe for oboe or violas. But this is just one of their sins."

This is why I didn't take notes, not wanting Trumpfl to think that I, too, had come there on some mission. Now I am trying to recall as much as possible, but the order threatens to be haphazard.

He went on to discuss beats, rhythm, and time. Regarding beats, he talked of consonants versus vowels, which represented the different durations of notes. This was his subject for days, to which he related all aspects of the voice, the derivations from it in instrumental playing, and the whole issue of legato playing. He described *k, d, b,* and *t* as hard consonants and *l, m, n,* and *r* as soft, while *j,* as it is pronounced in German, was the connecting consonant. At the end of notes, *m* and *n* were the pedal consonants.

He spoke lengthily of linguistic characteristics and their amusing carryover into music: for instance, how the Russians start with a "vowel" and delay the beat attacca, paralleling the pronunciation of their language. The pedaled *n,* excessively used by the French, reflects the nasality of French pronunciation. The strong first-beat accent by Hungarian musicians derives from their language, with its invariable emphasis on the first syllable of every word irrespective of length.

Above all else, by means of his oscillator, he showed me the consistent alternation of strong beats with weaker ones: how these formed units, constantly changing to prevent uniformity and the dullness deriving from uniformity; how long passages became virtuosic in sound when the strong accents which broke up the flow were eliminated. In the same demonstration, he showed how accents related to the inner notes supplied a motoric sense (as differentiated from a sense of rhythm, which was responsible only for the relative time-value of various note-lengths). He explained the need for unit consistency, which is inherent in all the movements of a true masterpiece and identifies the germinal idea underpinning an entire work. He played many tapes on which performances of the same work differed wildly. Then he put on the oscillator tape; mysteriously, the strong beats coincided! It was the inner notes that had the variety and individuality.

This led him to an explanation of agogic and its significance. I was unfamiliar with agogic, and had thought it to be a component of rubato. That was true, he stated, but agogic is rubato *within* a bar. Many musicians use rubato, however, as a free ticket to anarchy. He stressed that true rubato allows a freer emphasis on harmonic changes, melodic stresses, and emotional temperature within a phrase, yet never destroys the structure and balance of the phrase. Agogic is the same emphasis within a measure, yet never destroys the time-length of any measure. Almost limitless variations can be created within a measure (or within a bar) by lengthening, shortening, or stressing various notes. Some call for time variants, others for dynamic variants, but the structure must not suffer. When you lose time because of agogic, you have to make it up within the measure. When you lose time because of rubato, you have to make it up within the phrase. And this accounts for the coincidence of strong phrase-beats in otherwise startlingly different, but nonetheless equally valid, performances of the same music.

I asked why performances with radically different phrase beats were necessarily bad. He replied that a simple answer to such a complex question would be a sophistry, but he had deduced from his experiments that if someone consistently played bar-lines whose time span was either shorter or longer than the rest throughout, then the resulting performances could not be considered disciplined music making. Obviously, his machines measured discipline first and foremost. Just as obviously, music is one of the classic disciplines. It may expand to "free expression," but only within the boundaries of discipline created by composers. Never the reverse. Discipline relates most significantly to legato, which people speak of as either an unaccented note or a series of smoothly connected notes. Although this is partly true, legato is more comprehensively a musical concept wherein notes follow one another uninterruptedly—horizontally without dynamic change, upward with a continuous increase in dynamics, or downward with a continuous decrease in dynamics. These ascents and descents, which could be seen clearly on the professor's charts, represent the "diagonal" content of music, as he termed it.

"MOZART METER"—A STORY

These performance charts showed, even if I could not plainly hear, where a performer was preoccupied with climaxes in an excited, juvenile way—which was probably quite effective in a concert. People are flummoxed by loudness, by extremes of quietness, by violent speeds, and by excessive slowness. Small wonder that these extremes are the basic elements of popular music and the source of its appeal; we need only look at what goes on in rock music. The professor, however, expressed no qualms as long as these exaggerations were confined to popular music.

His overriding concern was to demonstrate that is was possible to measure right and wrong when music had been committed to tape, according to principles derived from the written texts of music—principles that most persons acknowledge, but interpret differently. He sought to show that masterpieces could be played without destroying the notes, phrases, and structures as written. While individual artists will vary their focus on the vertical, horizontal, or diagonal elements of a piece, basic principles nevertheless must be honored by all whose talent and responsibility oblige them to preserve artistic discipline.

I was instructed to watch the charts and listen to the tape, and I would see an infinity of variations in note lengths and dottings, staccati, marcati, spiccati, pauses, stresses, accents, along with sforzandi, forte-pianos, double and triple fortes and pianos. I explored the timing variations, positive and negative sounds, unit changes, and so much more! All fell within the expressive range from marvelous to superb, exciting, good, acceptable, passable, and finally to dull. What was inexact, haphazard, exhibitionistic, and undisciplined showed up clearly for the very first time. It took Professor Trumpfl hours and hours to explain to me all these details, with much pointing out of examples on tapes and charts and many references to the *Musicus Maximus* tapes. I worked hard to retain it all, and as the days sped by, my ears responded. I was able to detect all that he was elucidating.

I could not keep from questioning him during breathers about problems that had troubled me over the years, although they bore little direct connection to his research. For example, how important was memorization to performance? His reply startled me, especially when he played several recordings performed by artists from memory. "No one can really play a piece well unless he knows it by heart. However, the treatment of solo lines tends to linearity, without differentiation, when the end in mind is instrumental perfection. It tends to messiness when motivated only by emotion, and inexactness when the approach is properly multilineal. Using printed music in performances helps to control an excess of tension, and encourages better ensemble playing."

I asked whether performers were consistent in their use of the three elements—horizontal, vertical, and diagonal. "Absolutely not!" was his answer. He played recordings of the same work by the same artist at different times. The differences were audible and startling, demonstrating that the artist concentrated on different aspects of music making at various stages in life. Professor Trumpfl was particularly amused by demonstrating how a player's physical qualities—thin or fat, tall or small, male or female—could be ascertained by the sound they created. He accurately described musicians I knew, but whom he had never seen either in pictures or in person.

Too soon, the day arrived when my vacation was almost over and I had to return to reality, to work and my obligations. I drank my coffee in silence that morning, feeling as I had the day I left home to embark on my independent life. The professor sat opposite, deep in thought. To his left on the table was a small package, neatly wrapped in white paper. I looked up slowly after a time.

"Professor, why are you doing all of this? What do you intend to do with it?"

He seemed startled. "My boy, why have you stayed here almost two weeks rather than going to fish, swim, and climb mountains as you planned?"

"Because I love music more than anything else in life."

"So. You gave my answer yourself. Music is my life; knowledge is very important, but secondary. Together, the two mean everything to me. I have no illusions that people will believe I have answers to most of the mysteries in music. Actually, there are no mysteries. Everything in an unforgettable performance can be defined in terms of time, sound, and dynamics. The mystery, if any, is why some persons can hear and others don't; why someone thinks this way or that; why one person has me-

"MOZART METER"—A STORY

lodic, harmonic, and rhythmic abilities and the further ability to synchronize them, while another person is lacking in some or all. Not what human beings do, but why, is the only mystery.

"More than anything, I wanted to know what in music was bad; I forever keep wondering about the good and the beautiful. Music has come a long way, and so has science. I applied a bit of science to prove something that most people will nonetheless judge subjectively. I know the inconsistencies of my findings, as well as the indisputable truths. I am an artist, too; God forbid that I should become totally objective. I have taste and will try to develop it further, as long as I live. Whoever does the same, I respect him unconditionally."

Then he handed me the package. "For you, Bob." Inside was a study score of Mozart's *Jupiter* Symphony with an inscription by the professor: "The world without music is man without a soul."

We walked to my car, and I got in and started the motor. Professor Trumpfl waved, then turned, and with his head down, his turned-in right foot pushing ahead, he walked back toward the house. I looked at the number on the mailbox—5553—and whistled aloud the theme of Beethoven's Fifth Symphony.

CHICAGO, ILLINOIS, 1958/BLOOMINGTON, INDIANA, 1974

5   FRANCE

While recalling the past, and while reading biographies and autobiographies, I often find grey areas: flat statements of I went, we saw, we did, and so on. I can never help wondering, where did the money come from for train tickets, hotels, and food? Sure, most of the great musicians had musician parents and many had sponsors: princesses, presidents, governments, businesses, millionaires, and eventually billionaires. I had only my parents and Eva's, my father toiling again to make a living after the war and my mother saving a nickel out of every dime Father earned. Among the grey areas in my story are how we started our life in Paris, how we got permission to stay when we held only transit visas, and how we paid for a hotel. But we did. Probably we managed with the occasional money we received from our parents.

A fairly large group of Hungarian friends arrived in Paris at the same time we did. We all lived in the same area, commiserated together, and had some fun. Some of us were fairly well off, and some were struggling to survive. One day one of us, Francis Akos, reported that Alfred Indig, the original second violinist of the famed Budapest Quartet, now lived in Cannes. He was planning to form a quartet with himself as first violin. He knew all about managing a group, and could arrange for a hundred concerts in Germany. Akos could be second violin and I the cellist, and we had in our group another Hungarian, the violist Ìstvan Deak, who was somewhat older than the rest of us and had spent the war in France. His wife was something of a cellist; I had occasionally taught her in Budapest. We asked him for advice, and he said that we should go to Cannes, rehearse for a while, and then start playing all the concerts Indig could schedule. Indig suggested that we stay in the Hotel Meurice, where he had lived during the war. It was cheap, $10 a month for a room. We decided to go, not only Akos, Deak, and I with our wives, but also a couple who were good friends of ours, Paul Deri and his wife. Paul was from Szeged, where he had been a member of the Szeged concert series, Youth and Art, from 1941 to 1943. He wanted to be a singer. Thanks to his parents, he was the wealthiest of our group. His wife and he merit special mention, and I will pause in my own story to tell theirs.

Paul had had singing lessons in Budapest, and in 1941, when he was twenty, he was the envy of the rest of us because he had a car. His singing didn't get him anywhere, but he was a sweet guy, much loved. He survived the camps, married, and left Hungary without any plans. His wife, Zsuzsi, was a dancer as a kid. Around 1935 her father, a wheeler-dealer, was sitting one day on a bench in a public park when a little Gypsy kid, around six years old, faced him with fiddle in hand and played a tune. As the story was told, the boy wore nothing but a tie around his neck. Instead of giving him money, Zsuzsi's father took him home, bathed and fed him, and clothed him. Then he took the boy to his parents, who lived in the outskirts of the city in a hovel. He gave them some money, and they agreed that he could keep the boy. Searching among the Gypsies, Zsuzsi's father located twenty-three more musically talented kids; the oldest was around sixteen and played the cimbalom. Zsuzsi's father hired a teacher, who worked with them daily for several months. Then arrangements were made, a hall hired, and the famed Rajko (Gypsy kids) Orchestra was launched. Tours all over Europe followed, and the orchestra's adoring fans launched some escapades that match those of rock-and-rollers. Zsuzsi, who was about eleven then, occasionally danced with the orchestra's accompaniment. Living with those kids, she learned the wide repertory of curses for which the

Hungarian language is famous, and she often managed to shock the more inhibited around her.

When the war started, the Gypsy musicians, by then almost all grown, disappeared. Zsuzsi spent the war in Hungary. Afterward, in Paris, she rediscovered several of the former Rajkos, who were plying their trade all over town in top-notch nightclubs and restaurants. Some of them became lifelong friends of mine. Zsuzsi's repertory of curses did cause occasional troubles. For example, once in a movie house she did not appreciate the action and began swearing. Someone reminded her loudly that there were people in Paris who spoke Hungarian!

Paul Deri eventually became an excellent sound recording technician in Italy. He and Zsuzsi were divorced around 1956, and she remained in Hungary, where she was friends with my parents. They gave her their furniture when they left Hungary. Eventually she was convicted of selling passports with the help of a high functionary. She disappeared into Communist prisons and very likely died.

We were all installed in the Hotel Meurice: eight Hungarians, Akos's Austrian wife, and Indig's Dutch wife, whose family inheritance allowed them a modest income throughout the war and after. Indig augmented this income by spending an hour a day in the casino, for which he had devised a system which brought him slight winnings. Our first meeting was like that of long-lost friends reuniting. Indig was a sweet, lovely man. All of the quartet members were students of Leo Weiner, a bond that tied together 95 percent of all Hungarian musicians as if they were Freemasons. Indig owned a large collection of quartet music and proposed a starting program. We all knew the standard pieces—except for a Milhaud work he loved, which we were unfamiliar with—and agreed. We planned to rehearse in the largest room of those we were renting at three the next day. Why three? So Indig could go to the casino for his daily hour.

Here I must correct a serious omission in my recollections of my early youth. At fourteen, as I said, I stopped going to school, and a year later, when Schiffer retired, I left the Franz Liszt Academy. In spite of my busy schedule as a teacher, soloist, and ensemble player, I found myself with lots of free time. I was not a great one for practicing, usually doing so for only two hours a day. Playing poker, bridge, and blackjack with my former schoolmates (some still in school, some learning various trades) became one of my favorite ways to spend time—sometimes too much time. Gambling had a strong draw for me until I left the orchestral ranks in 1958.

When Indig described his roulette system, I volunteered to accompany him to the casino. After watching him for a few minutes I risked a huge amount, the equivalent of almost seven U.S. dollars. In half an hour I found myself with $12. Then Indig signaled it was time to go; he had reached his goal.

We returned to the hotel. The quartet sat down and the rehearsal began. And we were silently appalled; Indig played badly, like a singer saving his voice. We managed to spend three hours reading through two quartets. He told us jokes, and at the end we returned to our respective rooms. Indig said, "See you tomorrow" and asked me if I was coming to the casino. I told him I would.

The three of us gathered in my room. We didn't know what to do. He was *bad*. We wondered if he was just testing us; after all, he had toured the world with the Budapest Quartet. Then the others asked me what had happened in the casino. I told them, and they all asked me to play for them as well, giving me money.

The next day was the same story. In a half hour in the casino I won for the four of us, and Indig won as well. The rehearsal started on time, and Indig continued his substandard playing. I wanted to give my pals their share of the winnings, but they said no, just go on with it. So I kept the money in my pocket and felt rich.

We went on like this for four days, feeling that whatever happened we were getting rich, sort of. Indig sounded bad, but Cannes was a beautiful town. It was warm in November, and we enjoyed the sun, the sea, and the palm trees. But on the fifth day both Indig and I quickly lost the day's allocated betting money. We were supposed to leave and go rehearse. Instead we looked at each other and said, let's just pretend it's the next day. In short, in the next two hours we lost the four days' winnings and the original investments. We returned to rehearse with our dreams of riches gone belly-up.

We continued to rehearse into January 1947, when Indig managed to arrange a concert in a lovely church. We thought now he would play as

THE WORLD OF MUSIC ACCORDING TO STARKER

well as a member of a great quartet should. Sadly, his playing remained what it was at the first rehearsal. We woke up and realized that there might be a hundred concerts in Germany, but not for us.

The quartet was hopeless, and gambling had also failed us. Our finances reached their nadir, and we didn't have enough to buy food. One day Eva's legs gave out and she collapsed. What was wrong? Only that we hadn't eaten for three days. Another time, we pooled our resources with the Deris and bought one baguette and one can of food, which we split four ways. We had no idea what was in the can, some fish, but it was delicious and almost filled our stomachs. Then Deak, whose French was far more developed than ours, came to visit. We asked him to read the label on the can, and he said it was squid. Our acquaintance with squid derived only from seeing them on the seashore, being sold in their natural state: a rather unpleasant sight, though these days I am fond of fried calamari. Eva and Zsuzsi ran to the bathroom and got rid of it immediately.

During this messy stretch we developed a correspondence with Emil Tauszig and his wife, who was the sister of our friend Mrs. Naschitz in Temesvar. Both of them were originally from Temesvar as well, but had lived in France since the mid-thirties and were now in Limoges. He was a textile chemist and had been part of the Resistance. After the war he established a small firm preparing chemicals for textile factories. He was brilliant, winning regional chess championships and publishing chemistry journals; he also loved music. Eventually he became president of the Limoges Concert Society, and wrote concert reviews and philosophical treatises.

During the war the Tauszigs desperately tried to get news of their families. Finally they received a long letter from the Naschitz family. Obviously several earlier letters had been lost, because this one spoke eloquently about two Hungarian musicians, Gyorgy Sebok and Janos Starker, and not about the family matters they were anxious to hear. However, in a convoluted way, they established contact with Eva and me, and then with the Seboks, and invited us to visit them.

As the quartet's life was over and there was nothing to keep us there, we took the train from Cannes to Limoges. We hit it off with the Tauszigs right away. They asked me to play for a small group of people,

IN DEFENSE OF DILETTANTISM

For one whose greatest pride has been becoming an acknowledged professional in an area of artistic endeavor, the inescapable charge of dilettantism when dabbling in other creative milieus is sobering.

Professionalism: "Characterized by or conforming to the technical or ethical standards of a profession or an occupation . . . Manifesting fine artistry or workmanship based on sound knowledge and conscientiousness." These are two of the dictionary definitions; there are others. Exposure to many people whose creative or recreative work defies classification has brought me reluctantly to the conclusion that consistency is the only real definition of professionalism.

To avoid any misunderstanding, let me make clear that the professional and the dilettante are both paid for their services, unlike the amateur. But the dilettante's knowledge and conscience do not measure up to those of a professional. And the consciences and knowledge even of professionals (or supposed professionals) are often either unmeasurable or distorted by subjective considerations.

The musical community is heavily populated with celebrities whose output fails to meet the definition of professionalism, although they manage on occasion to produce a work, or performance, that awes listeners or reviewers. Their basic gifts, drive, and charisma, and current fads, account for much of their notoriety; but their lack of consistency demotes them to the status of highly gifted dilettantes. Many painters, sculptors, and composers whose originality earns them accolades also lack the basic skills necessary for them to be classified as professionals in their respective artistic communities. And this is so at a time when certifiable professionals are depicted derogatorily as thoroughly skilled and schooled but mechanistic and inartistic. Granted that professionalism in performance without the elements of artistry, imagination, and charisma is sterile, and that predictability, which is banal, replaces inevitability, which is creative.

The problem is not that dilettantism is illegitimate, but that its practitioners have pretensions of professionalism.

Reading both the classics and the contemporaries, I am filled with awe at the virtuosic manipulation of language, the construction and color of phrasing. I cannot hope to match that skill. Nevertheless, the joy of expressing my thoughts, of relating my life—even with minimal means and a technique that is often faulty and "out of tune"—helps me overcome the fear of being a dilettante, the while humbly accepting that satisfying classification.

BLOOMINGTON, INDIANA, 1980

and introduced me to the director of the town's conservatory. I felt that the Vienna fog had lifted. I was back as a performer. When Eva and I returned to Cannes to wrap up our affairs there, my old buddy Gyorgy Sebok and his wife came down to Limoges from Paris, where they had been among the large contingent of Hungarians in that city. They fared even better, also becoming great friends with the Tauszigs, who loved Sebok's piano playing. Someone proposed that we play a house concert in the mansion of the Haviland family, the porcelain makers, in a few weeks. We were paid with the proceeds from ticket sales, an expedient that was repeated with some frequency.

In the meantime we returned to Paris and found a hotel called Etna. We had a seventh-floor walk-up room with access to the roof. It turned out that we led a Hungarian invasion. The Deris came with us from Cannes. The Seboks joined us as well, and Livia Rev, one of the first pianists I ever played with in Budapest, moved in. Another cellist, Janos Liebner, who later became famous as a gamba player, took a room. Gradually a club atmosphere evolved, with other Hungarians showing up for visits: violinists, cellists, pianists. On occasion, though rarely, we even had non-Hungarians. We managed to convince the police to issue us residence permits, which had to be renewed every month. This was a hurdle I was very familiar with. Eventually we received a six-month permit, and also our Hungarian passport was stamped for a six-month extension of validity. Many of our colleagues were waiting for South American visas, and from time to time someone left for Venezuela, Chile, Brazil, or another such country.

One cellist, George Bekefi, became an important part of my life. We had spent time with him in Geneva, before he had gone to Paris with his cousin. On our return to Paris, he came to me and asked for help. His nerves were shot and he was unable to play. We had several sessions weekly. I wrote out exercises for him, left hand and right hand. He built up his strength and confidence, practicing like a fiend for four months. At the end of that time, his fiancée arrived from Budapest and he got married, played a small recital in Paris, received accolades, and left for Brazil, where he was immediately offered a post as principal cello. A few years later he came to the U.S., started teaching, and took the seat behind me in the Chicago Symphony.

Through the grapevine the news spread that I was a string specialist. Adolphe Mandeau, a Swiss violinist who was concertmaster of the Lausanne Chamber Orchestra, visited several times to work with me, sometimes bringing another Swiss violinist from his orchestra. They paid me in cigarettes, booze, chocolates, food, and nylon stockings that I could give to Eva or sell. Mandeau later became concertmaster of the Stuttgart Chamber Orchestra, then of the Düsseldorf Symphony Orchestra, and professor of the Volkwang Hochschule in Essen, where I eventually taught as a guest professor. We are still friends today. The other Swiss violinist, Anne-Marie Grunder, remained with the Lausanne Orchestra, teaching and performing as a soloist and chamber musician, and playing in festival orchestras.

On one of my visits to Limoges I was taken to a Jeunesse Musicale concert. The conservatory director was conducting and Paul Tortelier was the soloist. He played the Lalo Concerto admirably, as well as Paganini's "Moto Perpetuo." The children in the audience were told by the emcee that playing the piece was as difficult as climbing the Eiffel tower twice. When Tortelier finished, the kids cheered and applauded wildly. At the end of the concert we were introduced and the conductor insisted that Tortelier hear my playing of the Kodály Solo Sonata. As the concert was a matinée, we had dinner and he came to the Tauszigs' place, where I played it for him. He did not know the piece, and seemed nonplussed. My recollection of what happened next is hazy. Two weeks later in Paris, however, he introduced me to Pierre Fournier, and he must have spoken to many other people about me, as I was invited to play on the radio. In short, in my memory, he was responsible for my introduction to Paris.

Among our friends at the Etna was a Hungarian journalist, Andre Böröcz, who was working for Radio France's Hungarian news program. He also invited me to play and be interviewed on his show. Böröcz wanted to become a manager, and began by working on behalf of his pal Arthur Garami, an old colleague of mine from Budapest. He succeeded in getting him engagements, and went on to manage the Stuttgart Chamber Orchestra and found the Menton Festival, the Baalbeck Festival, and many others. He also started and ran musical cruises on the Mediterranean and Caribbean. These were the forerunners of all theme cruises.

Garami had been a star pupil of Geza de Kresz at the Franz Liszt Academy, along with Robert Gerle, who was also part of the Etna clique. Garami became concertmaster of the McGill Chamber Orchestra and then assistant concertmaster of the Montreal Symphony Orchestra, and taught at McGill University and the Conservatoire de musique du Quebec à Montreal. He died tragically in 1979: he killed himself. Gerle is one of the few of the Etna clan still alive. He toured the world as a soloist and conductor and taught at the University of Maryland and the Catholic University of America in Washington, D.C., as well as writing books on violin playing. Unfortunately, he now has an advanced case of Parkinson's disease.

In 1947 our friend Charles Bruck, who had conducted the failed recording by the winner of the Geneva Competition, was hired to conduct music for a film, and this led to the only time I have ever been paid to hold, not play, a cello. The film had some scenes in a restaurant where a Gypsy orchestra was playing. The music was recorded. In order to earn some money, Bruck signed up as an extra, and as what else but a Gypsy cellist! He borrowed my cello every morning, and for eight hours a day he sat, wearing a false moustache and a wig, pretending to play. In the evenings he brought the cello back. One evening he told me he had a conducting job the next day, but if he didn't show up at the film studio he would lose his job as an extra. So he asked me to stand, or rather sit, in for him, and I would get the money for the day. The only thing was that I shouldn't play, or even tell anybody that I could. So for eight hours I listened to the music and imitated cello playing. It was tough, but we needed the money, and it provided the gang with material with which to tease me. The next day Bruck went back to faking the cello himself. (A remake of this film was in production in 2003.)

The summer heat in Paris was oppressive, and there was nothing to do until September. Eva and I, together with the Deris and the Seboks, decided to go home to Budapest for a few weeks. It was lovely to see our parents. The political situation in Hungary, however, was a mess. The Communists had succeeded in stopping the devastating inflation and had introduced a new currency, the forint. But the ruling party was split into several groups in an internecine war.

Before we left Paris I had received several invitations to perform in Hungary, but while we were there, they were withdrawn. I only found out on the day we left that my appearances had been canceled because of remarks I had made in an interview in Budapest, speaking admiringly about Dohnányi. He was persona non grata to the increasingly Communist-dominated cultural organizations (something like unions), although by then he had been cleared by the Allied forces.

According to the law, we had had to turn in our passports at the Hungarian border. When it was time to leave, I had to run from office to office until I finally regained them. We boarded the train one day after elections in which the Communists gained control with 18 percent of the vote. Luckily, we were on our way back to Paris. The Deris and the Seboks stayed in Budapest until after the '56 revolution.

The second phase of our Paris life began. The Etna, where we had stayed before with the others, was on a quiet street near the Opera, but now we were alone in a less classy part of town, in the Kronstadt Hotel. The street was rather noisy and less than clean, lined with shops and eateries. We installed a hot plate, which was against the rules. There were no electric outlets so we had to take out a light bulb, screw in an adapter we had bought, and plug the hot plate into it. The hot plate often caused blackouts on our floor, and once the whole street went dark. After quickly hiding the evidence, we went out innocently for a stroll. By now we had learned to cook a few dishes. The specialité de la maison was layered potatoes: potatoes, eggs, and when we were flush, some sausages. It was cheap, filling, and tasty, often luring in friendly visitors to share the bounty. Before the Communists shut down the borders, Hungarians often stopped in on their way to wherever. Some stayed in our hotel while waiting for a visa or a boat. Otherwise, life went on as it does for any struggling artist, with occasional concerts and here and there some teaching. We made some trips to Limoges, and stayed slightly above water financially.

The next year arrived, but we were not sure what we were working toward. Victor Aitay was now in the Pittsburgh Symphony Orchestra with Fritz Reiner, and he wrote that Reiner would like to have me there as solo cellist. However, he couldn't do anything to help me get a visa. George Lang wrote that his uncle, a newspaperman temporarily turned impresario, would engage me for concerts. Nothing came of the offer, but the man reached some heights by managing a Hungarian tenor named Miklos Gafni. Gafni had an incredibly beautiful voice, a cross between Gigli and Caruso, the two greatest tenors of the past. When he came to Budapest from his home in northeast Hungary, with a few songs and popular arias in his repertoire, people went bananas over him. He had some vocal instruction, but because he was a Jew his opportunities were limited. He was sent to a labor camp during the war, where his singing talent helped save his life; he told the story of his survival in the short film *A Voice Is Born* (1947). He debuted at Carnegie Hall in 1947, and his great success there led to both nationwide and foreign tours. Because of his limited training and vocal range his success petered out, though at one point he was under contract to star in *The Great Caruso* (1951), the film that made Mario Lanza famous. He went on to build a successful paté business, and died in 1981 when he collapsed in Grand Central Station. He was a lovely man, generous to a fault, and a dear friend.

Andre Mertens, vice president of Columbia Concerts, looked me up in Paris. He offered to sign me up, saying that he would do the best he could for me but making no guarantees. I told him I had to think about it. (Forty-five years later I joined Columbia Artists for three years, and left in a hurry. Mertens had died years before.) I did, however, sign a contract with Pacific Records, which became interested in me as a result of my appearance on Böröcz's radio program. Until then my only experience with recordings had been a record I made for my mother in 1942. There was a business in Budapest called It's Your Voice, Take It Home, which would record something for a small fee, and I played two little tunes. Now I was led into a professional studio, with a microphone and machinery in a control booth. There were no tape machines as yet, only wax 78 R.P.M. discs, each of which could record about four minutes. With the Hungarian pianist George Szolchanyi, I recorded Manuel de Falla's *Seven Spanish Popular Songs,* then Paul Hindemith's Sonata op. 11. These recordings, to my knowledge, were never published, but I did receive some money for them. Then came the dramatic suggestion to record Kodály's Solo Sonata, op. 8, my big showpiece. The recording took only one day and filled four discs (eight sides), even after I had made two cuts to save time. When I listened to it, I noticed that the last side had an electronic hum and some vibration. I called attention to it and offered to rerecord that last four minutes, but Pacific balked. The recording was rushed into production and entered into competition for the Grand Prix du Disque, where it won first prize. Rave reviews appeared, but they also mentioned the noise on the last side. Eventually the company approached me to rerecord it. But this time I asked for payment, and the matter remained unresolved.

In the spring of 1948 Zoltán Kodály, on his way back from giving a lecture in the U.S., stopped in Paris. He was honored by the Hungarian ambassador, the Hungarian Institute, and many other groups, and wherever he went I was asked to be there and play at least part of the sonata. My acquaintance with Kodály was minimal. As a student I had twice attended his folklore class at the Academy. In 1939, when I started learning the sonata, my teacher asked Kodály to hear me. I played the first movement. Kodály asked if I planned to perform it, and my teacher said it was scheduled for a June 1 concert. It was then the end of April. Kodály only said good night. After the concert, while I was still responding to the ovation, Kodály was the first to speak to me. "First movement, too fast. Second, O.K. Third, don't separate too much the variations. Good night." I hadn't noticed as yet that they *were* variations. Now in Paris he basked in the usual celebrations, and the fact that a recording of his work, which until then had been obscure, received the prize was an extra bonus.

But the main event of that spring was meeting Antal Doráti. I knew little of him, but had met his violinist father, a friend of my teacher Schiffer, back in Budapest. Doráti had returned to Hungary for his first visit after the war to conduct. He was then music director of the Dallas Symphony. For his next season, starting in October, he needed a principal cellist. In Budapest he heard that the opera's first cellist was on a leave of absence, and when he found out that I was in Paris, he stopped over to see and hear me. Half an hour later he offered me the job. I told him about Reiner's invitation to join the Pittsburgh Symphony Orchestra, if I could somehow get a visa. Doráti said he would see what he could do and I would hear from him.

The terms he proposed were overwhelming, considering the situation I was in: a twenty-four-week season, during which I would be paid $150 per week, plus extra for recordings and solo appearances. In Paris we were scratching out a living on $10 or less a week. Musical life in the States was rather different in those days. The major orchestras had seasons of around twenty-eight weeks, and a few of them had a short summer season as well. In addition, the music directors had total control of hiring and firing. As I said goodbye to Doráti I was on cloud nine.

Early that year, my two faithful Swiss violin students had arranged some small concerts for me in Lausanne and Zurich. It took six weeks to obtain a Swiss visa, and I was only trying to spend a week in a country six hours away by train. And I was not happy with my status in France. I had finally obtained a permit to stay in the country as a resident alien, just as in my childhood in Hungary, but even friends who had lived in France for fifteen years could not become citizens. Because of this, I decided that, instead of pursuing some concert offers in South America, I would grab any chance I had to settle somewhere and become a citizen. So when Doráti turned up, I was determined that once in America I would work until I became a citizen, and then try to pursue my original plan of becoming a soloist.

Our lives in the months that followed resembled the script of Menotti's opera *The Consul*. The paper chase dominated our existence. American immigrant visas were allotted on a quota system, and one could spend years on a waiting list. Those whose professions were in demand, such as college teachers, could get priority, but not symphony musicians. Doráti had a friend, Wilfred Bain, who had been the chairman of the music department at North Texas State College. Bain's choir often sang with the Dallas Symphony. In 1947 Bain became dean of the Indiana University School of Music in Bloomington. Doráti told him about his dilemma, that he had to find a way to get me to Dallas by October. Bain in turn explained the situation to Indiana University's president, Herman B Wells. Wells agreed to appoint me as a lecturer in music. This made me eligible for a U.S. visa, though the application process was rather lengthy and cumbersome. Doráti, again passing through Paris, called up Gregor Piatigorsky, who also happened to be in the city, to ask whether he could speed up the process through his wife's relatives, the Rothschilds. One of them worked in the U.S. embassy in London. Doráti took me to the Rothschild Palace in Paris to meet Piatigorsky, whom we later came to call Grisha. I was not only impressed by both the place and him, but also saw the greatest collection of Impressionist paintings anywhere, with the exception of the Paris museums. Grisha tried to help, but was unsuccessful. Years later he mentioned that he had thought of bringing me to be his assistant at the Curtis Institute, where he was teaching.

One vignette of that day has remained with me ever since. When Doráti expressed his astonishment at the collection of paintings, Piatigorsky said they weren't his. I decided that whatever I attained in my life would have to come through my own efforts. No one should ever give me anything. Later, I sometimes felt that I was stupidly proud, but I was unable to change. One other aspect of that visit, as well, was significant. Grisha showed us his new Strad cello, the Lord Aylesford, and asked me to play on it. A year later he returned it to the dealer, Emil Herrmann, and in 1950 Herrmann loaned it to me. I played it for fifteen years.

The paper chase developed a catch-22. I needed proof that I was already a teacher. That I obtained from Limoges. But I also needed a valid passport to get a visa stamped into it, and that was tricky. My passport had to be renewed in order for a visa to be put in it. But the Hungarian government was now Communist, and if the Hungarian embassy in Paris renewed my passport, the U.S. consul might assume I was one as well. I could not tell the Hungarians who had admired me since my winning of the Grand Prix du Disque that I planned to emigrate to the U.S., while to the Americans I had to stress the fact that the day after the Hungarian election I had fled back to Paris.

The summer heat was on. Most of my time was spent going from office to office. Eva decided to go see her parents once more. It was a risky business, but she insisted. Our marriage was getting rockier as time went on. The living conditions were not favorable for a peaceful union. By September the quest for permits seemed to be succeeding and the necessary documents started to arrive, but there was no way to make the season's opening unless I flew to the U.S. Two very dear friends loaned me enough money to buy airplane tickets. When Eva returned we agreed to separate. By now we both had U.S. visas. We decided that I would go alone and she would decide whether to come across later and make her own life there, or stay in Europe. I packed my one suitcase, wrapped my cello in a soft sack, and went to Orly Airport, where for the first time in my life I boarded an airplane. I changed from Air France to KLM in Amsterdam, and after two more stops I landed at Idlewild, now called Kennedy, in New York.

6 UNITED STATES OF AMERICA: DALLAS AND NEW YORK

Arriving in the U.S. on a KLM plane is rather different from arriving on, say, the Mayflower. From above you gaze at the Statue of Liberty, skyscrapers, and the immense spread of Manhattan. Since I had spent twenty-six hours in a DC6 and gone through a six-hour time change, I felt some dizziness. We landed safely, and after a slight delay the immigration officer stamped my passport. I crossed through a door and I was in America. Eva Aitay greeted me and an hour later the Badgastein clan reunited, with Victor and George Lang joining us. It was Saturday and the Dallas rehearsals began on Monday, which meant I had to take a flight to Texas Sunday evening. There is one memory stamped into my brain of that one day in New York. I was taken for a walk on Sunday. We stopped at a restaurant bar on Columbus Circle at Fifty-ninth Street. There were tables stacked with herrings, sardines, sausages, pickles, and all kinds of condiments. We bought a beer for a dime and all the food was free.

DALLAS

The evening flight landed me in Dallas at 4 A.M. My instructions were to take a taxi to the Stoneleigh Hotel. When I got to my huge room there, I saw no bed, and was confused until I discovered the Murphy bed in a wall closet. I fell exhausted into it. The next morning I discovered my first drugstore and with considerable difficulty I managed to order, in poor English, a ham sandwich and coffee for breakfast. Afterward, a young woman came to the hotel, Wilma Cozart, who was then Doráti's secretary and who much later became vice president of Mercury Records, in charge of its classical division. She explained that my presence in Dallas had to be secret, because of the rules of the musicians' union, until my status was confirmed. First she took me to the immigration office, where I obtained my so-called first papers, which entitled me to apply for citizenship after five years. With these papers in hand she took me to the union office, where, after paying the necessary dues, I was issued a membership card. Now the Symphony was able to hire me. The rehearsals had begun that morning, and Ms. Cozart said she would come for me the next day.

So my professional life in the U.S. began at roughly 10 A.M., sixty hours after my arrival in the country. Doráti introduced me to the orchestra. The acting principal cellist, Lev Aronson, ceremoniously offered me the principal chair and moved to one next to me. He became a lifelong friend and took the post again after that season, when I left Dallas. He was a Latvian and a superb cellist. I had heard him on the radio, before the war, from what was then Leningrad. The war left him with emotional scars and it took years for him to regain his self-assurance. Among his students were Lyn Harrell and Ralph Kirshbaum.

The orchestra was excellent, with members from all over the country. I was the only cellist with a Dallas union membership. Doráti, a real disciplinarian, produced high-level playing, and I was kept busy learning repertory I had never played before. That was when I realized how limited was my knowledge of not only the symphonic literature but also that of the cello. My total experience performing with an orchestra amounted to having played the Dvořák Concerto three times, Bloch's *Schelomo* once, the Beethoven Triple Concerto once, Boccherini's B-flat Concerto once, and the Haydn D Major Concerto twice, and I was already twenty-four years old. I had only performed in public two Bach suites, two Beethoven sonatas, one Brahms sonata, a couple of Baroque

Dallas Symphony members: in the middle, Esther Shure, and far right, Lev Aronson (1948–49)

With Antal Dorati

sonatas, and a few trios and quartets. I was glad that I had said no to Mr. Mertens.

An orchestra member helped me to rent a room in the house of an old lady, where I could use the kitchen. Communicating with her was a bit problematic, as she spoke a mixture of Texan, Brooklynese, and Yiddish. My greatest linguistic feat was achieved at my first visit to a grocery store. I asked, how much? The cashier was stunned. He looked at me and said, "Man, you must be from very far away. Are you from Boston?" I have seldom felt prouder.

The rehearsals continued. I made some friends and received my first paycheck. I went to a bank, established my first account, and managed to get a loan sufficient to send back the borrowed sum to Paris, to my great relief. The season opened. I was treated like an exotic creature and received many compliments. Week after week, great soloists showed up. William Kapell, the stunning pianist, played with us. Jascha Heifetz came, and meeting him reinforced my awe and my determination to approach instrumental playing like him. Menahem Pressler and I became close friends. He was the only soloist I spoke to, due to our mutual lack of English. We spoke German. The orchestra went on tour. This meant three weeks of bus trips all across Texas and Louisiana, playing in halls and gymnasiums and discovering an aspect of musical life, if you could call it that, with which I was unfamiliar: crying babies, talking audiences, minimal facilities, hamburgers, steaks, shrimp, and whiskey. My taste buds were going haywire.

I had been alone, under such circumstances, for months when news reached me that Eva was on her way to New York on a ship. I cabled and proposed that she come to Dallas and we try to restart our marriage. I rented a primitive, but adequate, little house, and five days later, at the end of November 1948, I picked her up at the airport.

My first solo appearance in the U.S. came in a few weeks. I played the Brahms Double Concerto with Rafael Druian, who was the concertmaster. Luckily, I had played it as a trio around 1943 in our house concerts in Budapest, so I was up to it. I was also asked to play for a local radio show—naturally they wanted Kodály—and my name got around. A few people asked me for lessons, including a very young man sitting on the last stand of the orchestra, Jules Eskin. He is still the highly admired principal cellist of the Boston Symphony Orchestra. Since, as I mentioned, I was among the few local union musicians, I was also asked to play gigs, a term I didn't understand at first. (Similarly, I was startled when a colleague described a Heifetz concert he had heard and said that he had done "a good job.") At my first gig, I had to play trombone and bass parts, whatever music was put on the stand. On top of this I had to dance a czardas with the Viennese lady of the house, in whose honor the party was given. The pay was good, though, especially when converted into the French francs I still thought in terms of.

We had January off, and then the second half of the season started. Eva and I visited a Dallas couple one afternoon, and in their house we saw a huge piece of furniture with a five-inch screen. That was our first introduction to television. In March it was announced that Doráti was leaving Dallas to take over the Minneapolis Symphony. He asked me if I wanted to go with him, to work a longer season for higher pay. I said yes and we shook hands on it, no contract necessary. The last concert was around the beginning of April. After it there were many warm goodbyes, and I took a train to New York. I had to live there for six months in order to be able to join the union there, which would allow me to take a job anywhere in the U.S. and Canada. While I looked for an apartment Eva would wait in Dallas, with the Chihuahua dog we had acquired on one orchestra trip to the Mexican border. Eva was about four months pregnant.

NEW YORK

George Lang and I ran around for three days, and finally found an apartment for Eva and me on West Eighty-ninth Street. Eva joined me shortly after and we settled in. The dog stayed in Texas. A few days later the Metropolitan Opera returned to New York after their national tour. Victor Aitay was by then a member and Fritz Reiner one of the chief conductors. Reiner sent a message that he would like to meet with me—and my cello, if possible.

When the day came, I was ushered into a rehearsal room by John Mundy, the orchestra's manager, who was also a cellist. To my surprise, there was another cellist waiting who had already played an audition. I

THE WORLD OF MUSIC ACCORDING TO STARKER

At the Met with Fritz Reiner (1950–51)

had only meant to get acquainted with Reiner, as I already had the Minneapolis job. I shook hands with him and played something, and then Mundy brought over a stand full of music. He kept opening page after page for me to play, music I had never seen: Wagner, Mozart, Strauss. But from childhood I had been trained to sight-read anything, and I had a good time doing it. When I was finished Reiner mumbled something complimentary, and Mundy said that he would tell me about the details. I asked, what details? I said that I already had a job with Doráti, and Reiner said that he would see about that. I didn't know then that the two were distantly related via Reiner's first marriage, and Doráti still called Reiner "Uncle Fritz." In any case, I was glad to have met Reiner.

The next morning the phone rang, and an icy-toned Doráti said, "I hear that you've signed on to the Met. You must help me get somebody instead of you." I was dumbfounded. I told him that I had done no such thing; I had only gone, at Reiner's request, to meet him. "Yes, but he told me that he must have you, and I should get someone else. I can't argue with him. So call me about a cellist," Doráti snapped, and slammed the phone down. I sat there not knowing what to do. The phone rang again, and John Mundy said, "It's all arranged. Come to see me to sign a contract."

Two days later I became the principal cellist of the Met, to start at the end of September. I found out eventually that it was the best-paying job in the country, even though the season was only twenty-nine weeks long. We would spend twenty-two weeks in the city and seven weeks on tour, giving seven or eight performances a week, of which I was to have one performance off. On Saturdays the Met played a live radio show, sponsored by Texaco, and there was extra pay for the broadcast and for rehearsals. John Mundy became a lifelong friend, and even helped me survive the long wait before the season started, finding me work and even loaning me money. The other cellist I met at the so-called audition was a man named Zirkin, a cousin of Rudolf Serkin. He had a teaching post in Turkey at the Ankara State Conservatory; amusingly, our quartet in Cannes had considered a job offer in Ankara. I called Doráti, and he signed up Zirkin.

The summer New York heat was on and we spent many evenings in air-conditioned movie theaters until they closed. The little fan in our basement apartment provided barely enough cooling to let us survive. On occasion we played duets with Zirkin, and now and then we socialized with George Lang. The Aitays were working in Chautauqua for the summer. I met a few musicians, including Lukas Foss and Jacob Lateiner, and played some sonatas with them. Then came the most important event in my life, the birth of my daughter, Gabrielle. Looking at her fifty-three years later still brings back the thrill I felt holding her tiny body in my arms.

A few weeks after Gabrielle's birth, I walked to Thirty-ninth Street and started rehearsals with the Met Opera. The man sitting next to me was Engelbert Röntgen, probably thirty years older than I, a relative of the discoverer of X rays and a nephew of the Dutch composer Röntgen. He had been solo cellist of the orchestra for decades, but had to relinquish the post after having a heart attack during George Szell's tenure in 1942–46. I was warned beforehand that he would make life miserable for anyone who took the post, so when I greeted him I said that I was new at this and that he knew much more than I. I assured him that I would follow all of his markings, unless I felt strongly about some, and I asked him if he would help me. He became a devoted colleague and friend for the four years I was there, and literally saved my life during the toughest stretch of my entire musical existence. I saw him last shortly before he passed away in Switzerland, after his retirement.

What was it like being in the Met orchestra? I wrote about it for the *Opera News* many years ago, in a piece called "My Nights at the Met." The work was hard, but the weeks on tour in places like Baltimore, Atlanta, Dallas, Houston, Memphis, Chicago, Minneapolis, and Washington, D.C. helped me become acquainted with the real U.S.A. I also visited Toronto and Montreal. We played extra performances, matinées, and overtimes. There were some weeks I worked forty-eight hours, like a miner.

Edward Johnson was the director in my first year, but I never met him. Then came Rudolf Bing. Bing and I both had thin faces and were mostly bald, and in his first year I was often mistaken for him by people who addressed me as "Mr. Bing." (In 1956, when *The King and I* was playing in movie theaters, some people whispered that I was Yul Brynner.) Reiner was sort of the chief conductor, but Alberto Erede, Fausto Cleva, Fritz Stiedry, and on occasion Bruno Walter also conducted, as well as others. Tibor Kozma was an assistant conductor, and Kurt Adler was the chorus master.

In early 1950 a Hungarian named William Avar came to see me. In Hungary he had worked in a bank. In America he became a record salesman, a distributor for Vox Records, whose owner was George Mendelssohn, another Hungarian. I met George in Budapest during my opera stint there in '46. He tried to sign up the opera, all the singers and me as well, and pay us in the devastatingly inflationary Hungarian currency. His plan failed. By the way, he is supposed to have been the first person to tell the famed story about Otto Klemperer. According to the legend, Klemperer was in Vienna with George Mendelssohn and wanted to buy one of his recordings of a Beethoven symphony. He asked the clerk for the one with Klemperer. The clerk said he was sorry, but

A SOFT PITCH FOR THE PIT

As a member in good standing (by virtue of paying my dues on time) of New York Local 802 of the American Federation of Musicians, I am regularly sent copies of their publication *Allegro*. In the last several issues, the union's director of public relations has written a series of rather amusing anecdotes, aimed at debunking certain incidents related in *5,000 Nights at the Opera*, Sir Rudolf Bing's celebrated memoir of the Met. Having read both the book and the rebuttals by its comic antagonist, I felt impelled to make my own journey down memory lane. I know the union scribe well, whose pen is mightier today than his horn used to be. I had always enjoyed his wit, warm personality, and huge heart open to anyone in need, and was therefore saddened to see how long-borne grudges can distort memories of the past.

I turned my mental clock back to 1949. As an immigrant youngster recently arrived in the U.S., I landed (after a short season in Dallas) in the solo cellist's chair at the Metropolitan Opera. Edward Johnson was then in his final season as general manager, with Frank St. Leger and Max Rudolf at his side. Fritz Reiner, Fritz Stiedry, Fausto Cleva, Wilfrid Pelletier, and others of lesser note wielded batons. From time to time Bruno Walter visited us.

Then came the *big* change: Bing succeeded Johnson. I stayed at the Met until 1953, and today, looking back after twenty-one years, my memories of the old house on Thirty-ninth Street are at odds with those of a number of my fellow employees. Musicians who were little known when they came to the opera built careers there. Musicians who arrived already famous left when their careers had passed their zenith. A handful of the stars of the past still can be heard there, shining on in the firmament of opera. Many more, however, are in heaven (or hell, depending upon whose dedicated fans you listen to). But *very* few, on the stage or in the pit, who left the Met more or less anonymously were smiled upon subsequently by fortune.

I am one of the exceptions, and look back on my years there with pride, satisfaction, and plenty of smiles. The "good old days" far outweighed the "rotten old days." Time has hazed over the unpleasantnesses, and brightened even more what were then amusing incidents. I am not surprised that my memories are chiefly of adventures in the pit and in rehearsal rooms.

Back then, the blessings of "democracy" had yet to visit orchestras; we were hired and fired mostly on merit. The Lib movements, Black and Women's, had yet to be heard from (although an occasional second harpist was female). Musicians dreamed of a few extra weeks of work, longer rehearsals (meaning, at the Met, extra pay), a few additional dollars *per diem* on the road, fewer *rencontres* with dictatorial batonists, and of course the humpty-dumpty fall of anyone in control over them—which is understandably human. Pit musicians had no voice in matters pertaining to the stage, the budget, the repertory, or the board of directors. When a marvelous horn player swore revenge against a conductor, he vowed, "That s.o.b. will never catch me playing a wrong note!" (And he kept his word the whole time I played there.)

THE WORLD OF MUSIC ACCORDING TO STARKER

I recall the woodwind player with circulatory problems who plugged a foot-warmer into his music stand light, which triggered an occasional short circuit. But darkness didn't bother two first violinists, former members of the Vienna Philharmonic and the Vienna State Opera; once while on tour in Cleveland, on a bet, they played an entire week—nine different operas—without opening their music. Not only did they not miss a single note, they gave cues *and* sang the text. In German, *natürlich*.

Indeed, tours were a font of hilarity—two special trains of uncaged, unmitigated adolescents, releasing the pent-up emotions of a supercharged New York season. Only discretion prevents me from recalling capers involving specific individuals—which is why, instead, I remember the famous *Fledermaus* in Baltimore, when J. Strauss Jr.'s music aroused a real bat that scared performers and audience witless. Little wonder that the rumor spread everywhere that it had been a publicity stunt.

Less well publicized *frissons* happened regularly in Rochester's Eastman Theatre, where each year the spring tour ended. At the same time the Teatro Colón of Buenos Aires began its long season, which required the services of a number of the Met's personnel, in particular our beloved prompter. Had destiny placed him within the audience's sight, rather than hiding him away in a cubbyhole, he would have been hailed as one of the true giants of music in our century. His ability to cue soloists and chorus, all the while giving words and pitches to everyone—in Italian, French, even some German, and now and then English (ferociously accented)—endeared him to all whose professional lives he rescued. But the performances in Rochester were denied his guidance, and as a result their level of artistry often rivaled that of a recital by Florence Foster Jenkins. Ah, touring!

But New York City also had its moments. On one night, boring beyond tolerance, a question made the rounds in the pit. What would you do with a million dollars? (And a million dollars was a lot more money then.) We cornered every Stradivarius and Amati in the world and built business empires in our dreams, before tiring of the game. The next day, though, one violinist piped up, "I would restore all the cuts in the Wagner repertory all over the world, and pay for the resulting overtime." To which he added, after a pause, "I would also leave something for my cats."

During one rehearsal of *Die Meistersinger,* a very young first horn player made a mistake—considered unforgivable by most conductors, but amounting to a capital crime in the mind of Reiner. Said the player, one of the few anonymities at the Met who graduated to international fame, "Sorry, Maestro, it's the first time I am playing *Die Meistersinger.*" Reiner, whose sense of humor regarding music was minimal, put down his glasses (everyone braced for an outburst) and sighed! "What I wouldn't give for the joy of hearing *Meistersinger* again for the first time . . . Let's go on."

Another (more atypical) rehearsal stays in mind, however, during which appreciation of the science of conducting plummeted. Onstage were the chorus and solo singers. The "maestro" interrupted the music with a vehement command that the singers watch his beat instead of turning their backs, and follow his tempi as Mozart expressly instructed. The chorus master entered from the wings and attempted, unsuccessfully, to signal Mozart's devoted servant. Finally the "maestro" turned to him and yelled, "Don't bother me! The chorus was all right." "Yes, Maestro, thank you . . . but we, uh, forgot to sing."

This same conductor's disdain for downbeats approached the status of legend. When one night he startled us with the most authoritative beat he had ever given, our only problem was that the music had come to a general pause. The silence was broken by a crashing timpani beat. The player, who'd only recently joined the orchestra, hadn't had time yet to understand the "maestro's" beats or their significance.

I also vividly remember the excuses I came up with for arriving late. The fifth time this happened, I was changing into my tuxedo while the overture played without me. Dear John Mundy, the personnel manager, interrupted my colorful fiction with, "Don't, Janos. I know how unpleasant it is for you to be late." More than two decades later, I can't recall ever again being late for any professional obligation. I also recall the night when my chair had been moved from its customary position and put smack in front of the conductor's podium, meaning that my back was to the stage. I was told why later: The conductor had had enough of my watching the ladies on stage instead of his hands.

In those years, we were remote from the mechanics and machinations of the opera and its directors. We had a grapevine—we knew who slept with whom, who would get what part in which opera, and why (or why not). Most of us, though, just played the best we could, fought for improved conditions, took our skills elsewhere if asked to leave, and seldom cried foul. We had our favorites and our nemeses, cheered and booed like others, and prayed for four of a kind in our ongoing poker games. But whatever our likes and dislikes, we rarely envied those in power. We knew what it meant to run the Met, to work with hundreds of people including an underpaid chorus, an abused ballet, overpaid stagehands, self-centered stars (perhaps justifiably so—their presence guaranteed sold-out houses), and innumerable other vexations.

Which is why, from the distance of those decades, I cannot help but wonder about those whose game it is to muckrake, and thereby tarnish or obscure the true and lasting achievements of Rudolf Bing's regime. Opera is *not* a democratic institution: the hand on the helm must be firm and decisive, or the ship will founder. For myself, I salute all those who ran (and run) such a fragile ship; and for my friends and soul-brothers in the pit I wish continued health, strength, and dedication to opera.

BLOOMINGTON, INDIANA, 1974

THE WORLD OF MUSIC ACCORDING TO STARKER

he only had it conducted by Bruno Walter, Toscanini, and a few others. Klemperer insisted that he had to have it, because he *was* Klemperer. And the clerk asked mockingly, "Of course, and the other gentleman is Beethoven?" "No," retorted Klemperer, "he is Mendelssohn." Eventually George altered his name to de Mendelssohn-Bartholdy and documented his collateral descent from Felix Mendelssohn.

In the late '40s, William Avar decided to jump the Vox ship. He established his own label, Period, and started to record. His ace in the hole was the Vox distribution list he took along. The LP era had just begun, and for a while the fight was on between 45s and 33s, although 33s quickly became the clear winners. Tape recorders began spreading around the world, together with quickly obsolete contraptions like wire recorders. Many new record companies were established; record players were flooding the market and the public was hungry for things to play on them. Even the big companies could not meet the demand. Musicians could buy an Ampex recording machine and a microphone and make recordings in their basements. The companies that printed the records had ample capacity to handle the independent producer's material. The costs were minimal. Any record that sold 500 copies made some profit, very much as CDs did in their first few years. University libraries were all trying to build their collections, so at least minimal distribution was well-nigh guaranteed.

Avar's visit was prompted by his acquiring the rights to the Kodály recording I had made in Paris. I told him that it would be risky to publish it on an LP because of the electronic disturbance at the end, and also because of the cuts we had had to make to accommodate side changes and time limits. He asked if I would be willing to record it again, along with whatever else I liked. He offered some minimal payment per record and, of course, eventual royalties. I agreed, and eventually made fifteen LPs with him. Working with him also allowed me to meet Peter Bartók, the son of Béla, who was a sound engineer. He was a top recording engineer, quite inventive, although his knowledge of string playing was limited at the time. As years went by he developed a keen ear and could detect the tiniest intonational discrepancies, and he also invented a gadget to facilitate tape editing that became a standard feature on recording machines. Typically generous (or perhaps naive), he sent the gadget to Ampex, and they thanked him for it.

Our collaboration started with a ten-inch recording of a Corelli sonata and Vivaldi's D Major Concerto with piano. The pianist was Marilyn Meyer, who eventually settled in England. The next was Kodály's Sonata op. 4, Bartók's First Rhapsody, and a violin piece by Leo Weiner called *Wedding Dance*. These recordings prompted a call from a Hungarian pianist living in New York, Dr. Otto Herz. One could compare him to Gerald Moore. In Hungary he had been in great demand as an accompanist, not just among his compatriots but also among artists visiting Hungary, such as Pablo Casals. Aside from that he was the president of the Budapest Magicians' Club, and had the most prodigious photographic memory; he knew the entire Budapest telephone book. When I was a youngster at the Academy, Antal Molnar, one of the teachers, told the story of how Herz had substituted at the last minute for a sick pianist in a performance of a twelve-minute ballet Molnar had written. Herz sight-read the score at a rehearsal the day of the performance. He did not like to have a page turner, however, and that evening, as he turned the first page over, the music fell to the floor. Molnar froze in the box, but Herz played the entire piece from memory, and the composer said that he only changed four or five chords. I had only once had the pleasure of playing with him before the war.

His voice on the phone sounded full of hurt. "How dare you record Bartók, Kodály, and Weiner without me," he asked plaintively. I stuttered and told him the pay was very small. After a short silence he said, "That doesn't matter." And we began to work together. Scheduling the sessions was a bit complicated, with my Met job. We met between rehearsals and on my occasional free nights in Peter Bartók's studio in the Steinway building on Fifty-seventh Street. Peter ran the machine and my wife, Eva, acting as an AR person, marked notes for correction and picked the final takes. By then I was playing the Lord Aylesford Strad, and the results were highly satisfactory. When the recordings were issued they received kudos, especially the Kodály Solo Sonata with its second side, the Duo for Violin and Cello, op. 7. The violinist was Arnold Eidus, a superb player who won first place in the Paris Thibaud competition in '46 and became the leading commercial violinist in New

York, working in radio, TV, and films and making all sorts of recordings.

Peter Bartók's studio consisted of two rooms, one for the machinery and one for the microphone, which was the unidirectional kind you see in old movies. The room held one and occasionally two pianos, and was jam-packed with boxes and paraphernalia. Reverberation? Who had heard of it? When we started on the recording of the Solo Sonata, we found that the tape sounded lousy. For an hour we kept moving both me and the mike, but it was still no good. Not only was the mike unidirectional, its height was not adjustable. Finally I asked Peter if he had a back-up mike. He said yes, so I suggested that he put a chair next to the first mike and lean the second against it, so that there was one mike for the high notes and one for the low ones. Years later, on a visit to the Massachusetts Institute of Technology, I was told that they had used this record as an excellent example of high-fidelity recording. Some went so far as to call it the forerunner of stereophonic sound, along with Stokowski's multi-miked orchestra recordings. I wonder!

Avar became a good friend and an occasional bridge partner. He also asked my advice in planning repertory, not just for me but also for singers, pianists, quartets, and the like. His business was thriving and he sold rights in England and elsewhere. Through his sales to a British company named Nixa, my name slowly became known in England's musical circles.

I returned from the Met's spring 1950 tour to face months of doing nothing. Fortunately a friend of a friend, a violinist named Jesse Birnbaum, called and asked if I could help him. He was playing in and acting as contractor for Menotti's opera *The Consul* in a Schubert theater on Broadway. It had been running for months, but the second cellist had recently gone as an extra with Toscanini's NBC tour, and the union wouldn't let him back to continue. The violinist asked me please to come down that night as a stand-in. I did and sight-read the opera, the first ever produced as a Broadway show. I was asked to continue, and agreed; I had nothing else to do, it paid fairly well, and it solved the summer financial dilemma.

The orchestra for *The Consul* was astonishing. Birnbaum, an enterprising young man, had approached Menotti with the idea of hiring

Juilliard and Curtis graduates in addition to the contracted house musicians. Menotti told him that if he could swing it Birnbaum would be the contractor, not just a player, which meant double pay. Birnbaum assembled a group that included future international prize winners; future concertmasters for the New York Philharmonic, the Dallas Symphony, and others; and musicians who would go on to become first winds and brass players in major orchestras. My partner was Shirley Trepel, a great cellist, a great lady, and thereafter a lifelong friend. Life in the orchestra pit was hard, but often amusing. We sometimes played poker during intermissions. One day the fiddlers were standing around the pot, cigarettes dangling from their mouths and instruments tucked under their arms, looking at their cards and laying down their bets. One player folded and started playing Waxman's *Carmen Fantasy*, one of the toughest pieces ever written for the violin. A second player joined in. By the time we had to return to the pit five violinists were playing the piece in unison, complete with its double stops, harmonics, trills, and runs. The next day I suggested playing some chamber music, and a couple of times we gathered on our free day for a Brahms sextet or a Schubert quintet, works a few of them were familiar with.

As the weeks went by, I began to get frazzled. The heat and the rote work of playing Menotti daily got to me. Fortunately, the phone rang again. It was Nicholas Harsanyi, a violinist and former senior colleague of mine at the Liszt Academy. He had gone on to become the violist of several string quartets, among them the famed Léner Quartet, with which he toured the world until the death of Jenö Léner in 1948. (During the quartet's last two years, Laszlo Varga was its cellist.) Harsanyi at that time was teaching and conducting in Princeton's Westminster College. In the summers he was teaching and conducting at a Saranac Lake music camp. He had stopped playing the viola and even sold his instrument. The story he told me went as follows.

Feri Roth, the founder of the very successful (but sadly now defunct) string quartet bearing his name, had called him from Los Angeles. In 1938 Roth had brought Pro Ideale, Harsanyi's quartet, to the U.S. (The other members were Michael Kuttner, Paul Rolland, and George Barati.) Now Roth was asking for his help. He had managed to get an engagement to perform Roy Harris's quartet arrangement of Bach's *Art*

Roth Quartet: with Nicolas Harsanyi, Jeno Antal, and Feri Roth in front (1950)

of the Fugue at Tanglewood on the bicentennial of Bach's death. He had also booked two earlier concerts at Williams College, playing six Mozart quartets. But he had no quartet, only the name and the stationery. He had contacted his original second violinist, Jeno Antal, now a member of the Cleveland Symphony, who agreed to join him. Then Roth called Mexico, where Joseph Smilovitch and Imre Hartmann had settled. Hartmann was the former violist and cellist of the Léner Quartet, and like me had been a student of Adolf Schiffer. I had met him once, in 1936, in Cortina d'Ampezzo.

Both Hartmann and Smilovitch agreed to play, so Roth printed the programs and arranged for a couple of days of rehearsals prior to the Williams College concerts. Then, four days before the concerts, Hartmann and Smilovitch canceled. Roth frantically called Harsanyi, who told him that if rehearsals could be held at Saranac Lake he could get away for the few days needed for the concerts, though of course he had to get a viola. But Roth needed a cellist as well, and asked Harsanyi for help. Harsanyi reached Laszlo Varga in Chautauqua, but Varga was not able to get away from the orchestra and told him to try me.

When he called, all I asked was, when? He said I had to be there the next day. Then he called Emil Herrmann in New York to borrow a viola. Meanwhile I called Birnbaum and explained the situation, and he agreed to let me out of the *Consul* for a week. The next day I landed at Saranac Lake's tiny airport. Roth was beaming with joy that his quartet was on again, and the famed Mrs. Coolidge, who had sponsored him twenty-five years before and now was doing so again, would have him back as planned. We rehearsed at a leisurely pace for two days, six Mozart quartets and Bach, bathing in the glory of the works and the fact that all four of us were Leo Weiner's students and spoke the same musical language. We had a ball.

We drove to Williams College, where we played two very good concerts. In the program I was Imre Hartmann and Harsanyi was Smilovitch. Then we went to Tanglewood. The venue was the then famed shed. It was packed. There was oppressive heat, listeners with pocket scores, and old ladies with silk ribbons around their necks. Things went surprisingly well for a while, but when we began one of the mirror fugues, Roth closed his eyes and started to play the wrong version. Four bars later Antal's violin was supposed to enter, followed by the viola and eventually the cello. But how could we enter? Roth was playing away in a world of his own. Antal's glasses fogged up; Harsanyi started to giggle and looked at me. I was facing the audience, and I saw people turning pages in their scores, trying to find out what Roth was playing. Finally Antal decided to start playing his part anyway. Cacophony ensued for a couple of seconds that seemed an eternity, until Roth came to himself and stopped, took off his glasses, wiped them, and restarted correctly. The rest of the concert went on acceptably. After it was all over, George Lang, Lukas Foss, Robert Gerle, and other friends came and greeted me with straight faces, saying, "Bravo, Mr. Hartmann." I was greatly relieved that my name was not on the program.

The next day I was back in the pit of *The Consul*. After I had played it for the 120th time, the Met season began. I left my new friends, bought a recording of the opera, and swore that if I ever complained about hard work I would listen to it to remind me how I felt then. To this day I have never put it on.

It was the fall of 1950. The Aitays were living on Long Island. We

THE WORLD OF MUSIC ACCORDING TO STARKER

rented an apartment in nearby Jackson Heights, and also became the proud owners of our first automobile, a Hudson. I could now either drive or take the subway to the Met. The routine continued: rehearsals at 10 A.M., private lessons at either 8:30 A.M. or 3 P.M. at home, then the performances. As time went on more and more recording gigs came my way, and, of course, I continued making my Period recordings in studios and churches, often at night when the opera was finished.

By an amusing coincidence the Italian cellist Antonio Janigro was recording the same works in Vienna as I was in New York: Beethoven and Brahms sonatas. My partner was Abba Bogin. Then Period began a project called "Around the World with Starker," recording French and Spanish music with Leon Pommers as the pianist. The project ended before we embarked on Italy and Russia. Instead we went on to issue four Bach suites, six Mozart piano trios, and Beethoven's *Archduke Trio*. The pianist for these was Agi Jambor, with whom I had played Beethoven's Triple Concerto years before in Budapest for a one-dollar fee. The violinist was Victor Aitay, by then the second concertmaster of the Met. These records are not among those I am most proud of, though years later they were reissued as by "Starker's Trio" because my fame was spreading.

Work with the Met continued to be rewarding. There were stunning singers like Jussi Bjorling, for me the greatest of all tenors. Fritz Reiner conducted superb Strauss and Wagner operas, and Eugene Ormandy conducted a memorable production of Strauss's *Die Fledermaus*. The job was originally assigned to Reiner, but then Bing signed a recording contract with Columbia. Because Reiner had an exclusive contract with RCA, he reassigned the conducting to Ormandy, who was the musical director of the Philadelphia Orchestra. Ormandy's manager, Arthur Judson, told him to do it for free as a promotional step. Ormandy, who was not familiar with operas, kept asking Tibor Kozma in Hungarian about tempi, details, and so on, not realizing that two Hungarians, Aitay and I, were at arm's length from him. When the stage rehearsals started, his well-known habit of expecting maximum body gyration from his players became evident. For a lifetime I have been known to use minimal body motions. My section and I played fortissimo, but with no swaying, and Ormandy kept gesturing toward me for more and more. Finally I asked him if there was anything wrong. "Oh," he said, "I am so accustomed to my great Philadelphia cello section." That rubbed me the wrong way. I said, "Mr. Ormandy, you don't have a better section than us. However, we sit to your left while Philly sits on your right." He was at a loss for words, then, "Oh, maybe it's the basses." I said, maybe. The next day he wrote a letter to John Mundy complaining about lack of cooperation by some, and he carried a dislike of me, bordering on hatred, to his last days. I did not make my debut with the Philadelphia Orchestra until after he retired. At the end of the season we recorded *Die Fledermaus* with him for Columbia and excerpts with Reiner for RCA.

One of my more memorable recording gigs was for Decca Records. Leroy Anderson, a composer for the Boston Pops, was to conduct some of his latest jewels: "The Syncopated Clock," "The Waltzing Cat," "The Typewriter" (I think), and so on. The time and care spent on that LP was only matched once, when Reiner and Heifetz recorded the Brahms Concerto in Chicago. The quality of the orchestra was summed up in the four cellists: Frank Miller, Leonard Rose, either Harvey Shapiro or Bernard Greenhouse (I cannot remember), and me.

It was a joyous day when, after a short correspondence, Joseph Szigeti came to visit us. He wrote, "I heard about your string method and I would like to know what it is." Szigeti was one of the giants among the violinists I had heard from childhood on, and my admiration for him is undiminished up to this day. He invited me to his recital in Town Hall. The experience was akin to the evening I spent at Enescu's home in late 1945. The first few minutes were excruciating; as I saw later, his fingers had deteriorated to the point that he had almost no flesh on them. But once he loosened up a bit he produced heart-rending beauty. I transcribed the Schubert D Major Sonatina for the cello because I had heard him play it.

I invited him to dinner, and picked him up at his hotel. He was carrying his fiddle and a bag. On the way he asked me to stop at a deli, where he bought something, and we continued. Once at the apartment he soon sat on the floor playing with Gabrielle. Dinnertime came and he produced some lean ham he had bought at the deli, saying that was all he was supposed to eat. We had made chicken paprikash, with cu-

cumber salad and dumplings. He sighed and said he couldn't resist the meal, and proceeded to have three helpings. "I'll pay for this tomorrow," he said, and ceded the ham to the fridge. He went to the bathroom and reappeared in a sweatshirt, picked up his fiddle, and said, "Now show me." I explained my system and he took copious notes for the next hour.

Years later, after a Chicago Symphony concert, he came to dinner again. The same scenario was repeated, sweatshirt and all. He had played a Mozart concerto that afternoon, and it wasn't that good. He was scratching all over the place. After dinner he took out his fiddle and said, "This is how everybody plays Mozart." And he played it superbly. "But that isn't what Mozart wanted; I must make my life difficult." I saw him again in Switzerland shortly before he died. He was a great musician and a rare human being.

In looking over my life, I sometimes think of myself as having reached great heights against all odds. Well, my time at the Met Opera represents those odds against returning to the solo stage; four years of forty-eight-hour work weeks, with commercial recordings on top of them, are not the road toward playing concertos and recitals on tour. In the summer of '51, when we returned from the Met tour, came a week that almost killed me. For six days I spent from 10 A.M. to 1 P.M. recording *Carmen* for RCA, from 2 P.M. to 5 P.M. recording *Faust* for Columbia, and from 7 P.M. to 11 P.M. recording Mozart quartets for Mercury Records. I slept for forty-eight hours when it was over. In fact, that was the system I used for all four years. Around January I called in sick and slept for twenty-four hours. The rest of the season I lived with six hours of sleep a night, if I could get it.

My friend Janos Scholz, who was the cellist of the Roth Quartet until it broke up, told me before I joined the Met that two years there is the end of real playing. I heard stories of some of my predecessors breaking down after one year. I set a limit of four and trained myself not to stuff my memory with operas. When Feri Roth again asked me to play some summer concerts and recordings in 1951–53, I said yes. Just clearing my head of the Met and making my own recordings helped my sanity, besides the fact that they put my name on the map.

Sometime around 1951 I had a night off, and Eva insisted that we go see a movie our friends were saying was terrific. After a while she began

UNITED STATES OF AMERICA

nudging me with her elbow, telling me to watch, which I was already doing. She said, "Don't you see?" Slowly it dawned on me. In Paris I used to amuse myself by writing short stories or vignettes and reading them to friends. One day a friend's relative came for a visit from London. She told us about her job at Rank Studios, which was to reduce books to synopses to be considered for filming. She worked for a very successful scriptwriter and was the daughter of a fairly well known Hungarian novelist. I was urged to read her one of my stories. She asked me what I planned to do with it, and I said, "Well, if you think you can show it to somebody, take it. If you can sell it we split fifty-fifty." Four weeks later she wrote from London that they liked the story, but it had to be published as a short story to protect the copyright. I couldn't do it in English, so I asked her to do it, and the fifty-fifty deal would still stand. She didn't write back, and I forgot about the incident. The movie Eva and I were watching now was *Kind Hearts and Coronets*, with Alec Guinness. My story had been a ghost story, and the movie was written by the man who read my tiny synopsis. The ghost was omitted, but most of the funny murders were adopted. I don't necessarily suspect foul play; rather I believe I triggered a thought that six months later came to fruition. Strangely I felt almost cheerful. It was a great movie and I may have had something to do with it. About forty-five years later I heard from the woman again, when she asked me to comment on the playing of two of her grandchildren, a violinist and a cellist.

In the summer of '51 Avar wanted to do some orchestral recordings with a small ensemble. The budget was tiny. I chose the Boccherini Concerto and the Mozart-Fischer Horn Concerto. Somehow he managed to book two concerts at the Castle Hill Festival on the Crane estate in Massachusetts, working through a young, aspiring Romanian conductor who was a protégé of the estate's owners. The arrangement was that fifteen musicians would come from New York, perform the concerts, and then return to New York and make the record. The orchestra was called the Castle Hill Festival Chamber Orchestra, and it was led by a former New York Philharmonic concertmaster, Max Pilzer. Unfortunately, the conductor was so inept that we barely escaped disgrace at the concerts, and we had to ask him not to conduct the recording. Once in New York, we assembled in a downtown studio for two three-hour

THE WORLD OF MUSIC ACCORDING TO STARKER

THE WORLD OF MUSIC ACCORDING TO STARKER

THE WORLD OF MUSIC ACCORDING TO STARKER

THE WORLD OF MUSIC ACCORDING TO STARKER

please help with the Elgar we were to play in September. I had never performed it and I wasn't sure I had an affinity for it. He asked me when I wanted to see him and I said, "now!" I took a cab over and spent four hours with him. He grabbed the cello out of my hands and told me what Elgar wanted, note by note, covering the work. It was a unique experience. In September when I performed the work in Edinburgh, the reaction was pleasing. The *Times* expressed surprise that a Hungarian cellist understood the Elgarian spirit. On the other hand, the *Manchester Guardian* wrote, "Barbirolli tried to conduct Elgar, but the American virtuoso played something else." The *Herald Tribune* reprinted the reviews side by side. At the Festival I also played, for the first time in my life, all six Bach suites, in two matinees. True to form, the *Times* said, "We haven't heard such Bach since Casals," etc., while the *Guardian* headline was "Starker tackles Bach." I had to be successful, as by the time I returned to Chicago I had something like twenty concerts booked for the following season.

One aspect of these reviews followed me for decades. When the reviewer was complimentary, he referred to me as a Hungarian; when critical, he called me an American. For a while I became "the Hungarian-born American." Finally I was generally recognized as an American. It should be clear that my closest friends are Hungarians. I consider myself lucky that my musical education was in Hungary. My favorite foods are Hungarian, and I feel some pride when Hungarians' huge contributions to science, art, and music are lauded. But when I recall my twenty-two years in Hungary, I feel only joy and a sense of belonging in being an American. I criticize many aspects of U.S. life, which makes me even more American than most. I chose to come; I wasn't lucky enough to be born here. Having traveled on every continent, I am able to make comparisons. Whenever I criticize, there is an unspoken caveat that, nonetheless, the United States is unquestionably the best country of which to be a citizen.

(Many years later, a small event occurred that made me feel even more an American, while still reminding me of my Hungarian roots. In the early '80s I went to Austin to perform with the orchestra there. When I arrived at my hotel I was greeted by its general manager, and

With Carlo Maria Giulini, Walter Legg, and Eva Starker

after the concert he presented me with a paper from the state governor making me an honorary citizen of Texas. But the general manager was Hungarian, and we spoke that language to each other.)

While in Europe in 1957 I recorded the Haydn D Major Concerto and the Boccherini Concerto with Carlo Maria Giulini, a truly great musician. One day I walked in on a rehearsal. He was conducting Verdi's Requiem, and Joan Sutherland, whom I did not yet know, was singing. She and Elisabeth Schwarzkopf later signed with Colbert Artists Management, an American company, at Walter Legge's suggestion, as did I.

Except for an ill-advised three-year hiatus, I still enjoy a family-like relationship with them after more than forty years.

Before returning to start the 1957–58 season with the CSO, I had the joy of recording the Saint-Saens and Schumann concertos with Giulini, and I also appeared in the first public concert by the newly formed Philharmonia Hungarica, conducted by its founder, Zoltan Rozsnyai, in Vienna. When the revolutionary exodus from Hungary started, Rozsnyai collected anyone with instruments at the railroad station. With the help of Yehudi Menuhin, he obtained financial support to house the musicians near Vienna, and succeeded in developing an orchestra that became an important musical group, touring the world and recording. He passed away in San Diego.

A few weeks later, in Chicago at the start of the CSO season, Reiner asked me, "Have you ever heard of such a thing? I engaged this young man, Giulini, to conduct for two weeks. He sends me two programs, of which I already scheduled some works. He refuses to change those works." I mumbled something to the effect that Giulini was a very conscientious musician, but I thought he was excellent and he only conducted what he really knew. Giulini became a much-loved fixture with the CSO and elsewhere.

Once on a Friday afternoon in 1957, while tuning on stage before a concert, Bekefi nudged me. "Look." "Look where?" I asked. "Seventh row aisle." I looked and saw a very beautiful young woman, with dark hair partially covered by a hat. "Not bad," I told him. It was not my habit to exchange glances with audience members. The majority of the Friday crowd were to me, then, old ladies. On occasion some waved their hands at me, and I nodded if I recognized them, which sometimes happened, since I had spent four years sitting in the same seat. Actually, my seat was changed from time to time. Reiner preferred to have me in front of his nose, ever since our time at the Met when he moved me so I couldn't watch the stage or the audience. He blocked my view. Only when guest conductors came did I sit outside to the right, the place that grooms cellists to become conductors.

I resisted the temptation to conduct, as I was neither frustrated nor power-hungry. When I occasionally ventured into that field, it was to save money for the concert organizers; I would play a double role as soloist and conductor. The first time I did this was at Miami University in Oxford, Ohio, around 1960. I was to play two concerts. I played a recital, then I brought in fifteen members of the Chicago Symphony to play Haydn's Concerto in D. Next I played a Bach suite, and brought the orchestra back for Bartók's Divertimento for Strings. I had played the Divertimento in Budapest shortly after it was written, and this time I conducted it. Big deal! They knew it better than I. It sounded good and I was celebrated. I doubled again a few years later in St. Louis with the Symphony's Baroque Orchestra. That time I played two concertos and conducted Haydn's Symphony no. 55 (*The Schoolmaster*). I chose it to make clear that I had no ambition to conduct. The same program was repeated with the Stuttgart, Philadelphia, and Padova Chamber Orchestras. Eventually I was even offered directorships. I turned them down. I still believe that anyone with the type of musical schooling I had should be able to do a creditable job in conducting a program, but that does not make him or her a conductor. I was never frustrated by the limitations of the cello repertory, as were many of my distinguished colleagues. Certainly the conductor has a more prominent role in musical life than soloists or teachers, but I suffered through years of half-baked, ill-prepared maestros, and I did not want to join their ranks. The outstanding ones spent years and decades perfecting their art, an art vastly different from mine, an art that I respect and rejoice in when someone excels in it.

For weeks after Bekefi pointed the woman out, I kept looking for her in the audience. My home life was deteriorating, especially under the strain of having two sets of parents living with us. Eventually my parents moved to a hotel and then to an apartment. My father decided to take a job in a dry-cleaning shop as a tailor. I gave a monthly check to both sets of parents, so as to keep them from being embarrassed by having to ask us for money. Tension grew between Eva and me, and past problems resurfaced in our marriage. No solution was in sight, and the uncertain future once I had left the CSO loomed ominously.

In the 1957–58 season we repeated performances of the Hindemith Concerto, the Brahms Double Concerto, and Strauss's *Don Quixote*. Reiner still didn't believe that I would leave the orchestra. In the early

THE WORLD OF MUSIC ACCORDING TO STARKER

With Wilfred Bain

spring of '58 I received a call from Wilfred Bain, dean of the Indiana University School of Music, the man who in '48 had arranged a contract that allowed me to enter the U.S. He asked me to have lunch with him. We met in the Palmer House after a rehearsal. He proceeded to offer me a professorship as of September '58. I told him that I had a number of concerts booked. He said that was fine and quoted me a salary that was far less than what I was earning in Chicago. I told him that a professorship would tie me down too much and suggested something like a position as artist in residence. He cheerfully agreed. Only later did I find out that putting me in a nonacademic position allowed him to bypass hiring regulations, and that such a position didn't include a pension plan, insurance, or other benefits, issues I was totally unaware of. We shook hands, and now I had a job for at least a year—"just to see how it works," we agreed—as well as some concerts and recording sessions scheduled. So my professional future, at least, was a bit more secure.

The position meant moving to Bloomington, Indiana, a place I was vaguely familiar with, having made annual visits there with the Met Opera. Part of the agreement was that I would come for a quick visit to see the place and sign a contract. So Eva and I took the tiny fourteen-seat commuter plane. On arrival there was a huge crowd at the postage-stamp-sized airport. I wondered, were they there to see me? I asked Allen Winold, Bain's assistant, who had met us, and he told me no, the university's basketball team was about to return from a victory. We looked over Bloomington, and I signed the contract and arranged to rent a house in September.

Later in the season, I received a note from someone asking me some advice about buying my records. I didn't know the sender, but the letter referred to the Friday concerts. I answered, and it dawned on me that the sender might be the mystery lady. Next Friday a shy nod from her indicated that it was. I was fascinated by her, but had no idea of doing anything about it. My mind was overloaded with troubles: family, future, repertory, money, career, and travel. But after another Friday concert I went to fetch my car from the parking lot and ran into the mystery lady, who was doing the same. Up close she was even more beautiful than from a distance, her dark glasses giving her the appearance of a movie star. Her name was Rae. After a quick handshake, I asked to see her somewhere, sometime.

When I began these recollections I wondered how much of my privacy I should give up. I was and am a very private individual, and while I have attained considerable heights in my profession, my attitude has at times made my road rather strange. I sometimes assumed that most of my colleagues had similar attitudes. Because of this I never asked a conductor to engage me, or asked for favors from those in power. My feelings have also made it necessary to be selective in my recollections. I was never fascinated by the private shenanigans of prominent individuals, although I knew of the public's interest in such things. My belief was, and still is, that they should be admired for what they do or have done to enrich the world, and who they are or what they do aside from their work should be forgotten. But when on rare occasions a great artist also displays exceptional human qualities, we should rejoice. In other words, I decided that these memoirs should be honest, but omit the juicy or sordid details of my life. So I will simply state that my life was at a turning point, my marriage was an endless compromise, and I was vulnerable. I fell in love, but tried to preserve the status quo.

The season was coming to an end, and with it my life with the CSO. The penultimate program was Verdi's Requiem. In a rehearsal with the chorus, the orchestra had something like a 150-bar rest, during which I went into a dreamlike trance. Then, all of a sudden, I woke up and started with a fortissimo chord, one bar ahead of the orchestra. The orchestra broke up laughing, for in five years I had never made a noticeable mistake. Reiner threw his baton on the floor and shouted, "Why can't some people watch?" I said, "Am I not entitled to one mistake? I am sorry." He mumbled something and the rehearsal continued. I was hurt, but knew that he was mad because of my leaving. He was accustomed to firing people, but they seldom left on their own. In the last week my section gathered for a drink and presented me with a gold tie pin with a broken baton on it. The only communication I had with Reiner was a call asking about Mihaly Virizlay, who came to audition for my chair. I told Reiner that he was excellent but not as experienced as Reiner usually liked. A couple of hours later Reiner called again. He had just engaged Virizlay and asked why I had said that he wasn't good, which I hadn't. I was happy for Virizlay, especially because I had had nothing to do with his hiring. After the last concert I went to Reiner and thanked him for nine years of the greatest musical experiences I could ever have. We shook hands, and my CSO life was over.

In May I left for Europe, with concerts in England, Germany, and Portugal and several recording sessions. I started with the Bach suites, making two LPs with Gerald Moore accompanying me on the piano. Moore was a wonderful partner and a delightful man. At one session with EMI in London I hit a snag and couldn't concentrate. I asked for a break and wandered around the other studios. In the big hall the Philharmonia members were milling around. I asked what was happening, and learned that David Oistrakh was recording a Mozart concerto and the conductor had quit. Then Oistrakh appeared and suggested that they do it without a conductor. They changed the microphone's position, and Oistrakh faced the group and started leading them. I understand that this launched his conducting activities. In another studio Menuhin was recording the César Franck Sonata. I listened. He did a few bars, which sounded rather weak, but he cried out that they had got it. He was looking for just two notes, to be edited in. I returned to my studio and finished the recording. The next day I ran into Dohnányi. He was recording his second concerto, the one he played in Chicago. He scolded me for making a cut in my recording of his Concert Piece with Susskind. I pacified him by saying that it was necessary because of the length of the Kodály piece also on the album.

At an after-concert gathering during that last CSO season, Vitya Vronsky and her husband Victor Babin, the famed piano duo, had invited Eva and me to their home in Santa Fe. They would be away for the summer and we were welcome to stay there. This was the only time in my life I have accepted such an invitation. It gave me a chance to rest and work. Their home was delightful, packed with a few French impressionist paintings and a slew of works by Georges Braque, who had been the couple's good friend during their youth in Paris. One of them seemed to depict some chickens; it upset me after a while, and I removed it and rehung it when we left.

I played only one date during those eight weeks, Dvořák, in Chicago's Grant Park. (I also played a recital in Santa Fe's museum in thanks to

THE WORLD OF MUSIC ACCORDING TO STARKER

my hosts.) The papers reported that my audience of 7,000 had been the second largest ever in the park. I was surpassed only by Van Cliburn, who had just won the Tchaikovsky competition and given a concert right before mine. He had an audience of 70,000. My audience included Rae. I found out that she was married, but in the process of divorcing, and had a two-year-old daughter. I was troubled. I hated the idea of divorce. Gabrielle was nine years old, and Eva and I had four parents around us in Chicago. I was determined to save my marriage.

9

THE AFRICAN ADVENTURES OF LORD AYLESFORD

His Lordship was born in Cremona, Italy, in 1696—born, I say, because although his Lordship was created by man's hands, he definitely has a soul. He was made by that unique genius Antonius Stradivarius, and he is a cello. At birth he was possessed of merely a date rather than a name, but later he acquired the rank and title pertaining to an owner named Aylesford. I have attempted here to describe some of the hazards and adventures to which his Lordship (in the company of his present companion) has been exposed. Though his Lordship's soul may indeed be richer than mine, I have been forced at times to place emphasis on my own point of view—not immodestly, let me say, but simply for the reason that his Lordship's soul would not otherwise have the opportunity to express itself.

—The African Adventures of Lord Aylesford: Being the True Account of the African Tour of Lord Aylesford, Born in 1696, in Cremona, Italy, as Related by His Faithful Traveling Companion

As I washed down a last morsel of steak with Portuguese wine, my Portuguese manager addressed me from across the table.

"Janos, you want to go to Africa for a tour?"

It was 1958, and we were having supper after a Lisbon concert by his Lordship and me. The occasion was festive: the Calouste Gulbenkian Foundation of Music was hosting the affair. Our concert had been good, my spirits were high, and at that moment the idea of an African tour struck me as partly funny, partly unimaginable.

"A tour of Africa! Well now! Hunting, or what?"

"I am serious. A concert tour."

"Look," I said, "I know it is difficult to book cellists, but is it that difficult? Must we go that far? And Africa, by the way, is fairly large. Where in Africa?"

"Portuguese Africa. We'll talk about it tomorrow."

Later, in my hotel room, it dawned on me that he might have been serious. Only the other day he had mentioned that a well-known concert violinist had stopped over in Lisbon on his way to Africa. I turned off the light and let my imagination run free. I envisioned his Lordship and I playing Bach suites for native chiefs and naked slave girls, then following a jungle path to our next booking, I with his Lordship in one hand and a carbine in the other.

I recalled a friend of mine who had told me about his tour of Indonesia before independence. He had played for government officials, sometimes in private homes for fewer than forty persons, all of them starved for anything European. His description had evoked decaying colonialists listening to classical music with highballs in hand and tears in their eyes, moistly remembering the good old days in Europe. Well, I thought, should not the Africans have a chance to hear cello music, surely one of the most marvelous blessings of civilization?

One year later, at 8 P.M., Portuguese Air Transport announced the departure of their flight from Lisbon to Kano, Leopoldville, Luanda, and Lourenço Marques. The announcement to board the plane was, naturally enough, in Portuguese, a language of which I knew only a few polite phrases. I shook my manager's hand and remarked, as I picked up the cello case containing his Lordship, "See you in about three weeks.

THE AFRICAN ADVENTURES OF LORD AYLESFORD

It seems you weren't joking after all." My pianist, Gunther Ludwig, a thin blond German boy in his late twenties, took up his bag and started with me for immigration and customs. Suddenly I turned back and asked my manager, "You did call about Lord Aylesford?"

"Of course, old chap." He laughed, clapping me on the back, and added in a maddeningly precise Cambridge accent, "Don't worry, it is all arranged."

But I could not stop worrying. Old instruments, even those without titles, dislike changes of temperature. Since luggage compartments are generally unheated, the cellist who travels by air must insist upon keeping his instrument with him in the cabin. This invariably leads to an argument with airline personnel, who say a cello is too large to be considered hand luggage. Sometimes, in the past, I have resolved the problem by purchasing an additional half-fare ticket. Other times a place has grudgingly been made in the coat compartment, if one happened to exist. The problem of transportation is a constant challenge in the life of a cellist.

The moment Gunther and I entered the plane our stewardess rattled off something in Portuguese. I apologized and said, "Sorry, I speak English, or, if you prefer, French. But no Portuguese."

She replied in French, pointing to his Lordship, "Sir, we have no room on board for . . . that thing."

"Cello," I offered politely.

"Even then, we have no room."

Determined to be pleasant, I asked, "Miss, would you check, please? I have special permission to carry this instrument on board, since I have been invited by the government to play concerts in Africa."

She looked perturbed. "But we have no room!"

I removed my coat, put it on the rack above my designated seat, and began to look about for a place to settle his Lordship. The plane had no first-class cabin, and by this time all seats were occupied. There was not even a compartment for coats. My stomach began to churn. The stewardess reappeared with a ground officer, and a half hour of impassioned argument followed. The plane was already long delayed, and the other passengers had begun to hate me. So I took my coat and his Lordship, summoned Gunther, and left the plane to continue the debate in the terminal. Finally, after all arguments were exhausted, I could see there was really no room in the cabin for my cello. I agreed, albeit reluctantly, to bed his Lordship down in the mail compartment, where he rested atop mail sacks, carefully wrapped with four heavy blankets. By this time I was cursing eloquently in my native Hungarian. Gunther kept silent as he followed me back into the cabin. At long last the plane took off. The captain announced that our first stop would be Kano, in Nigeria, which was about an eight-hour journey.

Beyond the cabin window Lisbon was fading from my view. During the three weeks we had been there my home in Chicago had seemed awfully far away. Now, suddenly, Lisbon seemed almost like home.

Everyone used the first hour to settle down for the long flight, to meet neighbors, and to exchange itineraries. Most of the passengers were civil servants returning to Africa after a six-month vacation at home (with pay), furnished by the government as a reward for four years of colonial service. They were a quiet group. Those who had been home were reflecting on their farewells; those who were going to Africa for the first time seemed awed and a bit frightened by prospects unknown.

After the lights were turned off, I reviewed in my mind the events of the past year: how things had progressed from a casual remark by my manager to the actual start of our airborne safari. The Portuguese Circulo Cultura Musical had a policy of inviting internationally known artists to give recitals in Portuguese colonies, at high fees by European standards and with all expenses paid. "In regard to details," my Portuguese manager had said, "those will be worked out through your English manager." I hadn't known then that this meant practically nothing. I did receive some letters stating that the concerts were to be in Portuguese West Africa (Angola); then a letter of apology from England saying sorry, there had been some confusion, and that the concerts were to be in Portuguese East Africa (Mozambique). Finally, England gave up in embarrassment. I had signed the contract for this adventure only twenty-four hours before boarding the airplane; such is the way with many southern European managers, and I was not surprised. However, I didn't know my itinerary or even any program details. All I knew was

THE AFRICAN ADVENTURES OF LORD AYLESFORD

that the first concert would be in Angola on the day of arrival. There would be others in Angola, as well as some in Mozambique, all the way across the continent. Who was I to argue?

When the announcement came to fasten seat belts, it was 4 A.M., and our plane was circling over Kano. We had reached Africa! Gunther was like a fifteen-year-old on his first big date, trying without success to conceal his excitement. I recalled the first time I traveled from home without my parents, as a child prodigy of twelve. Naturally I had tried to behave like an experienced traveler, as if seeing Venice were a totally unremarkable event in the life of a Hungarian adolescent. Now, many years later, I could still manage the bored face, but as we touched down it hid disappointment, not excitement: nothing I saw seemed African. Like everyone else, I had decided in advance how Africa would look; but the Kano airport looked like any in Europe.

In the terminal we were offered a choice of tea, coffee, or beer. I looked with dismay at many fellow passengers gulping down glasses of heavy ale despite the early hour. I did manage to locate some orange juice, but before I could drink it, a local merchant in a turban offered to sell me a sweet-looking baby crocodile. True, it was stuffed, but it looked more alive to me than real ones I had seen in Florida. I don't know how other people feel about buying crocodiles at four in the morning, but I resisted the temptation. The temperature was already about eighty degrees. The terminal's huge ceiling fans were stirring the air sluggishly, but they only helped to extinguish our cigarette lighters. I tried, all the same, to summon a feeling of adventure. At the other end of the airport area there was a bazaar full of leather goods, carved wooden statuettes, and widely assorted gift items (some marked "Made in Italy" or "Made in Japan"). My crocodile merchant turned out to be only one of dozens. In true American fashion, I declared that all this was for tourists, not for me. By the time we reboarded an hour later, Gunther and I felt like African old-timers, and I was prepared to offer immediate solutions to the racial problem.

The equator is merely an abstract concept, and crossing it gave me no thrill. From thirteen thousand feet all continents look alike, and I still had no sense that I was on a strange new one. I still did not when we landed at Leopoldville. The airport was a replica of the one at Brussels, except that it was more modern. Only a few minutes after our arrival in the Congo, a young native approached us to sell what he said were his own paintings. They were fairly decent watercolors, but I had seen their like on sale everywhere from Greenwich Village to the banks of the Seine, and I still wonder about their true origin. No sooner had the boy disposed of a few choice items than at least fifteen other natives approached with identical masterpieces for sale.

It was only a short flight from Leopoldville to Luanda and our first concert. Airport and customs officials were strict, as we found them to be everywhere, yet courteous and efficient. To our great relief, a French-speaking lady, noting his Lordship's case, approached us and introduced herself as president of the local Circulo Cultura Musical chapter. With her was the secretary of the Luanda chapter. They led us to a Dodge of recent vintage, and we set off through what could have been one of the larger cities of Florida or the Riviera. There were palm trees, well-tended roadways, cars of all makes, and blue skies above us; the temperature was a pleasant eighty degrees. All of this struck us, at 1 P.M., as ideal, but we began to discuss our hopes of seeing wildlife—the Real Africa.

"Well," the chapter president said unenthusiastically, "we could go for a ride and see buffaloes and so forth. But it's about 150 miles into the interior." Her manner was such that we decided to postpone the Real Africa. The hotel, she informed us as we reached it, had been chosen for its proximity to the concert hall. It looked to me like any second-class, twenty-year-old establishment in the southern United States. To our great surprise there was no air-conditioning, nor did we encounter any during the rest of our trip. Lack of electrical power is one of the great unsolved problems in Africa. Our general impression of the hotel was that it could have been worse, and only because the rest of the city looked so modern had we expected something better. Our good shepherd asked us if we wished to see the hall and the piano, and this we agreed to do.

The hall turned out to be a modern movie house, in which the concert was scheduled for 9 P.M. To our amazement an announcement of it, with pictures of us, was prominently displayed. Once we were inside the place, someone went to locate the manager, who had the key that

THE AFRICAN ADVENTURES OF LORD AYLESFORD

opened a beautiful Steinway piano on the stage. Gunther smiled with happiness the moment he saw it—a Steinway concert grand in Luanda! Well, we might not be seeing the Real Africa, but it was going to be a joy to play the concerts. As we waited for the key, Mme. President informed us that this was one of three pianos built especially for the tropics, and purchased by the government for the Circulo at a cost of eighteen thousand dollars each. There was another in Mocamedes, where we were playing the next day.

"Oh, yes—" I asked, "where?"

"In Mocamedes. Don't you know?"

"Well, now we do. Is it near?"

"A few hours by plane," she explained, "and the program is the same."

"What program?" I inquired innocently.

"The one you play tonight."

"Oh, that one. Do you have a printed copy?"

"Certainly," said Mme. President, taking several from her handbag.

The program turned out to be one we had played a long time earlier, and to our relief we had all the necessary music with us. There were some preclassical works, then sonatas by Beethoven and Debussy, a few more short pieces, and, to conclude, one movement of the Kodály Solo Sonata. At this point the manager arrived and the piano was opened. Gunther, who had worried that the long trip might affect his hands, was overjoyed at the sight of the magnificent piano. Without waiting for a chair, or for me to unpack his Lordship, he struck a dramatic chord and began a scale. Immediately he stopped, thunderstruck, and I froze. The sounds we had heard were not merely excruciating, they were unbelievably bad. As if the piano were a hot stove, Gunther cautiously touched a random key; it sounded acceptable. Then another—and lightning struck again. We looked at each other incredulously. Throughout this horrid experience Mme. President appeared unperturbed. I asked her when the tuner was coming.

"The tuner?" She turned to the man with the keys, conversed briefly in Portuguese, and said to us, "He was already here and tuned the piano."

"There must be a mistake," I answered. "This instrument has to be tuned."

She looked about helplessly for a telephone. "He's the only one I know, and he tunes all of our pianos." She left to make a call, and soon returned. "We are trying to find him, but he's in rather bad shape. He isn't so young anymore."

"Can he hear?" I asked suspiciously.

"We have had many piano recitals," she answered, naming several major artists, "and there have been no previous complaints."

"Well, let's go eat," I suggested. "And then we will try to sleep before the concert; it was a long flight. The tuner will have plenty of time to put the piano in order. The concert isn't until nine."

Mme. President picked the best restaurant in town for our early dinner. It was a curious combination of a nightclub and a hamburger joint—plush décor, a bandstand and dance floor, but Formica tables and plastic-covered chairs. There was an upright piano on the bandstand. Simultaneously Gunther and I wondered: who tuned it? I tried the keys, and—guess who? Our mysterious deaf tuner. The three of us ate in silence, then returned to the theater. When we located the manager, he announced that the tuner had been back.

"He examined the piano carefully and found one leg crooked. This he fixed."

At this point Gunther and I conferred in German and decided not to get excited. I told Mme. President that it was in the society's own interest to get the tuner back; otherwise the noise that night would be unbearable. We bade her goodbye and went back to our hotel. At eight that evening, the alarm wakened me. I dressed, took his Lordship out of his case, practiced, and was ready to go when they called for us at 8:45 P.M.

"Did the tuner come?"

"Yes, he worked on the piano for three hours."

Although the concert had been scheduled for 9:00, it was 9:35 when we were permitted to begin. The hall was half filled with some eight hundred people. When Gunther played his first chord, the dinner of hours earlier rushed to my throat. The piano, incredibly, was worse than before. It is not possible to describe the concert that followed. Gunther didn't dare play chords: he just touched a key here and there, looking apologetically at me, while both of us dripped perspiration. Only one

THE AFRICAN ADVENTURES OF LORD AYLESFORD

thing kept us from stopping and walking off the stage; our ears had not recovered from the long flight, and the sounds we made reached us distantly, as if from another room. A sense of unreality seized me. Here we were, charged with the responsibility of bringing cultural beauty to this far-off place—and we could do nothing.

His Lordship and I survived the first half, though every time Gunther touched the keys I almost gave way to hysterical laughter. When we finally left the stage, the audience expressed—of all things—delight at what they had heard. As we looked at each other, an explanation occurred to me: the piano tuner had lived here a long time, and might have lost his sense of pitch years ago. Perhaps since then all the pianos in Luanda had sounded the way that eighteen-thousand-dollar Steinway did during our concert. Audiences had come to accept this as the way a piano normally sounded!

I was right. Again and again members of the audience congratulated us on the beautiful music we had made. Finally I had to stop them, unwilling to allow this absurdity to continue. At an after-concert party I began asking questions. It turned out that the tuner was not only the sole practitioner in Luanda but the only one in all of Angola. They told us he had gone to Mocamedes, where we were scheduled to play the following night, "to take care of the piano."

The good people who attended the party probably hate us to this day, since we talked until 2:30 A.M. about the disastrous effect the tuner was having on Angolan music lovers and on their children, who were just learning to appreciate the glories of music. We were taken back to the hotel in an atmosphere of chilly animosity. In spite of the mild African night we were given icy handshakes; everyone seemed delighted to learn we had to arise in three short hours to catch the plane for Mocamedes. It was small consolation to learn a year later that a tuner from Johannesburg was now being flown in from time to time.

Our alarm clock went off at 5:30 A.M., and an hour later—hating the world, music, airplanes, and my mother for encouraging me to become a cellist—I arrived at the airport with Gunther. Neither of us had uttered a word. The plane took off for Mocamedes about an hour late. We flew over desert, still without talking, until the seat belt sign lit up. I looked out the window and saw nothing but vast, sandy emptiness.

THE WORLD OF MUSIC ACCORDING TO STARKER

My first thought was that something had gone wrong with the plane and this was a forced landing. But we set down smoothly and taxied up to a wooden shack, in front of which a few people milled.

I collected his Lordship, alighted, and sauntered toward the ramshackle structure. A young man stepped forward and rattled off something incomprehensible. I did hear "Circulo Cultura Musical," however, and answered, "Si, Starker," at which some natives fell upon the luggage and threw it into a waiting car, an old Mercedes. To our dismay, the one-man reception committee spoke nothing but Portuguese, and when he stamped on the accelerator I embraced his Lordship and held my breath. Our speed was approximately seventy miles per hour over dusty, unpaved roads. I wondered at the rush, since the concert was not scheduled until nine, and here it was only 2 P.M. After a few minutes a village materialized ahead of us—narrow dirty streets, a few cars, and one or two lazing natives. We screeched to a halt in front of a hotel that was surprisingly European in appearance—similar, in fact, to many hundred on the Left Bank of Paris—and we were quickly shown to our rooms.

The first thing I did in Mocamedes, to whose culture-hungry citizens we were bringing beauty and joy, was take a shower. This turned out to be quite a hazardous undertaking, and no little exercise. If you are familiar with lavatories in provincial France and northern Italy, you know the basic problem. In plain terms, such bathrooms consist of a hole in the floor with two elevated stones placed strategically, one on each side, for the feet. Apart from the usual problems this presents of balance and coordination, the real difficulty is that flushing causes the water to rise ankle-deep. In Mocamedes, fortunately, this sanitary ingenuity was restricted to the shower, placed in the middle of the room without so much as a curtain, and only a trough in the floor to carry off the water. After I finished showering it was necessary to hop, kangaroo-fashion, out of the bathroom—and my slippers were victims of the flood. It was an hour before I could enter the room again.

Our next experience was a late luncheon. The service was rather bizarre, for every time we tried to speak in Portuguese the waiters doubled up with laughter. Even today I'm not certain what we ate. I recall some fish soup, then dried meat accompanied by boiled potatoes and a singular bouquet of vegetables. Everything tasted so much the same

THE AFRICAN ADVENTURES OF LORD AYLESFORD

that Gunther and I decided everything had been cooked in the same pot, though the flavor was not entirely unpalatable.

After lunch, despite the heat, we decided to take a nap. We awakened from a fitful sleep at 8:30 P.M., in time to dress. The only firm point in our correspondence with the Portuguese manager before the tour began had been that we play all engagements in full evening dress—tails and white tie. Thus bedecked we descended the stairs at five minutes before nine, his Lordship in my hand, the music in Gunther's. In front of the hotel a group of Europeans were seated on sidewalk chairs, drinking, while a horde of half-naked native children ran about with cleaning equipment. At our appearance everyone fell silent and stared at us, all with the same dumbfounded expression—stunned, I suppose, by the full dress and the huge cello case that might have contained, for all they knew, a machine gun or a dead crocodile. To complete the effect, I was wearing sunglasses against the lingering daylight. I've often speculated how the first man to reach an inhabited planet would feel. There in Mocamedes I knew for a moment what it would be like. After standing and waiting for several minutes, we finally sat down. This action prompted two fearless little fellows to jump upon our shoes and shine them. The spell was shattered. The drinking recommenced, and the noise.

Not until 9:30 did a taxi of sorts arrive, driven by the same daredevil who had whisked us from the airport. It took only two minutes to drive from the hotel to the white stucco city hall. Inside was a fair-size hall equipped with a small podium. On this was a twin of the Luanda Steinway. Yet the hall was absolutely empty, though by this time it was getting on toward 10 P.M. I retired to the mayor's office and unpacked his Lordship, whom I hadn't even tuned all day. As I started warming up, the door opened and a little man walked in. He spoke passable French, and introduced himself as the head of the local radio station. He had come to ask permission to record our concert. As kindly as possible, I explained that because of the previous night's experience with the out-of-tune piano we could not grant his request, but that at the end of the program I would play an unaccompanied composition, and this he could record. He thanked us, left, and returned in a moment

THE WORLD OF MUSIC ACCORDING TO STARKER

with a microphone, which he proceeded to set up on the stage. I stopped him, saying he should do this only after intermission.

He looked pensive for a moment, then said, "You know, the less you play, I think, the better. People here are not too familiar with good music."

Gunther and I huddled and decided on a program: the two preclassical sonatas on the printed program, then the Debussy sonata and intermission; afterward two short works totaling six minutes, and finally the solo piece—in all forty-five minutes of music as against the seventy-five that is standard for recitals. I asked the radio man if he would announce the revised program, in Portuguese, before we began. He assented, drew the curtain aside, and stepped out onto the podium. It was seven, perhaps eight minutes before he returned to say that everything was in readiness. Gunther and I shook hands solemnly, promising each other not to become irritated no matter what. We each took a long, deep breath and stepped resolutely onto the podium.

I heard something slightly resembling applause. Once my eyes became accustomed to the dimness, I saw some two hundred chairs. Jammed into them were all of twenty-five people. The suggestion of applause was a result of these Caucasian ladies and gentlemen, dressed impeccably, approaching one white-gloved hand ever so cautiously to the other. Their duty thus dispatched, they lapsed into dead silence, into a state of motionless disinterest. We had no other course, regrettably, but to start.

When Gunther touched the piano keys I began to feel hysterical laughter welling up within me again. "Hold it," I said to myself. "You've promised not to get upset. You must do the best possible under the circumstances." Accordingly, I kept my left hand sliding up and down the fingerboard, attempting here and there to approximate the noises coming from the piano. The first work, two hundred years old, had been composed in two short movements, and at their end I motioned for Gunther to rise with me. The audience, looking relieved, I thought, repeated their earlier exercise: one soft clap.

We resumed playing. The second sonata consisted of four short movements. A grand total of fifteen minutes elapsed from our entrance until we stood up a second time, to one soft clap. Our first group completed, we left the stage in unbroken silence. Back in the mayor's office, I noticed our friend the radio man heading toward the stage with his microphone in hand.

"What are you doing?" I asked.

"I'm setting up the microphone."

"During intermission," I reminded him.

"Isn't this intermission?"

I hesitated a second. "We haven't played Debussy yet."

"Oh, then why did you come out?"

"It is *customary* to stop between groups and rest a bit."

He looked incredulous, but left. We wondered whether, in far-off Mocamedes, preclassical and Impressionistic music sounded alike to listeners, but then we decided their inability to detect such subtle differences was excusable in light of the sounds we had made. We returned to the podium, this time, however, to no applause whatsoever. Not only was there no applause, there was no audience. I peered into the gloom and finally spied cigarettes glowing in the pitch black beyond a far door. For want of anything else to do, I started tuning his Lordship (born in 1696, for this) while Gunther decided to experiment with the piano.

The cigarette ends started moving in our direction, like fireflies. All twenty-five located their chairs in absolute silence, having discovered that our strange exhibition was not yet done. Now for the Debussy, which we cellists call a show number, full of opportunities for instrumental display. Hundreds of untrained audiences, struck by its colors and phrases, have responded enthusiastically to performances of it. The missionary awakened within me. Among our artistic obligations, after all, was to stir these people.

If I may say so, we managed to play the sonata as well as possible. I stood with Gunther at its conclusion to acknowledge our praise: one soft clap. The moment we turned to leave the podium the audience rose and filed out. I lit a cigarette, smoked half of it, then stamped it out.

"Let's get this thing over with," I muttered to Gunther, and signaled the radio man to set up his microphone. We went back to the podium and waited. The audience put out their cigarettes and returned. After six minutes of music, we had to leave the stage momentarily. The final

THE WORLD OF MUSIC ACCORDING TO STARKER

work, after all, was to be played without accompaniment. One soft clap. Again the audience filed out. I returned. They returned. I played. One soft clap. I retired. They retired.

I had believed that in my varied life I had experienced everything possible: often facing death, living in danger, living in comfort, playing as an artist in many countries, playing good and bad concerts to good and bad audiences. But this! Even children, who knew nothing about classical music or the cello, were always fascinated by the movement of the left hand up and down the fingerboard. Afterward they would ask questions: What is a sonata? How do you play? Why? Here, however, adults who were supposed to be the bearers of civilization reflected only disinterest and boredom. Suddenly I burst out laughing. Gunther thought I had gone quite mad.

"What's so funny?"

"Do you know," I said, "we've just made musical history? No cellist ever played a more expensive concert. Our fees, our travel expenses, and the hotel and food have cost the Portuguese government approximately three thousand dollars. Divide that by twenty-five listeners. Tonight each person who dragged himself to this place of desecration cost the government one hundred and twenty dollars! Even Callas doesn't do better than that!"

All I remember of our trip to the airport next morning is that once again we went at seventy miles per hour. The return flight to Luanda differed little from our trip out except that the weather was warmer. We stayed two days in Luanda, until the plane took us to our next engagement, in Lourenço Marques, across the continent in Portuguese East Africa. When we alighted from the plane we walked quickly to the immigration office, where a little gentleman greeted us in French. "Welcome to Mozambique! I am—" his eyes shone with joy, "—not from the Circulo Cultura Musical. But if you will permit me, I shall be happy to do anything for you. I am a music teacher here."

For the first time since we arrived in Africa, here was someone who had something to do with music. But we proceeded cautiously—after all, the piano tuner in Luanda supposedly had something to do with music—and asked only where the concert was to be played, and when. The little man, whom I shall call Mr. Sam, promised to supply all information within the hour. Lourenço Marques looked no different from Luanda except that it was larger and more modern. The hotel we stayed in was truly luxurious, eight stories high and circular. Each suite had a living room, bedroom, and terrace, with windows that opened on the Gulf of Mozambique.

An hour after we'd arrived the telephone rang with our second pleasant surprise: Mr. Sam was downstairs—on time! According to the schedule our first concert was to be three days later, on the Isle of Mozambique at the northernmost end of the Gulf; then a concert in Beira; and finally one in Lourenço Marques itself. At dinner that evening, I made passing reference to our unhappy experience with pianos in Angola, and received a third pleasant surprise. Smiling, Mr. Sam said not to worry, that a tuner came up from Johannesburg. "Conditions are different here than in Angola." How great the difference was we learned the next day, when Mr. Sam invited us to his home, produced an impressive record collection, and revealed a genuine love of music.

Most of the time we spent resting rather than looking around, and early on the third day we arose refreshed and ready for another trip. At the airport we boarded a ten-seat plane that did not go to the Isle, only to a place called Lumbo. From there it was an hour by boat to our destination.

Along the way the plane stopped at Quelimane, where we had our first sign of Real Africa. Palm trees and cactus were the only vegetation, the temperature was in the nineties, and in back of the small airport shack naked children played in a nearly dry river. One of the youngsters, a boy of about six, dangled an unlit cigarette butt from his lips; soon a girl of around twelve arrived smoking, and the boy helped himself to a light. A slow-motion convoy of semi-naked women, each with a bundle of branches on her head, came into view. None spoke. They were dry skin and bones, their ages beyond guessing, and seemed to be on the last lap of a journey to some crematory.

Eight hours after our departure from Lourenço Marques we put down in Lumbo, port of entry for our next musical adventure. The man who received us was evidently related to our guide in Mocamedes, as he displayed the same reckless anxiety to deposit us at the only existing hostelry. A ten-minute drive at seventy miles per hour through clouds of dust brought us to a house. Immediately the car was surrounded by a half-dozen native boys who grabbed whatever we possessed—including his Lordship. A brief scuffle ensued, during which I managed to recover possession of my noble companion. We then entered a well-tended garden, where a sign proudly announced this establishment to be the Grand Hotel of Lumbo. Past experience in Paris and elsewhere had conditioned me to expect, after such a pronouncement, the ungrandest quarters, and so I approached the place with some apprehension. Indeed, it was primitive. We learned from the man at the desk that we would leave for the Isle at 1 P.M. the next day.

It was early afternoon, and we had nothing to do but sightsee. The hotel was situated just a few hundred yards from the Indian Ocean. The heat was oppressive, so we walked toward the water. A pier, a long wooden structure no wider than ten feet, stretched into the ocean, and down its middle ran two narrow-gauge rails. Six natives were lying in pairs along the rails, dressed in what once upon a time must have been shorts. As we stepped onto the pier, the first pair raised themselves to a kneeling position; one began with a hammer to scratch at a spot where the wood was rotting away. The other produced a nail and in slow motion started to drive it in. They gave us a contemptuous look as we passed, muttering something between themselves. The next pair also became active as we neared; with pieces of cloth they commenced to rub at rust, producing two shiny spots, each the size of a fifty-cent piece. The third pair repeated the hammer-and-nail business. After we'd passed, each pair returned to their comatose state.

We had veal steak and potato chips for breakfast the next morning, and there was some time afterward for more exploration. We found a marketplace in which a couple of hundred natives milled about, shopping for bread, fruits, and vegetables. Flies and bugs and stray dogs were everywhere, but dirt was the master—dirt, and native fertility. There were babies all over the place, either on their mothers' backs or about to be born. At 11 A.M. a freight train arrived and discharged five natives, triggering quite a commotion. We saw nothing more, but the spectators were beside themselves, just as if the home team had won a game in the last half of the ninth inning. Since our departure time was nearing, however, we had to leave behind all this excitement.

THE AFRICAN ADVENTURES OF LORD AYLESFORD

I took his Lordship and my evening suit and walked with Gunther to the pier (passing the same natives, who performed their same little dumb show). At its end a clean-looking motorboat was moored, watched over by a spotlessly dressed officer who motioned us on board. At 3 P.M.—that African time again—the boat left for the Isle, which resembled, as we approached it, a Moroccan port mixed with a bit of India.

A gentleman waiting for us at the landing waved a greeting. Dressed in the latest Bond Street fashion, smoking a Camel cigarette in a gold-rimmed holder, he looked like a junior-size Walter Pidgeon standing in a garbage dump. In perfect English he introduced himself as Dr. So-and-So, president of the local Circulo chapter, and apologized for not having met us in Lumbo. He expressed the hope that we had met no difficulties and led us to an Italian sports car, meanwhile motioning a boy to pick up his Lordship and place him in a rickshaw. Gunther, without delay, joined his Lordship in it. I risked the car.

The concert hall was—where else?—in the town hall. The piano turned out to be a Bösendorfer, a make I had known only in Central Europe. Gunther, determined not to be distressed by what he might hear, touched the keys. We looked at each other incredulously; it had been perfectly tuned! He sat down and promptly lost himself in rapture.

We returned to the hall at 9 P.M. to give a concert, if need be, for ourselves. To my amazement, about a hundred persons had gathered, and they behaved throughout like an audience in any major European city. They listened attentively, enjoyed the music, later asked for autographs, and thanked us for the privilege of hearing our performance.

After supper we said goodbye almost reluctantly and boarded a little motor launch for our return trip. I secured his Lordship and settled back. It was past midnight, a quiet moonless night undisturbed by the noise of other craft. The sky was filled by a myriad of stars, and the motor purred softly like a contented cat. What earlier had seemed only bleak was now beautiful. I thanked my mother for wanting me to be a cellist, for giving me an opportunity to see the world and find such beauty as this, to bring pleasure to far-off people. As the boat approached Lumbo I wondered when I should again find peace such as this. I lifted his Lordship fondly, and we walked to the hotel through

THE WORLD OF MUSIC ACCORDING TO STARKER

the warm African night. I fell asleep feeling that it was indeed a Grand Hotel.

The flight next day to Beira was exhilarating, thanks to my newly gained equilibrium. At Nampula our thirty-minute layover became an hour and a half, though nothing more needed to be done than refuel the plane. It was just that our pilot and stewardess met some friends and had a visit. Time had ceased to be significant—one of the important African contributions, I believe, to white culture.

We found Beira to be a modern city with a huge harbor and the largest rail center in Mozambique. It also served as a shopping, entertainment, and vacation center for many Rhodesians. The Grand Hotel there was one of the best I've encountered anywhere, combining Old World luxury with an Olympic-size swimming pool, game rooms, and an extraordinary restaurant. Things obviously were looking up for us.

Here, as in Luanda, our concert was in a movie house that had a fairly decent piano. The only distraction was an adjoining hall in which, throughout our performance, an American gangster film was being shown. Whenever the film broke—and it seemed to quite often—the audience enjoyed the music, and we managed to adjust.

Our African adventure was nearing its end. We had one last concert, in Lourenço Marques, and then the prospect of a twenty-hour flight back to Lisbon. That concert turned out to be the artistic highlight of our entire cultural safari. On the afternoon of the performance we visited the hall, found the piano excellent, and sat down to play some. I was playing a bit casually when suddenly my eyes wandered to Mr. Sam, seated in the front row of the empty theater. His eyes were closed, and he was transported. Every phrase we played brought him convulsive pleasure. When we finished he came to us in tears and, unable to speak a word, shook our hands warmly.

Back at the hotel I unpacked his Lordship and spent the remainder of the day practicing. The concert that evening brought cheers from a grateful audience, and at the end more tears—and this time kisses on the hand—from Mr. Sam. His actions may have embarrassed us beyond words, but they made me wonder whether our trip hadn't a purpose after all. If only there were more Mr. Sams in the world.

Later, at the airport, there were more warm goodbyes and see-youagains. Departure time was midnight. The plane started down the runway; we had reached takeoff speed when suddenly the pilot hit the brakes. A motor had malfunctioned, and only by a miracle did the plane manage to stop short of the jungle. At noon the next day it finally left Lourenço Marques.

At Luanda a second motor went awry, and another twelve hours passed until we could continue on to Lisbon. By then the plane was jam-packed, which meant that his Lordship was practically sharing my seat. I do love him dearly, but the backache I got from fourteen hours in a straitjacket position led me to envy the flutist's fortunate lot. At long last, the illuminated seat belt sign meant Lisbon was below. Our Portuguese manager—his carefully cultivated Cambridge accent at full mast—had a fit when he saw me alight with his Lordship in one hand and in the other the little crocodile I had purchased for my daughter.

"Where were you so long?" he demanded. "You are twenty-four hours late!"

I just stared at him until we had passed through customs and immigration. Then, summoning up my own best Cambridge accent, I answered:

"Old chap, Mozambique is pretty demm far."

Originally published in HiFi/Stereo Review, 1962

10 BLOOMINGTON THEN

In September '58 we moved to Bloomington and I started university life. There were some superb faculty members at IU: singers, mostly former Met stars; the stage director Hans Busch; the conductor Tibor Kozma; my cello colleague Fritz Magg, who played with the Berkshire Quartet; and several musicologists. In his quest to build a great school, Dean Bain primarily focused on the opera department, but for that he needed a good orchestra, and therefore he recruited renowned instrumental teachers. Among the pianists were Menahem Pressler, the only one still alive and active, and Sidney Foster. However, my early days there weren't easy. I had only seven students, three of whom were weak. After one semester I advised two to leave.

I played some concerts in the U.S. and Europe, and Eva and I frequently went to Chicago to see our parents. Her parents continued living in our apartment, and her father tried all sorts of business ventures. One particular attempt involved an old friend whose activities had been affecting our lives since '47 in Paris. I once wrote about him in an essay called "How to Be a Hungarian." His name was Domokos Fekete, though he eventually changed it to Domingo Vargas, and he was called the great Hungarian imposter. He worked variously as a

Honduran envoy to the Vatican, an aide to the Haitian consul in France, an oil geologist in Mexico, president of an American-Panamanian oil company, and owner of a Brazilian shipping line, interspersed with jail terms in Belgium and in a detention center for illegal immigrants in California. I got him out of that one. He drove trucks loaded with explosives and sold gifts to sailors in a store on Broadway. He was an amusing liar with a brilliant mind, and was fluent in seven languages. Now he offered to ship lumber from Brazil, which my father-in-law would sell in the U.S. Nothing came of it. I saw Fekete/Vargas last in Berlin in the seventies. I wonder if he is still alive.

Tension continued between Eva and me in Bloomington, and I suggested a separation. Eva decided to go to Cuba with Gabrielle. I spent Christmas of 1958 in Chicago; I saw Rae, and the future did not look too bad. Bloomington offered some security, and I decided to stay. I was scheduling more and more concert dates. I finished recording the Bach suites in London, but my relationship with Legge soured and we agreed to an amicable parting. He found new enthusiasm for a slew of Russians, among them Mstislav Rostropovich, and history bore out his judgment.

I lived alone in Bloomington, and Gabrielle came to visit a few times. I tried to prepare her for the divorce that seemed inevitable. When my first year at IU was over, I left for Europe and Portuguese Africa, the trip I chronicled in the previous chapter as "The African Adventures of Lord Aylesford." On my return I went to Cuba to see Eva and decide whether there was a chance to save our marriage. After a few days I felt it was hopeless. Eventually I asked for legal advice.

Another family event happened in February 1959. I was in London, and a Swedish journalist came to interview me. One of his questions was, "Is it correct that your father was born in Zwierzinec?" I said yes. "And you are playing in Stockholm in two weeks?" "Yes," I said, "my first appearance in Sweden." There were some more standard questions, and he left. Two weeks later I got off the plane in Stockholm and found myself facing TV cameras, photographers, and a group of nine people with flowers: an older couple, two young couples, and three tots. The old man said he was my uncle Joseph, my father's brother, and he was there with his wife, their son and daughter, and their families. Joseph's children had ended up in Sweden during the war and married there, and their parents had recently joined them from Warsaw. I was thunderstruck. I had never known they existed. I found them nice but total strangers. My father had three brothers and five sisters, but the only one of them I knew was his brother Sam, whom I met briefly in New York in 1949. Joseph and his family were much like Sam; nice, but complete strangers to me. Years later I met one of my father's sisters and her descendants, and it was the same story. With the descendants of two other sisters, however, some rapport developed. One family, the Gerbers, are musicians and teachers, so we have a bond there. In December 2002 I met a cousin and his children and grandson in Israel.

The 1959–60 school year started on a sad note, with a memorial service for Ede Zathureczky, who had died on the last day of the previous semester. He was president of the Franz Liszt Academy after Dohnányi, a great violinist and an admired teacher. He joined IU in '57 and fell victim to the immigrant syndrome, unable to adjust to the new world, missing his status in his native land, not performing, and stunned by the different attitudes of American university students and administrators. He would call me for help: "What am I going to do? A student is chewing gum." I told him to tell the student to spit it out. He asked if he could do that and I said yes. He cheerfully reported that it worked. Or he would call in despair that a student wanted to leave him. I said, "Be glad, one less in your class." One night he practiced, went to bed, and died while making love to his wife.

The good news for me this year was that I had eleven students in my class and plenty of talent this time, which allowed me to really teach. I moved into a small apartment in the university's Union, which meant I could walk to the music school and had no household duties. By this time I had signed with Colbert Artists. Van Wyck organized my European activities, and I had French, German, Italian, Spanish, and Portuguese managers. The Colberts offered a ten-concert tour in Japan for the fall of 1960. Van Wyck offered a number of concerts in South Africa, Spain, and Germany, which turned into an around-the-world trip. My records kept appearing on the market, though the EMI contract had expired. I was teaching, playing, and driving more and more often to Chicago to see Rae. In the spring she drove my mother down for a visit, and I introduced her to Bloomington. My divorce was granted in May, and five weeks later we were married.

That summer I was teaching in Bloomington, and as my class grew to eighteen, I asked for a one-third appointment so I could fulfill my obligations elsewhere. Bain hired Leopold Teraspulsky from Chicago to fill in, and he began to build his own class. My friendship with Bain stabilized after a few bumps. In my first year he called and told me that I had to play in the opera orchestra, as there weren't enough good cellists for the yearly performance of *Parsifal*. The prospect of returning to the toughest Met times, with their *Ring*s and *Parsifal* marathons, rubbed me the wrong way. He insisted, saying that Fritz Magg, who preceded me by two years at the Met, had already agreed to help. So I agreed, but I refused to participate in rehearsals, only the performance, and specified that both Fritz and I would sit on the last stand. I also said that if he ever asked me again I would quit. The second year he called and said that I was away too much and what if some legislator came down from Indianapolis and wanted to see the big-shot cellist? I told him that in that case I would just have to arrange bookings as a full-time soloist. Bain pacified me, and I was also notified that I had been appointed a full professor. That was the last time my outside activities were ever questioned.

In '59 Gyorgy Sebok managed to get out of Hungary with his second wife, Eva, and settled in France. Within a few months he was discovered as a superb pianist. I was in Europe that year, and saw him for the first time in twelve years. In minutes our friendship was reestablished, and it continued until he passed away in 1999. I asked him to join me in '60 for the Japanese tour, and for several concerts in Europe in '61. Erato, the record company for which Sebok was pouring out LPs, asked us to record all the Beethoven sonatas and variations and the Brahms sonatas. As my EMI contract had ended, we taped everything in one week.

The 1960–61 season was a turning point. I spent a few weeks teaching, and the rest of the time in practically uninterrupted traveling. I had what was called a New York debut in the Metropolitan Museum, although I had played before in New York without being reviewed. Mieczyslaw Horszowski was the pianist. He had been the pianist on the first recordings I ever heard of Casals. He was a superb musician, who at the age of sixty was willing to learn a new sonata by Bernhard Heiden, my colleague, who wrote it for me. The rest of the program was the Beethoven A Major Sonata, Debussy, and the Brahms E Minor Sonata. When we started rehearsing the Brahms, I felt trouble coming after only two bars. He played so slowly, holding me back, that I couldn't imagine how we could play four sonatas without some catastrophe. When the first movement was over I lit a cigarette. He looked at me and I looked at him. "Excuse me, but is that the way you used to play it with Casals?" I asked. He said, "Yes." I asked him if he liked it that slow and he answered, "Not really." "So why don't we play it the way we both like it?" We were both glorified in the reviews and I was discovered in New York. My U.S. engagements doubled the following season.

I received an invitation to play Prokofiev's Cello Concerto with the Berlin Philharmonic, conducted by Karajan, in '61. Shortly afterward a cable came asking to replace the concerto, which I already knew because I had recorded it, with the *Symphony Concertante*. But I had a year to learn the symphony, so I agreed, and just to be safe I scheduled it with the Johannesburg Orchestra. The tour started. I played in Europe and went on to South Africa, and on arrival in Johannesburg I was told that the Prokofiev material hadn't arrived. We settled on Hindemith, but I was a little worried about playing Prokofiev's symphony for the first time in Berlin. Luckily two rehearsals were agreed upon.

The South African tour, through Johannesburg, Pretoria, and Cape Town, was only O.K. I was accompanied by Sequeira Costa, a Portuguese pianist. As the papers reported, I treated the journey more like an extended honeymoon than a concert tour, discovering the rare beauty of South Africa and especially Cape Town. Unfortunately, our plan to visit Kruger Park was quashed. The park was closed shortly before our arrival after a tragic car accident in which Matthias Seiber, a Hungarian-British composer, was killed. The biggest success of that tour was the beauty of my wife, which overshadowed my cellistic prowess in all the papers and made me proud.

We went from South Africa to Spain, and from there to Japan. Just before we began the long trip east, an urgent cable arrived. The Japanese audiences desired my rendition of Bruch's *Kol Nidrei*, a piece I had taught but never played. I managed to locate a copy in Madrid. Our first stop after leaving Spain was Rome, where Sebok joined us. Between Rome and Beirut I memorized the piece with Sebok holding the music, conducting silently and from time to time asking me to name the notes. In Beirut we had a six-hour layover, and the airline took us on a sightseeing tour. Those were the days! It was a formidable city then. In Karachi, however, we were not allowed to leave the plane. We went on to Tokyo via Hong Kong. A young man with cursory English greeted us and deposited us in the Frank Lloyd Wright Imperial Hotel. We could barely see anything after almost two days of flying. Luckily we had a chance to sleep, as the first concert was not for three days.

The next day, as Rae and I walked through the lobby, all we heard was English being spoken by American businessmen. I said that I wanted to learn about Japan while in Japan. So we moved to a Japanese hotel, which had a traditional part and a Western-style part. We chose the traditional one, tatami, paper walls, and all. In the middle of the night we woke up. In the rooms surrounding us were a group playing poker, an excited couple making love, and a family with crying children. The next day we moved to the Western wing.

The first concert was rather shocking. After the opening piece, the polite applause died away by the time we reached the stage door. After the second piece it was the same. In the intermission we wondered if they didn't like us—maybe we might as well go home! But at the end the applause, though quiet, went on and on. We kept returning for bows and then started playing encores. Finally we stopped and a huge line formed to get our autographs, take our pictures, trace the outline of our hands on cardboard, and give us flowers and presents. When we asked about our cool reception at the beginning, we were told that Japanese audiences are polite. They knew we were coming back and didn't want to tire us with unnecessary bows.

Several concerts and interviews followed, including one performance that was broadcast on television. Some of the concerts required train rides to towns where there were only Japanese hotels. We took overnight trains, where first class meant four people to a sleeper. Rae had to share the cabin with me, Sebok, and the man who was supposed to be our manager. The manager's wife shared the next compartment with three

THE WORLD OF MUSIC ACCORDING TO STARKER

men. Each car had a Japanese toilet—a hole in the floor—and a Western one with a porcelain seat, but no cover. Some of the hotels also had Western facilities, but the small spaces still caused us a bit of consternation and discomfort. Forty-two years ago the majority of Japanese people were quite a bit shorter than us, though we weren't giants. Plus, it took us a while to realize that one sits reversed.

The halls were cold. The audiences wore heavy coats, and we kept our hands functional with electric heaters backstage. The language problem was constant, especially one evening when our manager didn't show up. At the end of that concert, however, he arrived proudly carrying a toilet seat wrapped in newspaper, which improved our wellbeing for days. By then we had learned that our young man was not a manager, but an employee of a major newspaper, which had guaranteed six of the concerts. The other four were subcontracted by a bona fide manager, but as it turned out he was a crook. He signed a contract for a concert in Osaka to be broadcast on television, saying that it would be the first televised performance in Japan, but when the local organizer found out we already had done a TV recital he canceled the date. He had already paid the fees to our crook, however, who promptly disappeared. Years later I heard that he was in jail for similar activities.

When we arrived for the last concert in Tokyo, the hall was jam-packed but our young man was nowhere. Since we were supposed to get paid, I delayed the start. The stagehands kept urging us to begin. I remembered sitting in a concert hall in Budapest in the mid-'30s, waiting for Casals to start his recital, which he did forty minutes late. I turned to Sebok and said, "This is so provincial. We have to start. We are musicians. Never mind. We will play in bigger places yet." Sebok nonchalantly replied, "Not possible. Tokyo is the largest city in the world. Let's get started."

Years later I learned the reason for Casals's delay from the organizer of the concert—Imre Kun, the same man who had paid me $1 for a concert after the war. He wanted to pay Casals in Hungarian currency before the concert, but Casals said his contract called for U.S. funds. Kun told him that it was Saturday and he could only get dollars on Monday. Casals said no way and that he wouldn't play. Kun, in desperation, remembered that the president of the National Bank, a great music lover, was in the audience. He went to him and explained the situation. Mr. Fellner called his driver, drove to his home, took the necessary American money out of his safe, and returned to give it to Casals. Casals counted it, and the concert began.

The end of our first Japanese tour was not as felicitous. Our young man arrived while we were playing, but he had no private means to make up the stolen funds. He managed to give us some pearls instead. I used some to pay U.S. commissions, and my wife still wears some. The around-the-world tour still had a Hong Kong date a few days later, but I had had enough. For the first time in my life I canceled my appearance, and by Christmas we were home, covered with glory and with beautiful memories of the sights and sounds of strange cultures, as well as the sour taste of the hazards.

When I remarried I inherited a beautiful four-year-old girl, Gwen. While her mother and I were away she was tended by a gem of a black lady named Willie. Within the shortest possible time, Gwen became as much my daughter as Gabrielle, and ever since has called me Papa. Still, I missed Gabrielle. While she was in Cuba in '59, I was rather concerned about what would happen to her. Castro had taken over and the Communist reorganization had begun; I was familiar with what that could be like. Luckily Eva and her friends went to Mexico and eased my worry.

Our accommodations in Bloomington were rather hilarious. Carelessly, I didn't secure a house in time, and the only available housing was a small apartment in a graduate student building. We were surrounded by struggling students. The poor souls couldn't figure out what a professor was doing in their midst, with a child, a wife, a nanny, and two cars. In addition, the place consisted of two bedrooms, a living room, a kitchen, and a bathroom all squeezed into a space roughly the size of an RV. It was rough, though I was teaching eight to ten hours a day and spending a lot of time on the road, so I wasn't there much. Of course Rae decorated the tiny place like a boutique, and even arranged small dinner parties by which she established her reputation as the great cook and hostess of the town.

Starting in 1960, several former colleagues from the CSO moved to Bloomington: first Philip Farkas, horn, and Jerry Sirucek, oboe, in

With Menahem Pressler and Joseph Gingold

1960, then Leonard Sharrow, bassoon, in 1963. Even more significantly, Josef Gingold came to IU from Cleveland. It is rather difficult for me to speak about Gingold. I consider him the greatest violin teacher I have ever known, and among the greatest musicians I ever met. Beyond that he was the most honest, decent human being, and he was like an older brother to me until the day he died. His death left a huge void. For decades we played a concert together every year, eventually donating the receipts to a variety of causes: scholarships, the United Negro College Fund and other black college funds, Poles suffering under Soviet occupation, and from '79 the Eva Janzer Memorial Cello Center. We also recorded the Kodály Duo.

In the summer of '61, after playing some European dates, I did my second tour of Portuguese Africa, this time with Sebok. We visited villages in Angola and a wild park (was it Gorongosa?) in Mozambique and had a great time. I needed it. The European dates included probably the worst experience I ever had, my long-awaited debut with the Berlin Philharmonic. When I arrived in Berlin a message greeted me, canceling the first rehearsal. The orchestra had just returned from an all-Beethoven tour in England, and they were tired. The entire three-hour rehearsal would be for the Prokofiev, as the rest of the program was the *Eroica*, which the orchestra had been performing on tour. My stomach was not happy, considering this would be my first performance of such a demanding work. The orchestra was in place at 10 A.M., but there was no sign of Karajan. We waited. He blew in at 11. Without any explanation, he said, "Are you playing the first movement at the end?" I thought I had forgotten my German. "What do you mean?" "I think it's better that way," he said. My answer was, "Both versions of this work are printed in the same order."

The rehearsal began and it was a disgrace. He kept comparing score notes with the orchestral parts and was obviously unfamiliar with the concerto. Whenever an extended solo passage came with minimum scoring, he stopped. "We don't need that, you know it." It was a sight-reading exercise for both him and the orchestra. By one o'clock we had scrambled through the piece once. "See you tonight," Karajan said. I was inexperienced then. I should have canceled, but, stupidly, I went through with it. The first concert was a disaster. I played acceptably, but the orchestra sounded like a rehearsal. I stayed on to hear the *Eroica*. It was stunning. I felt sick. The second night sounded like a general rehearsal. The third night was first-class, as by that time they had all learned the piece. Each night Karajan mumbled that the first movement should be at the end. The reviews, naturally, were from the first night. I wasn't panned, just ignored, and the *Eroica* and Karajan were deified.

One month after that debut I was back in Berlin to play and record the Brahms Double Concerto with the Rias Orchestra, Wolfgang Schneiderhahn, and my old Budapest friend Ferenc Fricsay. They had just returned from a tour with Menuhin, and I went to their concert. Menuhin played Bartók's Concerto. It was the best playing I had heard from him since his days as a child prodigy. Fricsay, by then ailing, had turned into a great spiritual musician in the Furwangler mold. Recording the Brahms with him was a revelation and a great joy.

I had lunch at one point with a former Berlin Philharmonic cellist whom I had met at the Geneva Competition in 1946. When the conversation turned to my disgusting experience with Karajan and his sug-

THE WORLD OF MUSIC ACCORDING TO STARKER

gestion of changing the movements' order, my colleague burst out laughing and told me Karajan had put the records on the turntable in the wrong order. Well, true or not, no better explanation has been found since. It could be argued that the second movement ending is more effective than the third, but that the first is? No way. I was not invited back to the Berlin Philharmonic for twenty years. But that's another story and just as unpleasant.

Later in '61 I made my first visit to Israel, with the Israel Philharmonic conducted by John Barbirolli: eight concerts in Tel Aviv, Jerusalem, and Haifa. The experience was varied and rich. It was a high-class orchestra and hall; the atmosphere was weird, and everyone in the string section acted like a concertmaster. Barbirolli, the kindest conductor alive, smilingly tolerated the total lack of discipline and the concertmaster's smart-aleck remarks: "Sir John, you can't do that, it's too fast." Barbirolli replied, "Sure, my dear, we will take it a bit slower." Great musician as he was, he never took such things to heart. He was an insomniac and drank whiskey and water throughout the day and night. He was never more than a bit tipsy, though, and he was always kind. He had his oboist wife with him. After-concert dinners were at the Philharmonic's guest house, where the Barbirollis and I were staying, and they often lasted long into the night. One night, after I had finally fallen asleep, he knocked on my door. "Are you awake?" "By now I am," I said. He asked if he could borrow my cello. I gave it to him, and he practiced till about 6 A.M.

On the ride to Jerusalem we saw reminders of the '48 war: tanks, ruins, Arab fortresses, and soldiers with machine guns, as well as flourishing kibbutzim and hordes of settlers planting trees and turning deserts into gardens. New Jerusalem was in a building boom. Beyond the walls separating Israel and Palestine there was nothing but arid land and the sacred part of old Jerusalem. We spent two hours sitting in on the trial of Adolf Eichmann, the man who was responsible for the murder of the majority of Hungarian Jews. It was a dreary day. Eichmann was sitting in a glass cage, and the prosecutors and defenders were droning on and on. I was glad to return to Tel Aviv. I did not return to Israel until after the '67 war, when the land was very different.

I went back home to Indiana to start full-time teaching again, in my new studio in a new building which had been finished in 1960. Rae and I moved into a rented house on a dead-end street, small with beautiful trees. Compared to graduate housing, it was a palace. Life went on: I taught huge classes, traveled, toured Europe, and made short trips within the U.S. and to Canada. This was to be my routine for the next thirty-five years. The composers among my fellow faculty were writing more and more works for me. Bernhard Heiden wrote a sonata, a cello duo, a concerto, an aria with orchestra, and a cello quartet, and he arranged "Lilliburlero" for solo cello. David Baker, who occasionally took cello lessons with me, wrote a sonata, a concerto, a duo for cello and percussion, a cello quartet, a two-cello quintet, and a cello duo. And Juan Orrego-Salas wrote a concerto and a duo for tuba and cello. These works have been performed in Paris, Tokyo, New York, Pittsburgh, Oakland, St. Paul, and many, many other cities around the world. They have been an ideal form of collaboration with colleagues and friends.

The school grew and its standards rose. In '62 Bain called. He said he had hired a pianist but the man had just canceled, and he asked about my friend in Paris, Sebok. I told him I could find out if Sebok was available, and he insisted I call right then. I did. Sebok asked, "When?" and I said, "Now." He asked about our concerts in Europe and I told him I would find another pianist for them, and that the dean needed an answer in twenty-four hours. Seventeen hours later he called back and said O.K. It took a month for him and his wife to get visas, and Rae and I left for Europe just as they arrived. They moved into our house and became surrogate parents to Gwen for life. When we returned they rented an apartment. For two seasons the programs of all my U.S. recitals were changed to sonatas, and we performed together. No other partner has ever given me as much joy in making music. Though we are completely different, he a philosopher and I an ideo-realist, an idealist without illusions, we were in total agreement about everything musical. We performed across the country to considerable acclaim. But because of the peculiar way he was classed as an accompanist rather than a pianist, we came to the conclusion that it would be better for his career if he went his own way. On occasion, I performed with Charles Webb who took over the deanship of the School of Music from Wilfred Bain and led it to greater heights for twenty-four years.

With Juan Orrego-Salas

With David Baker

The Nerikis: Shigeo, Sho, and Reiko

For years I played with Leon Pommers, an excellent pianist and a lovely man, who also partnered with such violinists as Erica Morini, Nathan Milstein, and others. In later years my partners included Stephen Swedish, Ralph Berkowitz (Piatigorsky's partner for years), Helena Costa, Helen Taverniti, and Alfonso Montecino. In Europe, Gunther Ludwig was my partner for many years and a top-notch musician, as was Alain Planes. Then in the '70s Shigeo Neriki, a Sebok student, showed up in my class to play for my cellists. I asked him to travel with me, and not only did he live up to the highest expectations, but he became like a son to us. And as the icing on the cake, his wife, Reiko, also a Sebok student, appeared on the scene. She used to assist me in class, and when Shigeo is touring on his own, she plays with me at the highest level. On occasion I have played with Menahem Pressler (a great musician of the Beaux Arts Trio), with Rudolf Buchbinder, and with Julius Katchen. On Japanese tours I have played with Shirley Yamaguchi and Shuku Iwasaki, and I have also recorded with Iwasaki. In the last few years I have played some concerts in Europe with Denis Pascal, an excellent pianist, who traveled the same route as the Nerikis, from Sebok to my class. He even had his wedding in our home. His wife was my student and assistant and, on top of that, a superb singer. They are also like family members.

In '62 Mercury Records offered me an exclusive contract. The head of their classical division was Wilma Cozart, wife of Robert Fine, the inventive genius of stereophonic recordings. She was also the lady who greeted me in Dallas in 1948. For the sonata recordings they signed up Sebok. They had just signed Henryk Szeryng as well, and considered having us establish a trio, but the plan was quickly shelved after an impromptu tryout. We felt it was just as well, considering our initials: the three *S*s. The first Mercury recordings were with the London Symphony Orchestra, conducted by Stanislaw Skrowaczewski: concertos by Lalo and Schumann. Then Chopin and Mendelssohn sonatas with Sebok. I continued with Antal Doráti and the Dvořák Concerto, Bruch's *Kol Nidrei*, Saint-Saens's Concerto, and Tchaikovsky's *Rococo Variations*. Then, with Sebok, I recorded the Brahms sonatas, a mixed recital LP, and the three Bach Gamba Sonatas. After the Italian cello sonatas with Stephen Swedish, I went on to the six Bach suites. In '65, in the middle of recording the Bach, I lost the use of my Strad, as I described in chapter 3. Half of the suites were recorded with the Strad, the rest with my new partner, the Matteo Goffriller.

In 1966 I discussed future repertory with Mercury. I felt that I had already covered the major repertory, and even repeated some of it, so an exclusive was not really desirable any longer. I was stupid, of course, since when I was no longer under exclusive contract Mercury's promotional budget for me promptly became nil. On the other hand, I could pursue making recordings that the big companies were not interested in. One of my lifelong regrets is that I missed recording *Don Quixote* with Reiner. When the CSO called EMI about it in 1959, someone mechanically answered that Starker was exclusive. They signed Antonio Janigro.

So now I was free, except for the usual five-year no-repeat clause, and until 1990, when I signed a ten-CD contract with RCA, I was free to record almost anything for any company. Probably the most enjoyable of these recordings were those I made in the late '60s. For a few years I spent about two weeks every summer in the Adirondacks, helping to

THE SAGA OF THE STARKER BRIDGE

The year was 1965. I was returning from a trip to Bloomington. I attended a concert of the then-called Leningrad Philharmonic with David Oystrach as conductor and soloist. In our huge auditorium I was seated in a back row, and listening to him I was struck by the sound of his violin. It seemed amplified. During a sleepless night the words *amplification* and *preamplification* kept me awake. The next day I called a cello student who I knew was handy with tools and owned an electric drill. We took off the bridge of my cello and drilled holes in its feet, and with a knife widened the entrances to make the holes conical shaped, thereby acting like mini-preamplifiers without any alteration to the instrument itself. The experiments were repeated, by then with the help of our resident luthier, Ole Dahl, on cellos, violas, violins, and basses about two hundred times. A letter S replaced the traditional fleur-de-lis design in the middle of the bridge so as to make it recognizable. A patent was applied for, and the patent office asked for more precise data as they found an early-twentieth-century right to drill holes without the conical specification. I let the claim drop but the bridges were produced in Germany. In 1966 *Time* magazine called it a major discovery in 300 years of instrument making. This is a claim I do not own up to. Research showed that the bridge helps in activating overtones. I have used it ever since, and so do a few thousand people around the world. The jury is still out in judging its ultimate value.

build the Adirondack Festival, headquartered in Saranac Lake. One day the American pianist Julius Katchen showed up. I had met him passingly in Paris in 1948; he moved there just as I was getting ready to leave. He had already recorded for Decca all of Brahms's piano works, and now proposed that we collaborate on the piano chamber music. I was about to leave Schroon Lake, so we agreed to meet somewhere in Europe and see if we fit. A few months later he came from Paris to Rotterdam, where I was playing. We sat down and played through a sonata and agreed to start the project. In '68 we met with the violinist Joseph Suk in Aldeburgh, and after a performance in London we recorded the three Brahms trios in the hall that Benjamin Britten built. There was a slight hitch when U.S. Air Force jets took off nearby, and we had to interrupt the taping. The three of us spent a pleasant evening

With Josef Suk, Rudolf Buchbinder, and Zdenek Kostler

with Britten and Peter Pears. Katchen and I had by then recorded the two Brahms sonatas.

We planned to continue with the piano quartets and quintets in the following season. Invitations poured in for the trio to perform at festivals, tour South Africa, and so on, and to rerecord the E Minor Sonata, with which we were not quite satisfied. All of this was to start in the spring of '69. But a cable arrived with awful news: Katchen had died. After the shock wore off, one of our German managers, Hans Dieter Gohre, tried to salvage some of the booked concerts as a memorial to Katchen. Suk and I played in Hanover with Gunther Ludwig, my partner at the time. The results were not satisfying. We played in Munich with Claudio Arrau, a great pianist but less good as a trio member.

Gohre also represented a young Viennese pianist named Rudolf Buchbinder, twenty-one years old. He had begun performing with the Vienna Trio at age ten and traveled the world with them, and had just left them to launch a solo career. Suk and I met him in Strasbourg, where the three of us had only three hours of rehearsal before our concert. The results were gratifying, and we agreed to meet every year for a few days and enjoy ourselves. Suk had his own traveling trio, named after his composer grandfather, and Rudi knew the trio literature inside out. I was the oldest and least experienced trio player, but enjoyed it immensely. Suk is a great violinist and also a superb violist, and, I hear now, a conductor as well. Buchbinder, though less known in the U.S., is one of the great pianists of our time.

On another tour my wife and I did in the '60s, our itinerary called for recitals in Belgrade and in Skopje, Macedonia. It was the height of Communism and Titoism. The pianist was a Hungarian-speaking Serbian. In Belgrade we were entertained by the U.S. consul general, Andor Clay, the son-in-law of the pianist Otto Herz. I have already told of recording with him in New York. From Belgrade we took an overnight train to Skopje. We arrived at 10 A.M. and were greeted and walked to the hotel a few hundred yards from the station. On the way we passed a cinema, and my wife noticed the poster outside. *The Old Man and the Sea,* a film based on Hemingway's story, was playing with subtitles. We had been traveling for weeks, and my wife felt hungry for anything English. "It's a pity, but we have no chance to see it, with the concert tonight," I said. We registered at the hotel and were told they were sorry but our rooms were not ready. So we had breakfast, mentioning the poster to the pianist, and he said that they might have a matinée at 11 A.M. Sure enough, there was a short line at the cinema. We bought tickets and entered to find out that the program had changed; no *Old Man* but a Walt Disney cartoon festival. Still, we decided to stay rather than sit in the hotel lobby. As usual in those days, the show started with a newsreel. The date was May 7 and the newsreel showed the May 1 military parade in Belgrade, with Tito saluting the troops, tanks, big guns, planes flying overhead, all to celebrate Yugoslavia's military power. All of a sudden my wife started to poke me. "Don't you hear it?" she said. "What?" "The background music. It's *God Bless America,*" she said. It startled us. No one else noticed it. When we were back in Belgrade we told our story to the Americans, but they knew nothing about it. Months later we heard that Louis Armstrong had been touring the U.S.S.R. a while before. The band had run out of encores and played

CONCERT HAZARDS IN SPAIN

The schedule called for a sonata recital with Rudolf Buchbinder in Marbella, on the Costa del Sol in Spain. The mostly English retired settlers had organized a society that held a prestigious concert series in a resort hotel there. The program was three Beethoven sonatas. I had a date the night before in Germany, and so did Rudi somewhere else. Until then we had performed only the A Major Sonata together in public. We met at the Frankfurt airport and calculated that we would arrive at four o'clock, which would allow a two-hour rehearsal prior to a late concert, as is usual in Spain. A nice lady met us at the airport and we boarded her car for the forty-five-minute drive to the hotel. Her driving made us a bit queasy. She tried to pass trucks and invariably slowed down when she was alongside them. Eventually, with trepidation, she asked a few questions about our needs, explaining that she was substituting for the society's president, who was in England. We mentioned the need for a page turner, a music stand, and a solid chair. She almost ran off the road, but promised to try to solve these horrendous problems.

When we reached the hotel a young woman came to help us register. She was the public relations person for the spa. We asked to go to the hall to rehearse. She looked perplexed, but walked us to a freestanding banquet building fifty yards from the lobby. About five hundred folding chairs were being set up, and there was a makeshift podium barely large enough to house a Steinway grand piano. A group of workers were fixing up colored lights around the so-called stage. I quickly stopped them. A piano tuner was busy tightening the piano chair and getting ready to tune the piano. When we asked for the artist's room, they looked puzzled. We were led to the back of the hall, where there was a serving kitchen, stacked with hundreds of dirty dishes left over from lunch that day. Any chance of rehearsing was shot. The conditions were ridiculous. Moreover, we were hungry. The plane schedules hadn't allowed us to eat anything.

The PR lady led us back to the hotel and asked if we wished something during the concert. Jokingly we said scotch and soda, and went to the restaurant to have a steak sandwich and a drink, knowing that we could at least have a shower and a nap before the 9 P.M. start. At nine we met in the lobby. The PR lady showed up at 9:30 and told us not to worry, that they were not particular about punctuality. Vague memories of Angola came to me as we walked into the filthy kitchen a half hour late. A distinguished old gent greeted us. When I responded, "How are you," he put both hands behind his ears to indicate hearing problems. He was there to turn pages for Rudi. Our apprehensions increased.

We entered the so-called hall and walked up a small aisle toward the stage. All the seats were occupied by well-dressed ladies and gentlemen, plus a fair number of children under the age of ten. When we took our bows I noticed that the first row, a few feet away from us, contained a group of seven- and eight-year-olds. We launched into Beethoven's Second Sonata. We both knew the piece, but had never rehearsed it together. Still, the fact that we had often played trios together helped us coordinate ourselves. We did our best, so to speak, by the seat of our pants, but to anyone with trained ears the discrepancies must have been obvious. I saw several kids rhythmically kicking their chairs, and invariably syncopating. On top of everything else, at one point I sensed trouble. I looked back and saw the page turner stand, turn, and start to sit down again, but his chair leg slipped off the edge of the improvised stage. Miraculously, and accompanied by a big sigh from the audience, he managed to lift it back into position.

We got to the end of the sonata. Huge applause! After we took our bows, instead of retreating for a few minutes to the "artist's room" as is customary, I announced that the unappetizing kitchen and the walk through the hall forced us to continue. It was appreciated. The fourth sonata followed, with its sensitive ensemble problems, and the two of us were less than happy with the result. The response, though, was satisfactory. At intermission we had to return to the kitchen. Lo and behold, the PR lady had taken us seriously and there was the scotch and soda. We looked at each other and said, what the hell, and we lifted our glasses and took a swig. It was the only time we had taken a drink during a concert in our lives, and we never have again. Rudi chatted with the page turner, I lit a cigarette, and the door opened. Two elegantly coifed and dressed ladies entered. One looked familiar. The other said, "Bravo. I am Mrs. Arthur Rubinstein and this is my friend Madeleine Carroll." Then I realized why she looked familiar! I had admired the great French movie actress since childhood. Rubinstein, that great pianist, had a villa nearby. There I stood, with drink in hand, speechless for a moment; then I turned to Rudi, who idolized Rubinstein, and said, "Come and greet Mrs. Rubinstein." His hand that held the drink started shaking. After a few inane sentences the ladies returned to their seats. We quickly drank a couple of glasses of water before returning to the stage.

Luckily, we had already performed the A Major Sonata together, and we came up to our accustomed standards. That evening reinforced our belief that there are no unimportant performances. You never know when or where someone will show up, however unexpectedly, who knows and hears.

My other Spanish experience reminded me of a peculiarly South American archetype. The world is composed, as many have often said, of all different kinds of men, a fact particularly noticeable in the makeup of international musical life. There are the artists and the audiences, and then there are those who organize the meeting of the first two. Among these organizers we find a well-known specimen, occasionally loved, but feared by all artists who travel in Europe south of France, and whose American grazing is the South of the U.S. He is the Southern Concert Manager.

The chief characteristics of a member of this species are, of course, identical to those of his compatriots everywhere. In addition, he maintains a sacred belief in God's guidelines for Sundays, and religiously observes siesta hours.

THE WORLD OF MUSIC ACCORDING TO STARKER

He mixes his great capacity for procrastination with a lack of concern for trivia. Trivia, for globe-circling artists, means plane, train, and car transportation between engagements, hotel reservations, programs, rehearsal time, and starting hours. Among most Southern Concert Managers, lackadaisicalness is an entrenched tradition of long standing. They assume that convincing a musical society, or several societies, in their territories to engage an artist and sign a contract constitutes a major managerial achievement. But if an artist's transit from one place of endeavor to another is not guaranteed, then everyone's work is jeopardized.

A case in point. My friend Gyorgy Sebok and I, together with our wives, arrived in a Spanish town called Gijon, where he and I would perform Beethoven's cello and piano sonatas in two recitals on successive nights. Since this was not our first visit to Spain, we automatically assumed there would be difficulties, and examined daily the latest correspondence from our English-speaking manager. To one letter he added a P.S.: "Please, please keep your sense of humor." Our schedule called for a concert in Barcelona on the day following the pair in Gijon. We could get there only by taking a night train to Madrid that connected with a flight to Barcelona, not an unusual scheduling. Our itinerary failed, however, to mention the starting time of the Gijon concerts. Programs in Spain start anywhere from 5:15 to 10:15 P.M., depending on the location, so we were not too disturbed by our train's 9:30 P.M. departure time. Imagine our astonishment when we learned that the second Gijon concert was to begin at 7:45 P.M., meaning we had just one hour and forty-five minutes to play the program and encores, receive the crowd backstage, sign autographs, change clothes, pack, get to the station, and board the train with twelve pieces of luggage and a cello case. We also had to consider the legendary tardiness of Spanish audiences, and the lack of a dining car on Spanish night trains. Needless to say, there was no alternative means of travel. It was either board that train or miss the concert in Barcelona. And so we were forced to adopt extreme measures.

There was one small loophole. Sebok and I could catch the train twenty miles away in the next town. This distance could be covered easily by car in half the time that it took the Spanish express train. Our attempt to change the starting time of the concert failed, of course, but we did manage to place a notice in the local paper requesting that the audience be punctual, *por favor*. Before the performance, we packed all twelve suitcases and checked out of the hotel. During the afternoon, the Mesdames Starker and Sebok shopped for a picnic dinner that could satisfy two hungry husbands in the sleeping car. We decided that the ladies should leave the concert at intermission and board the train with all of our baggage. Sebok and I planned to join them, either at the Gijon station or at the town twenty miles distant.

We went onstage that evening only three minutes late. The hall was half-empty, but it filled up during the first sonata. Gradually we eliminated all repeats from the music and glanced nervously at our watches whenever possible. Each additional bow required by enthusiastic applause made us shiver. Every ritardando became a masochistic exercise in self-control. We did succeed in completing the concert twelve minutes before train time. The applause continued. I made a motion with my hands that implied utter despair, and the clapping ceased. We grabbed our music, our coats, and the cello, waved goodbye to a surge of autograph seekers, and jumped into a waiting taxi. The driver, properly coached beforehand, careened through all traffic and stop signs to deposit us, brakes screeching, in front of the station. Three minutes before departure time we climbed into the sleeping car. Our respective spouses were astonished, and, in fact, so were we.

On a little table they had laid a rich spread of cold cuts, complete with wine and candles. Immediately, we raised our customary after-concert cognac glasses and tried to relax, exhausted but content. Mrs. Sebok said that all had gone fairly well, except that the conductor had been highly dubious: two ladies in full regalia, occupying two compartments, preparing a cold but lavish supper—that was hardly traditional. They had explained, however, that their husbands would be joining them at the next station. A few minutes after we boarded the train, there was a knock on the door. The conductor appeared, hesitated, then stammered, "The train is leaving! You gentlemen had better get off." We stared at him speechlessly. Then he haltingly added, "Their husbands are joining them at the next station!" When we reached Madrid we were handed a note saying that the Barcelona concert was postponed for a day; belch, sigh, and a silent Hungarian anathema on all Southern Concert Managers.

On another occasion, the Dvořák Cello Concerto became a vehicle for a performance by a solo cellist and a conductor, which was unique in my experience. The orchestra was the Las Palmas Philharmonic, since disbanded and rebuilt in the Canary Islands. As the long orchestral introduction began, only every tenth note was audible. The conductor, formerly a cellist himself in Pablo Casals's eponymous Barcelona orchestra, made the most musicianly gestures to his players, but his apologetic expression conveyed no hope that the notes would be played. Bows were moved left to right across stringed instruments, and wind instruments were held properly to lips, yet only an occasional gurgle escaped. Infrequently, someone tried to play but seemed frightened by his exposure and so abandoned the enterprise. My poor wife nearly fell out of her box in an attempt to see where the occasional audible note was coming from. I played the solo part with a feverish conviction while the conductor waved his hands and followed me with ecstatic joy. Later at supper, a band in the restaurant greeted me with the main theme of the concerto. They were members of the Philharmonic, as were the police and firefighter bands, not to mention the rest of the Las Palmas nightclub musicians. All were passably good at their daily chores, but in the Dvořák their playing could only have been compared to that of the diva of legend, Florence Foster Jenkins.

God Bless America. Someone taped it and it became an underground best-seller. Who in the newsreel studio had the nerve to use it as background music for the May Day parade remains a mystery.

During those years I continued my recordings for a variety of companies. Philips asked for the Brahms Double Concerto with Szeryng and me playing with the Concertgebouw Orchestra, conducted by Bernard Haitink, and also the Beethoven Triple with Szeryng, Claudio Arrau, and the New Philharmonia Orchestra in London with Eliahu Inbal. Playing the Triple was weird. At the pre-rehearsal Szeryng kept suggesting changes he had found in the Urtext, which he didn't have with him. Arrau suggested tempo changes by dangling his pocket watch. I burst out laughing, and we quit and went out for a lovely dinner. At the session, after all the microphones were set, Szeryng appeared, picked up his mike, and put it next to the concertmaster. With his back to the conductor, he kept changing bowings and literally conducted the violin section. After a while Inbal stopped and offered his baton to Szeryng. "Would you like to conduct, Mr. Szeryng?" "No, no, no, you are doing fine," Szeryng responded. The circus atmosphere continued, though everyone was playing reasonably well. By the time we reached the last movement, with Szeryng still changing and penciling in different bowings in the concertmaster's part, I couldn't help myself. I stood up and said, "I hope you all know that the charm of this recording lies in the diversity of views." The orchestra broke up. Szeryng, in dead earnest, whispered to me, "Why did you say that? Of course they know."

This goofy performance of the Triple Concerto had a quality of déjà vu for me. In the '60s Walter Legge had had a brainstorm. He asked Otto Klemperer to conduct three soloists and the Philharmonia in three concertos and nothing else. To everyone's surprise Klemperer agreed: there would be no orchestral part, no overture. Legge asked the great Hungarian pianist Annie Fischer to start with a Bach concerto; Szeryng and I would do the Brahms Double, and all three of us the Beethoven Triple. It was the first time this kind of program had ever been performed. There were to be a pre-rehearsal and two orchestra rehearsals, but the day of the pre-rehearsal Annie called to say that she had just arrived, was dead tired, and couldn't come to rehearse. So Szeryng and

I just went through the Brahms. The next day, with the orchestra, the three of us played like children, not knowing who did what. That was the first time Fischer and Szeryng had ever played the piece. I tried to pacify Klemperer by saying, "Don't worry, we will rehearse this afternoon." But Szeryng sheepishly announced that he had a concert that night in Birmingham and had to leave, and Annie said she couldn't because she had to sleep.

When it came time for the performance, London's Festival Hall was sold out. Legge asked for dates for the following seasons so as to make it an annual tradition. The Bach and Brahms went on famously. Beethoven didn't go quite so well, but the public went wild nonetheless. Then the traditional handshaking began, complicated by the multiple permutations of conductor, concertmaster, and three soloists. Klemperer was waiting to get offstage. When Szeryng arrived at the center the maestro reached for his hand, but Szeryng grabbed mine first. Klemperer shoved his music stand and it fell. The violists were scrambling to protect their instruments. Klemperer grabbed his cane—he was quite handicapped by then—and hobbled offstage. No one had taken a bow yet, but we had to follow him. Klemperer disappeared into his room. The audience was screaming. I ran to Klemperer and said we had to take a bow. He yelled no and that he would never again be on stage with that . . . Whatever followed was a rather uncomplimentary epithet. Eventually the three of us took some bows and went to supper, but Klemperer didn't show. The concerts continued for a few years, but the cast changed.

In later years I did participate in similar programs often, with Joseph Suk, Franco Gulli, Arthur Grumiaux, and eventually my son-in-law William Preucil. The pianists were Sebok, Buchbinder, and the conductor and pianist Dennis Russell Davies, a man I admire unreservedly as a musician and friend.

In 1964 Jean Martinon, a great conductor and composer who was then musical director of the Düsseldorf Symphony Orchestra, wrote a concerto for Pierre Fournier. At the time I was playing with the Düsseldorf orchestra and also teaching classes, as I have done on occasion in Rotterdam, Rio de Janeiro, and elsewhere. Martinon showed me the manuscript and I suggested many changes. Fournier played the work's

THE WORLD OF MUSIC ACCORDING TO STARKER

With Dennis R. Davies

European premiere, and I did the U.S. premiere in Ravinia with Seiji Ozawa conducting, in New York with Martinon, and in Honolulu with George Barati. This is a work that should be in the repertory. Antal Doráti also showed me a cello concerto he had been commissioned to write in the late '40s. It wasn't good. He rewrote it and dedicated it to me, and I recorded it in 1978 with the Louisville Orchestra and Jorge Mester. With Mester I also recorded Peter Mennin's cello concerto in 1969. Mester is one of my favorites and a friend.

A funny thing happened when I premiered two concertos, by Bernhard Heiden and Miklos Rozsa, on consecutive days, Rozsa's in Berlin followed the next day by Heiden's in Paris. To have time to prepare I went to Paris and rehearsed the Heiden there, then left for the Berlin

With Miklós Rózsa and Harry Newstone in Sacramento

performance. After that I flew back to Paris for the general rehearsal and concert. When I arrived, I found that my suitcase was lost. I bought a shirt, walked onstage in a sport jacket, and took it off for comfort. After the concert the suitcase arrived at the hotel. The Rozsa concerto was recorded in Munich by the Munich Philharmonic and Moshe Atzmón. I premiered it in San Francisco, then in Chicago with Georg Solti. After that performance Rozsa gave me a pair of gold cufflinks, and to this day I wear them at all my concerts.

I became friends with Gerald Schwartz, conductor of the Seattle Symphony and a man I admire for much more than his top conducting skill. We made a number of CDs together, including Dohnányi's Concert Piece, David Diamond's *Kaddish,* and Alan Hovhaness's Cello Concerto. With the Scottish Chamber Orchestra we did the two Haydn Concertos.

In 1967 I recorded etudes for the cello, a fairly novel idea then, as *The Road to Cello Playing.* In 1969 Decca recorded my performance of

Bloch's *Schelomo* and *Voice in the Wilderness* with Zubin Mehta and the Israel Philharmonic in Rome. In 1980 I recorded some of my colleague David Baker's works: his duo for cello and seventeen percussion instruments (with George Gaber, the great master of that field) and his cello and piano sonata. And my attempt to revive the works of my cellistic grandfather David Popper, who had taught my teacher Adolf Schiffer, resulted in a 1988 CD called *Romantic Cello Favorites* with Shigeo Neriki. On my visits to Japan I have recorded recitals, Beethoven sonatas, and the Schubert Arpeggione with Shuku Iwasaki and Shigeo Neriki, as well as the last version of the Kodály Solo Sonata. In Milan, I recorded the César Franck Sonata with Sebok, to complete the Schubert disc begun in Tokyo.

In the '80s I made a series of recordings for a Canadian company called Sefel, which was founded by a Hungarian engineer who made a fortune and asked the pianist and conductor Arpad Joo to help him build a record company. I recorded the Brahms Double Concerto and the Kodály and Ravel duos for cello and violin with an excellent violinist, Emmy Verhey. I also recorded a concerto record with the Santa Fe Chamber Orchestra, and the fourth version of the six Bach suites. But then Mr. Sefel went into bankruptcy and the company sank. The Sefel recordings were directed by my old Mercury friend Harold Lawrence, one of the legends in the recording industry. Arpad Joo built a huge catalogue of superb records, held major posts in Spain and Holland, and then disappeared. I hope he will reappear, as he is supremely qualified. I played a number of recitals with him as well. Several of the Sefel recordings were later published by Delos.

The last chapter of my recording life, with BMG-RCA, should wait till later.

11 𝄢 "L'ART POUR L'ART: WALDO CAPER, 1926–1960" — A STORY

"News flash! An airliner bound for South America has crashed near the Azores. Search craft have sighted a few scattered fragments of wreckage in the turbulent waters of the Atlantic, but it is now thought that there were no survivors. The last radio contact was at 9:25 P.M. local time. The pilot said, 'Explosion in the rear area of the craft. Mayday! Mayday!' Then the transmitter went dead. The airline has furnished a partial list of passengers. There were seven Americans on board, including the world-renowned concert pianist Waldo Caper, en route to his first tour of South America after triumphs in Europe—"

I snapped off the television and tried to control my breathing. I poured a strong drink and tried vainly to hold back tears. Waldo was one of my truly dear friends. Immediately I placed a call to his wife. Her father answered and said that Lucy wouldn't be able to talk to anyone, not for a while at least. She was close to hysteria, under a doctor's care. "The children?" I asked, and he said they would be staying with him for the time being.

"How are they taking it?"

"They don't really know what it's all about. They're watching TV as if nothing has happened."

"Please tell Lucy that I called. If there's *anything* she needs, I'll be there right away."

"Thank you, George. I'll tell her when she wakens."

I tried to work but couldn't concentrate. I'd known Waldo since childhood. We were born in the same Oklahoma town, went to school together, and began piano lessons at the same time, with the same teacher. We played baseball and basketball, were constant companions . . . Until this moment I had been spared the agony of losing someone close. Both my parents were still living, and my grandparents and other relatives, even during their lives, had been little more than pictures in a photo album. I had imagined that when someone close to me died, it would be as if they had gone on a long trip and eventually I would see them again. But now . . . How could I adjust to Waldo's untimely death?

All the newspapers carried the same headline: "No survivors in Azores crash." All printed photos of Waldo, Lucy, their children. Two days later, the Philharmonic announced a Waldo Caper memorial concert. Across the country, symphony orchestras dedicated a piece on their programs to the memory of Waldo Caper. Radio stations broadcast special programs of Waldo's recordings. Three music schools announced Waldo Caper scholarships. CRC—Classics Recording Company— sent out a press release announcing that all of Waldo's unpublished tapes would be issued as soon as possible in a memorial album.

This last irritated me particularly. I remember Waldo saying how he'd argued with company officials about those tapes. He had made them, as stipulated in his contract, but was told the time wasn't ripe yet to market them. The public wasn't ready for so much Caper in a short period of time. Besides, sales were down, the budget was tight; they wanted to wait. And now they would release them! Meanwhile, record shops everywhere decorated their windows with Waldo's picture, outlined with black ribbon and surrounded by all of his recordings.

Wire-service obituaries all said much the same thing: "Waldo Caper, the shining star of American pianism, died in the flaming plunge of a plane into the ocean. He served his art and his country faithfully. He spread the gospel of American culture wherever he traveled. Audiences cheered his performances of the classics, as well as the romantics and

L'ART POUR L'ART

the moderns. His technical powers were unquestioned. His artistic maturity exceeded his years and defied explanation. He was one of the select few blessed with inexplicable genius. Music was his means of communicating with us. Even as we mourn, let all be grateful for the unforgettable time span during which he gave us music . . ."

Similar lamentations appeared in all of the papers; CRC's public relations office had flooded the news services. Eulogies by actual music critics were less flowery, perhaps, but their tone left no doubt that Waldo Caper was a truly great artist. What a pity Waldo could never read them. I remembered what the same reviewers had written about his last concert here: "No doubt Mr. Caper has talent. In a few years, if he applies himself to the real message of music, he may join the exclusive club of great pianists . . ." "Waldo Caper is basically an intellectual musician. He displays himself well in the contemporary repertoire. His Bach is logically conceived, yet cold, rather removed from the sensuous reality of the master's style . . ." "What a shame that Mr. Caper concentrates solely on his instrument. Certainly his pianistic feats are laudable, but these should be subordinated to musical purposes and not amount to an end in themselves . . ." Yet the eulogies of these same master judges were completely free of criticism. Waldo had made it; he had finally entered that rarified sphere of art where only a few are ever permitted to tread.

A memorial service was held, with the president of the local musicians' union, no less, in attendance. The conductor, general manager, and director of the Philharmonic came in person to pay their respects. Lucy was present, supported by her parents. Waldo's own manager had to miss it, though; he was working nonstop to find replacements for Waldo's bookings. But he sent a large wreath and a poignant cable. The union president praised Waldo in a short speech as a great American artist and a member in good standing; he concluded by announcing Waldo's election by unanimous vote as an honorary member of the union. There were other speeches. I saw Lucy only for a few seconds, and held her hand. She looked at me through tears, then was led away.

Two weeks passed. I was opening my mail one morning—bills, charitable solicitations, a couple of postcards, and then a thick envelope with Portuguese stamps, but no sender's name or return address. I held it in

THE WORLD OF MUSIC ACCORDING TO STARKER

my hand and tried to guess the contents. I didn't know anyone in Portugal. Sent by surface mail? Must be some kind of advertisement.

A strange sensation seized me as I ripped the envelope open. I started to shiver when I saw, in the familiar and unmistakable handwriting of Waldo:

> Dear George,
>
> I wonder, old boy, if this will ever reach you? I'm not sure yet why I am writing in the first place. Let's call it self-analysis! I am sitting in one of these dull hotel rooms where I spend most of my life now. I leave tomorrow for my first South American tour. Remember, George, when I told you . . . time? Time is all we need? And patience, too. When you have the goods, no one can stop you except yourself. Well, no one stopped us. You quit the piano, but succeeded otherwise. You have a career, a lovely wife, and a future. You have a home in which you belong.
>
> My life? The one I wanted more than anything in the world? I have the present. I have a future. But a home? That's something else again. For that matter, what about my present and future? No other person knows more about me than you, that's why this self-analysis is addressed to you. There *is* another reason, but that must wait upon the outcome of this self-investigation. As I said, I am—

The phone on my desk rang. The day had to start. I put the envelope in a pocket and went through my necessary tasks automatically. All through the day, Waldo's face kept flashing through my mind, looking at me with penetrating cold eyes. Phlegmatic eyes, but twinkling sarcastically somewhere deep within them. The cigarette perpetually dangling from his lips. Smoke incessantly and acridly surrounding his person.

What kind of being was Waldo? True and dedicated, a real man and artist. His basic honesty earned him a great many enemies. He was never able to congratulate a fellow artist unless he'd really and deeply appreciated the performance. Otherwise he would walk into the greenroom and say, "Lousy concert! Aren't you ashamed of yourself? Are you drunk or something?" Small wonder that he accumulated so many adversaries. He refused to attend after-concert parties, remaining in the hall to practice for his next performance. That brought his manager

L'ART POUR L'ART

plenty of angry letters from local organizations. It also explained why Waldo wasn't reengaged by a lot of towns. This had only delayed his acceptance; however, sooner or later, everyone was obliged to acknowledge his power, authority, and unquestionable sincerity.

At the age of twenty-four, he met Lucy—a lovely girl—at a cocktail party. He sat silently in the corner for maybe thirty minutes, watching her every move. When anyone attempted to talk to him, he said, "Sorry, not now." Finally he got up, walked over to Lucy, and asked, "May I talk to you? I'm Waldo Caper." Before the surprised girl could answer, he continued, "I believe you are the woman I must marry, and I mean to marry you!" Three weeks later he did. First came the twins, then Waldo Jr., who's now five.

Waldo Jr.? Funny, Waldo Sr. wasn't "Waldo" at all when his mother gave birth to him. He was christened Walter, but a gradual twisting of the pronunciation finally produced Waldo. To his first manager this sounded very artistic (I hate to admit it, but I was that first manager). When he'd won competitions around the country, including at state and national levels, he landed a scholarship to the Curtis Institute.

My wife put dinner before me, and I ate absent-mindedly. Then I asked her to pardon me, and went to my study.

> As I said, I am absorbed in this self-analysis. What has caused the need for such study or reflection? Music, career, private life, the world around me. Not that I feel the world revolves around me, far from it. For many years the world meant nothing to me, except a place in which to attain my imagined and desired goal. You might say I lived a sheltered life for too long. I never knew hunger or real suffering—the kind, it turns out, more people than not are exposed to. Beginning in my childhood, I played my piano and nothing else mattered. First I strove for technical proficiency through practice and more practice. I learned every kind of music there was. I had all the talent required and then some. I never knew those difficulties my friends struggled with. I quit the game of competition early—my overwhelming concern was the message I could express through music, the expression of my world, my ideas, and my ideals.
>
> But the time came to ask a question. Is this world of mine valid? What did I know, after all, of the world? I was too young to fight in the war, and I had not yet fought for a living. Since I had no time for other people, very little emotional turmoil reached me. The only dis-

turbance was an occasional sneer about my being a 'sissy musician.' But I knew I wasn't a sissy and developed an attitude of superiority rather than inferiority. At most I felt pity for those who ridiculed my art; I thought only that their lives had less beauty than mine. But I didn't know the world, and so I read and read, anything in sight: history, biography, classics, romantics, moderns, everything. I also read papers, magazines, mysteries, even comic strips and pornography. For months I hardly slept.

What I learned was shattering—meaning that I wasn't ready yet for all that information. I put off drawing any conclusions, though I couldn't help but notice an absurd repetitiveness down through the ages. You know how I dread the monotony of unrelieved repetition, yet it is everywhere, in history as well as in art. The same criminals. The same geniuses who obtain power and then use it for destruction. The same dedicated scientists who constantly discover new ways to benefit mankind, but are condemned for their findings sooner or later and die, whereupon ruthless individuals adopt their discoveries to further their own ambition. Leaders-to-be of armies and nations utter words full of nobility on their climb up the ladder of success, but once they reach the top, they cause the world to suffer. In art, all those who stepped onto new roads, found new shapes, colors, and sounds had to fight alone; seldom, if ever, did they gain the recognition in life that accrued to them after death.

In my early years it was easy; I didn't care. I wanted to make music only for art's sake, not for recognition. This is a phrase often carelessly used, but I believed that it had real meaning for me. I felt I had integrity and that nothing could take it from me. Nothing! But I realized that my artistic goal would take me to a level that audiences would have little chance of understanding, much less reaching. As a concert pianist, I had to communicate with people. The best solution seemed to be to preserve and develop enough of music's graspable language so that audiences could appreciate me and eventually come to recognize what I really stood for.

What elements in musical language do I mean? Above all, technique—speed, clarity, tonal colors—and this did seem to work; I was successful on one plane, no doubt. Engagements multiplied, and I had basically good reviews—if they were a bit patronizing at times, they all predicted a great future. Often I laughed when the know-it-alls criticized my Beethoven performances; after I had studied it for years, a sonata finally took shape. Yet they babbled about tempi, dynamics, and style, as if they knew what the words meant. But their

L'ART POUR L'ART

babble had for me no real meaning. I always considered music reviewers to be reporters who had the right to express an opinion. Freedom of the press and all that.

The trouble first started, I think, with my marriage. In the beginning I was as happy as anyone could dream of being. Lucy is the most wonderful creature I've ever met. She is beautiful, and her beauty stems from an inner balance—I've never found this quality in any other person. She is the perfect wife, mother, and friend. I love her and have no doubts whatsoever that she loves me. Time and again I've said to myself how fortunate I am to have found such a human being and have her as my wife! But, my dear George, *do* I have a wife? Not quite. She is a partner, rather, in correspondence. When we traveled together, that was the most wonderful period of my life. We had no home and rented furnished places; my piano went with us. Most of the time we lived in hotel rooms and motels, yet any place became home when we occupied it. A train, a car, we were together—in *our* world living *our* life.

There were of course the usual difficulties, meaning money. Originally $10 problems, then $100 ones, and finally $1,000 ones. At first we worried about paying grocers and the rent. When we could take these for granted, the big issue became Lucy's travel expenses; we managed, however, until the twins came. We'd said we wanted eleven; who should have children, if not those so much in love? Now we have three beautiful children, as you know—healthy, intelligent, loving, all anyone could wish for. But they put an end to Lucy's and my traveling together. I could afford to take her along; my fees had increased that much even after all the percentages, publicity, taxes, and God knows what. I even began to pay off all those old debts incurred on the way up. But what kind of life is it for children to be dragged all over the world? And we couldn't leave them with nurses or aunts or maids. What sense of belonging can children have if they don't grow up with their parents nearby? Even the poor have this. But I had to travel. And so Lucy stayed at home.

As my success increased, my tours became longer and more frequent. I was absent for weeks. Our phone bills skyrocketed. But there is a limit to communication when you tour other continents. I was sick from loneliness, hated everything and everyone, and didn't want to see any of the famous sights. I hated women who tried to throw themselves at me; I'm a healthy male, but it wasn't me they wanted. They wanted the 'famous artist.' Any man alone on a stage, watched by thousands, is bound to be idolized by at least a small percentage of those out front. *Any* male in tails under stage lights looks better than the snoring husband in a lukewarm marriage.

So the years passed. We built that magnificent house—nothing but the best for the children. Yet more and more I came to hate home. I could hardly enter it before it was time to leave again. And the cost of this lifestyle added a new element to my artistic pursuits. I *had* to play concerts whether I liked it or not. Bunched-up concert dates, insane travel connections, bad planes, conductors who could hardly read a score, programs I detested—it all became necessary to meet expenses. Some of my record jackets sent me into convulsions. But integrity, George, is a lopsided proposition. You've read those eulogies about our dead greats: 'Unflinching integrity.' What I feel about that is too disgusting to write. Sure, they had integrity, but when? I'll tell you— when they reached such heights that they could be independent and others, in turn, had to adjust their integrity to suit the whims (I beg your pardon, principles) of the great ones.

I found myself with less and less time to work in privacy. Over and over I kept repeating the same repertory. When I had a rare vacation, I tried to cram every second of it with my family and then live for the next miserable, lonely, deadening months on this. But let's not be slapdash or maudlin. I still loved music. I still had the urge to spread the message. When I sat on a stage, the world was light-years away and nothing mattered but music. But when the concert or rehearsal came to an end, I couldn't bear any more of the same jokes, stories, and gossip, repeated tiresomely in every town or city. As you well know, musicians are a race, not a profession. We would don uniforms and kill each other if our leaders commanded it (the alternatives being desertion or treason), but we speak a similar language. We agree or disagree on the same ridiculous details in Bach, Beethoven, Brahms, and Mozart. The fourth-stand bass players in Leningrad, Kalamazoo, Boston, and Johannesburg have similar idiosyncrasies and may even resemble one another.

I preferred instead to eat, walk, read, and go to movies alone, until one day I found myself having dinner with a beautiful young woman. She looked a bit like Lucy and was intelligent and free. The next morning I woke up and said goodbye to her. I didn't know how to adjust to this experience. I loved my wife and wanted to be with her. So why did I do it? Loneliness! But I couldn't tell Lucy about this. And what about her; was she lonely, too? I became insanely jealous, couldn't sleep, had nightmares—I kept seeing Lucy in the arms of other men. I played bad concerts after sleepless nights. I started drink-

L'ART POUR L'ART

ing and found myself more and more frequently in bed with women whose names I didn't even know. And I didn't have to lie; opportunities were plentiful, I needed only to be careful. Rumors about artists abound, and whether they're true or not, they make good party conversation. I simply reconciled myself to phony mirth at any veiled reference.

At home, all seemed lovely on the surface. But I watched Lucy and believed her to be watching me. I had visions of mental illness and went secretly to a psychiatrist. But I knew I was healthy; I had no hidden fears or ghastly experiences from my childhood. My guilt complex was recent, obvious, and curable. I was not neurotic beyond the requisite sensitivity of any artist. And I knew what I wanted—my family. My wife, my children, and my music—all that I really needed. But that order is meaningless; which one first? Who knows? I cannot live without being productive, and Waldo Caper's only destiny is to play the piano.

My next thought was to tell Lucy it's no use, we must divorce. The *Who's Who* of musicians includes only a few whose first wives stood at their gravesides. We must accept the maxim that marriage is not for concert artists. Other professions are equally cursed, but few are more connected to predestination than the instrumentalist's. How, though, could I do such a thing? What could I possibly say to Lucy—go marry someone else even though I love you? She always said that we needed to survive the hard years; the children would grow up and go to school, and then we could travel together again. It sounded so logical, so right, when she'd say this at home, but thousands of miles away I found myself in total emptiness.

Remember I said earlier that you have a home where you belong? I lost all sense of belonging—no real home, no real family, and for that matter no real country. Mind you, our beloved U.S. of A. is celebrated for its dumbness in not using or reaping the full propaganda benefits of its artists' successes abroad, as other countries do. We American artists go around the world, but invariably it is a French or British cultural attaché who invites us to a party in our honor. Their American equivalents don't even show up at a party, much less at a concert. When by chance you meet one of these brilliant emissaries, they all but brag about their musical ignorance.

It wasn't very long ago, George, that I found myself in emptiness. I pictured my future: the years ahead, my own home becoming just another hotel, my children treating me like some visiting uncle who tries to make conversation about subjects he knows only from letters.

I saw myself growing increasingly apart from Lucy, her world, her friends, while she herself became only snapshots in my wallet. I saw myself cheered all over the world and smiling victoriously on the stage, but crying helplessly in hotel rooms alone. I saw myself sending alimony checks to Lucy and wondering who would be a father to my children. I saw myself falling in love, from sheer desperation, with someone, anyone, and starting the whole vicious cycle again.

Yes, others do it—some more successfully, perhaps. But I'm not cut out for it, or so it seems. The world is ready to blow itself up, and it may just deserve that. At one time I felt that my knowledge of books didn't entitle me to hate the world, but I must tell you now that I've seen enough. I feel today that I have the right to say that the sights around me are repellent. There was a time when I persevered and tried to fight—but I'm just plain tired. The psychiatrist said I should take a long rest. And what after? Will my integrity rekindle? Will my family problems be solved? Will the world be better if I am less tired? Will audiences suddenly discover true values and throw their millions into art instead of hipwiggling young punks who pander to the libido of adolescents? Will my children have a better father if I take a sabbatical rest? No, dear George. I can defer the agony, but solve it? Never.

This is my problem and mine alone. No one can help me. The world will go on, with or without Waldo Caper. There are all those others with a gleam in their eyes and the world at their feet. I've had my share. I didn't live in vain; I made a mark. For a while at least, my name will be remembered through recordings, reference books, and the few who understood my mission. I've known happiness in my comparatively short life, more than most persons in a full lifetime. My family is secure; I am insured to the hilt.

As I said at the start of this letter, I have another reason for writing all this to you. The light is coming up outside my window. Lisbon wakes to another day. A few hours from now I will be on a plane bound for South America. In my luggage is a clever little gadget—I purchased it from a drunken Moroccan in a dive in Marseilles. It was stolen from a shipment to Algiers. Believe me, I paid a nice sum for it! I do feel sorry for a cargo of innocent people, none of whom I know. But any other way involves the risk that my family will lose the insurance money.

I searched all of my life for beauty. I found it, and it destroyed me. I choose an ugly way to die—by killing other human beings. But thousands, just as innocent, are killed by ambitious and power-hungry criminals every day. Fellow passengers must be killed for the sake of four people I love. I, Waldo Caper, have thereby invested myself with powers that higher authorities ordinarily arrogate to themselves. You may say, my friend, that I am sick. Maybe. Or perhaps a coward. I prefer to say that I'm simply exhausted and repulsed beyond description by the repetitiveness of the world, by my family life, by my career struggle, and above all, by my nonsensical effort to reach a majority of the people with my artistic message.

I am sending this letter by surface mail. Please, I trust you—you must destroy it after you've read it, no need to tell you why. The last page is a predated letter to you—June, 1959—in which I refer to a will deposited some time ago at the Gotham in your name. Please, give it to Lucy, saying that you found it among your papers with instructions in the event of my death.

Forever,

Waldo

The legend of Waldo Caper exists in the pages of music history.

Reading through the gossip columns the other day, I noted the following.

"Hugh Rodell, talented young painter, married Lucy Caper, widow of the great American pianist who died last July in a tragic plane crash. It has been rumored that he left her half a million dollars in insurance, not including recording royalties and property."

ON TOUR, 1961

12 BLOOMINGTON NOW

Many things happened in the '60s that are worth remembering. In '63 Zoltán Kodály was invited to Indiana University. He had recently remarried and came with his bride, who was sixty years his junior. Those of us who had known him as students were amazed at the change in him. The clipped words became sentences and even jokes, prompted by a visit to the university's swimming pool. In describing his various visits to other campuses, he said that from every bush a Hungarian had jumped out. Three years later I was asked to participate in a Toronto festival where he was awarded an honorary doctorate by the Toronto Conservatory of Music (now the Royal Conservatory of Music). After my performance of the Solo Sonata and Duo with Lorand Fenyves, he complimented me with what was, for him, unusual approbation. I used the opportunity to ask about a dubious note in the score: was it a G or a G-sharp? He thought for a few seconds, and then said, yes.

The year 1965 was particularly memorable for my acquisition of the Matteo Goffriller cello and celebration of my parents' golden wedding anniversary, together with Father's seventy-fifth birthday. We held a surprise party in a Chicago restaurant. Father's brother Joseph came from Sweden, and friends arrived from all over the States. Special news-

*With Zoltán Kodály
and Lorand Fenyves
in Toronto*

With Mother and Father on their 50th wedding anniversary in Chicago (1965)

papers were printed. Sebok and I put on wigs and short pants and played Mother's favorite tune. My daughters also played and sang for them. There was a wedding ceremony to make sure that I was legitimate, a lottery, dancing, and a coronation. The speakers included the congressman who helped them come to America.

In '66 I became a homeowner for the first time in my forty-two years: a little ranch house in a new development, tiny trees, but beautiful roses and cows marching along the fences. Since then the house has grown to five times its original size, and the cows have turned into humans and homes.

The touring continued. In '67 I was offered Japan again, and with that tour I began an association with Yoshiro Kambara of Tokyo that has lasted ever since, through roughly ten visits to Japan. He is an honest and decent man, and a concert manager of great efficiency. Rightly or wrongly, around this time I adopted a strict attitude toward long tours. I did not tour in the U.S. I went in and out of Bloomington so as to take care of my classes. Tours to places such as Japan, Israel, Australia, and South America I undertook only once every three years. I refused six-week tours of Australia and New Zealand. I felt that they would turn into business trips, and that didn't fit my idea of music making. I limited all tours to three weeks, and traveled to Europe three or four times a year rather than stay there for weeks on end.

I began my combination of teaching and performing in Europe with the Luzerne Festival, where I played recitals and concertos (such as Prokofiev, with Zubin Mehta) and taught a week of classes. Many of my colleagues were there as well: Fournier, Enrico Mainardi, Gaspar Cassado, and others. One day in the early '70s, Werner Krotzinger, former concertmaster of the Stuttgart Chamber Orchestra, showed up in Luzerne. He was by then the director of the Volkwang Hochschule in Essen, where for years Paul Tortelier had taught. Paul was having health problems in Essen; he resigned, and Krotzinger offered me the job, a special professorship. I told him I couldn't leave Bloomington, but he said that I spent enough time in Europe, and their school year was different enough, for me to take the job. I was having some misgivings about Luzerne, so I said I would think about it. Two days later I called him and proposed a plan. I would spend twenty days a year in

Essen, fitting in the time before and after my European concerts. I would take twelve students (they had seven cello students at the time) and teach six hours a day, so that each student would have ten hour-long lessons. But I proposed that Maria Kliegel, a young German cellist who was finishing her Artist Diploma in Bloomington and had been my assistant for two years, move to Essen and teach the rest of the time when I was away; I also suggested that Tortelier take my place in Luzerne. The deal was set. After four years the cello class had grown to seventeen, and I left. Maria became a celebrated cellist and teacher, and in 1981 she won the Rostropovich prize.

My sabbatical leaves from IU offered me the chance of unusually long tours. So when a trip to Japan, Taipei, Korea, Hong Kong, and Manila was booked in 1967, I mentioned that I would like to go to India while I was out there. My managers at Colbert Artists asked if I was sure and I said yes. But I had forgotten to look at the map! Only when my wife and I boarded the plane in Hong Kong for Calcutta did I realize the immensity of the distances.

Our flight stopped en route in Thailand. While we were waiting to take off again, it was announced that there was rioting in Calcutta and martial law had been declared; there were no flights in or out, and of course my concerts were canceled. So we spent two lovely days being tourists in Bangkok, then flew to Bombay, our second stop in India. Recitals were scheduled in Bombay, Poona, New Delhi, and Madras. I ended up canceling the Madras recital and cutting the tour short. I wasn't enjoying myself; the pianist was mediocre and I was shaken by the contrast of unbelievable poverty and immense wealth. I saw half-dead paupers lying on the pavement in front of a luxury hotel. We were stunned by the magnificence of the Taj Mahal, but the corpses of cows rotted on the highway (if one could call it that) to Agra.

The trip's highlights were a boat trip through caves and lunch with the great writer Santha Rama Rau and her mother. The latter was president of India's family planning organization, but was resigning because the job was hopeless. In Bombay we had an evening of sitar and traditional dances in the home of a rich disciple of Ravi Shankar, and we visited a school of music and dance. In retrospect I am glad we went there, but I have not wished to return.

THE WORLD OF MUSIC ACCORDING TO STARKER

ON BOBBY KNIGHT AND HOOSIERS

My claim to basketball fame. One day when I returned home from concert performances in, I think, the fall of 1985, Charles Webb, dean of Indiana University, rang me up in great excitement. He said that coach Bobby Knight had called and asked if I would speak to his team. We both were flabbergasted. It was the first time that an athletic department, let alone the legendary head coach, had ever contacted the School of Music, except about the band. I hadn't had any experience with basketball since age fourteen. Every student at the Franz Liszt Academy had to have two hours of sports activities per week, and I was assigned basketball. My ten-year-old grandson is a fanatic and talented player; I wasn't. I ran after the older and taller musicians and grabbed their pants in desperation. I did not last long. So why would Mr. Knight want me to speak? It turned out that he had read an article about me being a strict disciplinarian as a teacher, and that appealed to him.

I was invited to the locker room. The team sat on benches, and they were still taller than I was standing. Mr. Knight gave some brief complimentary remarks about me and sat down. Attempting to be funny, I started out with a story told to me by one of my students: "Three cellists were traveling in a car, and they all died in a fatal crash. Trying to enter heaven, they knocked at the Pearly Gates. St. Peter inquired as to who they were. When he heard they were all cellists he asked the first one, who did you study with? Rostropovich, came the reply. St. Peter said no way, you have to go to hell. The next replied that he studied with Leonard Rose. He also had to go to hell. The third said he studied with Starker. St. Peter thought, then said he could come in, as he had already gone through hell."

There was dead silence among the players, though a few of them exchanged glances. Mr. Knight hid a faint smile.

For the next twenty minutes or so I spoke about discipline, concentration, dedication, and team spirit as it is expressed in ensemble playing in music and other contexts. Afterward, I was invited to watch the practice session. I saw fascinating footwork, passing, faking, and dribbling. But when it came to sinking the ball in the basket, the team was cold. Being a maniacal teacher, I took a deep breath and said to Mr. Knight that if I wanted to practice hitting the basket, I would sit on a chair and inhale before throwing, and also keep moving the chair. He looked at me and said, "Oh, yeah. Maybe we will try it." He thanked me for coming.

That year IU came close to winning the championship, and John Feinstein published *A Season on the Brink*. A year later the Hoosiers won the nationals. Friends told me that in an interview Steve Alford, the star scorer, said that he practiced shooting from a chair. I was proud that they had won, as I am when a student wins a competition. It is the student who wins, not me. I can assist and teach, but cannot give talent. I made a second visit to the team two or three years later and gave a similar speech, but that visit was not followed by glory, though I still proudly wear the team shirts I was given. However, let it be said that Coach Knight is one of the greatest teachers I have ever met in any field.

Around the time of my basketball adventure, another event firmed my identification as a Hoosier. A frantic phone call from New York asked for my help. A TV producer friend had just finished his six-part series on Muncie, Indiana: Middletown USA. They used "Back Home in Indiana" as the theme song. A cellist had recorded it but he disliked it, and he asked if I would please do it. I wasn't familiar with the song, so he quickly mailed it to me. I made a sort of arrangement for solo cello, and realized that I was the right person to do it, considering that, with all my travels, I come back home to Indiana fifty to sixty times a year. The series was controversial because it covered some sensitive subjects, and because the credits showed me playing, I was teased and heard across the country.

The Philippines surprised us with two symphony orchestras, music schools, an active musical life, and an art industry. Hundreds of painters sold their works, sometimes while they were still wet, on the streets and in galleries. I was to perform with one of the orchestras. Ed Laut, a former student of mine who was now principal cellist of the other orchestra, after waiting excitedly for a year to greet his teacher, overslept and missed the concert. He is now a professor at the University of Kansas, and after twenty-five years he still blushes when reminded of it.

My first visit to Korea was far less satisfying than subsequent ones because of the lack of high-quality hotels. It was one of the rare occasions when I agreed to stay in a U.S. embassy, partly because we had met the ambassador in Tokyo in 1960. When we arrived, the entire airport reeked of garlic. Only after generous helpings of kimchi did we grow accustomed to the nation's scent. I played a solo recital in an immense hall, and the program called for a Bach suite. I felt I was betraying Bach's basically intimate work, a feeling I still have in such venues. The best part of the Korean tour was meeting Wonsik Lim, the Korean conductor who established the Korean Broadcasting Orchestra after World War II and also founded Seoul Arts High School, which has trained many of the gifted Korean musicians who have enriched the world's musical life. Lim passed away in August of 2002. I returned to Korea, and to Japan, at my planned three-year intervals, and learned the beauty of the land and the talent and drive of its people.

A comical event surfaced in my memory while I was in Seoul that first time. In 1938, when I was called at noon to substitute in a performance of the Dvořák Concerto at 6 P.M., a Korean conductor, cellist, and composer named Ahn Ektai was visiting Budapest. He conducted a symphony he had written, which was Mahlerian in scope; a part of it is the Korean national anthem today. After my performance he came to me and said that I must come to Korea, play, teach, and marry a Korean girl. The last was tempting; I had seen pictures of beautiful ladies in exotic dresses. Alas, at age fourteen I was not yet a free agent.

The year 1969 brought troubles. My daughter Gabrielle, by then a college student and filled with wanderlust, decided to travel through South America, heading for Amazonia. She was in Ecuador for the moon landing, and heard it reported on the radio. Her next stop was Peru, where she took a job teaching English; by then she was nearly as fluent in Spanish as in English. On her twentieth birthday, while riding a motorcycle, she was hit by a car. A doctor who had trained at the Mayo Clinic managed to save her leg by the barest margin. I was near the end of a European tour; I canceled the London and Paris concerts and flew to Lima to bring her home on crutches. Fourteen operations later, she was well again. She returned to Peru three years later, and has grown to love it as a second home.

In 1971, I finally returned to Hungary. I had been receiving invitations for years, but I stuck to my decision; twenty-five years had to pass before I would return. I had no real relatives there, but some surviving friends and colleagues. The country was under Communist rule, but I had no qualms about politics. I had already performed in Czechoslovakia, Yugoslavia, and Bulgaria, and when the musicians' union asked musicians not to perform in Greece, which was in the grip of a Fascist junta, I did. Obviously I did not approve of the Hungarian government's policies, but I do not play for governments. I play for the people. However, I insisted on payment in Western currencies. That was why I refused to perform in Soviet Russia and China; they paid visiting performers in nonconvertible local currency. Meanwhile the Soviet and

Chinese governments sent their people to the West, where they collected huge fees, eighty to ninety percent of which went into the government's coffers and was used for armaments. I strongly objected when the State Department sponsored American artists performing in those countries, and refused repeated offers.

But Hungary was different. I only needed time to forget, and after twenty-five years I was ready. I arranged the schedule so that I wouldn't have time to reflect before I played. On a Wednesday and Thursday I played the Hindemith Concerto in Stuttgart, Germany. After the concert I was driven to Frankfurt, where Rae joined me from Bloomington, and on Friday we went to Budapest. We arrived a few hours later than planned. In the hotel I took a shower and a nap, and at 7 P.M. I sat on the stage of the Franz Liszt Academy. I looked up at the teacher's loge and did not recognize anyone but my beautiful wife. I was greeted noisily, and when the hall quieted I played two Bach suites and the Kodály Solo Sonata.

Afterward I gulped down a huge dose of scotch, as was my habit, and started greeting people—hundreds of people. As well as the usual requests for handshakes, autographs, and photo opportunities, I was barraged by "Do you remember me?" and "When can we talk?" When I had a vague notion who the person was, I told them to come over to the hotel the next day at three. Eventually I started saying four. After an hour we left and were driven back to our hotel. I said, let's have dinner, and we went to the restaurant where, in 1944, a policeman recognized me but was too lazy to arrest me. We had a feast and the great Hungarian Gypsy primarius, Sandor Lakatos, played his heart out for my wife. We returned to the hotel. Our terrace looked out on the Danube. I broke down and wept, then slept.

The next day Rae arranged a cocktail party. Seventy-five people showed up and I recognized most of them. "When are you coming next?" they wanted to know. I said I would return in three years, the same tour schedule as for Japan, Israel, South America, or Australia. "But this is your home." I told them, not anymore. I come and play in Hungary as anywhere else, as long as they want me.

The next day there was an orchestra concert conducted by György Lehel. As a young student in 1945 he dreamed of becoming a maestro, and used to listen to me practicing. He became one of the best, and we played together a few times elsewhere in Europe.

On our next trip to Hungary Rae and I took along our two daughters. We went to see the houses I grew up in, and visited Gyömrö, the village where we used to spend our summers. I showed them the lake, and the trees under which Mother sat and served us fried chicken. I even found the cabana, with its nails on which we hung our shirts when changing. Gradually Hungary became a regular stop on the touring schedule, though on each visit I found fewer surviving acquaintances. In '91, while I was there, the Communists were ousted and a democratic government was voted in. The next day I left.

I also toured Australia under the aegis of the Australian Broadcasting Corporation and Musica Viva Australia. Musica Viva had been founded by Richard Goldner, a Viennese violinist and inventor. He developed violin shoulder pads and mutes and a zipper that was bought by the Australian army. With the proceeds he established Musica Viva and introduced chamber music to his new homeland. He toured all over with a string quartet and also invited internationally known performers. Later, when he was living in the U.S. with his wife and former student Charmian Gadd (an excellent violinist and a former disciple of Josef Gingold), I asked him to help me create an organization intended to put music back where it used to be, in the salons: elegant supper parties in large homes, with top artists performing ad hoc programs for large fees after the meal, both audience members and artists dressed to the hilt, and the artists as well partaking in the feast. In addition, the artists would perform free concerts for high schools the next day. Goldner was both teaching and conducting at the time, but he listened to my proposal. The organization never got off the ground, but symphony supporters here and there raised funds in these ways. Goldner died in Australia, after having received high honors in Austria as well as Australia.

I visited Adelaide, which felt like Texas in 1948. In Sydney I participated in a guitar congress, teaching Bach to guitarists. I was among the first musicians to play in the newly built Sydney Opera House before its official opening in 1973. I always considered Sydney the second most beautiful city in the world, after Rio de Janeiro, and I was impressed with the Opera House's architectural beauty. But I was unimpressed with the new hall's acoustics and practicality. Steep, narrow passageways lead into the hall from bars; Australian audiences are known for imbibing before, during, and after performances. I think it was in the mid-1970s that I spent a New Year's Eve listening to Sandor Lakatos and renewing my old acquaintance with him. Canberra struck me as an imitation D.C., and Melbourne as England transplanted. Years later, playing in New Zealand, I had the same impression. There I saw more sheep than people, and more open spaces than in Alberta, Canada.

I was in Paris early one summer in the mid-'60s, premiering a newly discovered Janson concerto at the Festival de Paris. Several IU friends showed up. We were walking on the Champs-Élysées looking for a place to have lunch when Bernhard Heiden turned to me and said congratulations. I asked him, "For what? What did I do now?" "Don't be modest. You and Gingold were named distinguished professors, the first ever in the music school." My wife asked prophetically, "Does that mean we can never leave Bloomington?"

I had spoken to Andre Böröcz of my idea for concerts in private homes, and he crystallized it and made history as the music director of a cruise company, Paquet Voyages, when they announced the Mediterranean Music Cruise aboard Paquet's ship *Renaissance*. Böröcz contacted his festival friends, Jean-Pierre Rampal, the Vegh Quartet, and me. We were to sail, and Byron Janis and Arthur Rubinstein were to give occasional guest performances in ports. The menu was one day at sea with a concert on board, and the next day in port with a concert ashore. The ship offered luxurious accommodations for about 200 and top chefs providing superb meals, and passengers could listen to rehearsals and mingle with the artists.

The cruise sold out in days to wealthy music lovers from four continents, including eighty-five people from the U.S. The passengers could board in Marseille, but the cruise's official start was from Monte Carlo. My wife and I boarded a plane to fly to Nice, from where we would be driven to Monte Carlo, but a few hours into the flight the pilot announced that France had been hit by a general strike, and no airports were open. We would have to go to Barcelona instead of Nice, and somehow join the ship two days later at its first stop, in Mallorca. One

THE WORLD OF MUSIC ACCORDING TO STARKER

hour before we were to land in Barcelona, the pilot said that the weather was perfect, visibility limitless, and he would try to land in Nice without radar. He managed it, and we took a taxi to Monte Carlo. Böröcz thought he was seeing ghosts when we arrived.

All eighty-five American passengers canceled, but the others made it. That night Prince Rainier and Grace Kelly hosted a gala concert in the palace, with Byron Janis as soloist, but supper was on the ship. At 2 A.M. the cruise got under way. With the reduced passenger list, the people aboard became like a family, practicing, performing, swimming, playing Ping-Pong, and skeet shooting. François Reichenbach, the famed filmmaker, was on board collecting material for a profile of the music cruise. Also on board was France's leading music critic, Bernard Gavoty. Gavoty acted as emcee, giving lectures and introducing the programs, a role that was taken over on later voyages by America's favorite radio man, Karl Haas, who has hosted *Adventures in Good Music* since creating the show in 1959.

Rubinstein played a recital in Mallorca, and we continued on to Tunis. Everywhere we went, onshore events were free for local people; there was outdoor dancing and roasting of lambs. In Messina I attended a concert with the Virtuosi di Roma and Jean-Pierre Rampal in the open-air Greco-Roman theater, which had incredible acoustics. Mount Etna was active, making the scene something that could have been staged by Hollywood. Dubrovnik was next, and the Zagreb Philharmonic was brought in to perform in the old fort, with me playing the Dvořák concerto. There was a small hitch, though. I dressed for the concert on the ship, while the passengers were driven to the fort. When the overture started they noticed that they had forgotten to bring me along! There was a mad dash back to the ship to get me. I walked through the audience, unpacked my cello, and went on stage. This added to the success of the evening.

Unfortunately, the cruise was a financial disaster. But Reichenbach's film went all over the world, and Gavoty's glowing articles blanketed France. The following year's cruise, and later ones, were immediate sellouts. There were new artists and new ports, as well as repeated ones, and umpteen other shipping lines announced music cruises and other theme cruises. A few years later, Böröcz launched Caribbean cruises;

(ABOVE) *With Martita and Pablo Casals in Puerto Rico*

(LEFT) *With Julius Vajda*

THE WORLD OF MUSIC ACCORDING TO STARKER

the first one included Casals in the audience in Puerto Rico. The flutist James Gallway, clarinet king Benny Goodman, and the English Chamber Orchestra were among the artists. There were families who attended year after year, almost religiously. The ship's crew knew everyone by name. Because of my increasing obligations, however, I joined the cruises for fewer and fewer days each year. My last performance with them was in Greece; Menuhin was to conduct me in Delphi, but he arrived late and sat in the audience. It was a windy day, with music flying and stands falling, as if the Greek gods were not fond of the music or the tourists.

My experience of South America started in Colombia and continued in Costa Rica, Venezuela, Brazil, Argentina, Uruguay, and Chile with orchestral performances, recitals, and classes. Luckily I managed to miss the region's frequent eruptions of violence; revolutions had been suppressed or had not yet started when I visited. I chronicled some of my experiences in my Dvořák Concerto recollections, where I stated that no traveling cellist ever lived who didn't have a slew of stories concerning that work. I enjoyed São Paulo the most, rediscovering many old Hungarian friends: musicians, amateur partners of my childhood, and Dr. Julius Vajda, an old friend of mine from school. On one trip I was accompanied by my daughter Gabrielle. She lived in Peru at the time, and traveled with me to Brazil, Argentina, and Chile. Because I have so often been an absentee father I have tried, from time to time, to have my daughters join me when my wife has not felt up to some tours.

In '73 I sent Gwen for a summer to study violin in Banff, Canada, with Lorand Fenyves. She came home raving about the beauty of the place. Shortly afterward the Banff Centre called to ask if I would consider teaching. I agreed to two weeks. We ended up spending seventeen summers there. Beginning as one of many average festival and educational centers, it grew into one of the best, and also developed an excellent year-round program. When a new president downgraded music in favor of theater in '91, however, I quit.

I continued to visit Israel at three-year intervals, playing with the Philharmonic, the Israel Chamber Orchestra, and the Beersheba Chamber Orchestra, and teaching classes in Jerusalem's Mishkenot Sha'ananim. We traveled daily and spent a lovely New Year's Eve in

1988 in Beersheba, with Arabs and Jews drinking, singing, and dancing together as they did in eleventh-century Spain. Gradually we came to understand the insoluble problems of Israel and the Palestinians: a striving modern state surrounded by a sea of hatred and animosity, millions being used as political footballs, and extremists on both sides screaming for revenge. It brings to mind the killings at Kent State, for which the National Guard soldiers were blamed. The day afterward, however, a student told me about a phone call he had received from one of the organizers of the demonstration, who told of throwing firecrackers from the back of the surging crowd. It was after that that the soldiers fired. We never read a news account of that part of the scenario.

My father and my father-in-law both died in 1976, and that year Rae and I brought our mothers to Israel. We spent Christmas and New Year's in Tel Aviv with the usual daily concert and daily sightseeing. On January 6 we went to the Al Aqsa Mosque in Jerusalem, to the Wailing Wall, to Golgotha, to the site of the Last Supper, and to Bethlehem. As we came out of the Grotto of the Nativity we watched a Greek Orthodox procession. We had seen the holiest of holies of the three major religions in one day, with no bombs, no suicidal killings: only believers following their "isms."

In 1974 Rudi Buchbinder and I were scheduled to play two evenings of romantic cello sonatas in Ravinia. Two months before the concerts, Rudi sent me a cable from Vienna saying that a new Brahms sonata had been discovered, and should we consider playing it? By the time I called him, more details had emerged. Professor Gottfried Marcus, at the Vienna Musikhochschule, had come upon a first-edition transcription for cello of the G Major Violin Sonata. He was so startled that no one knew about it that he spent six months researching its origin. It was published in 1897, the year Brahms died, and Simrock's catalogue calls it simply Brahms's Sonata in D Major, op. 78. In interviews the professor described the over 200 modifications he found, and stated that he had located a receipt showing that Brahms had been paid for the transcription. Buchbinder obtained a copy of the 1897 publication and mailed it to me, and I called Ravinia and proposed a change of program. They accepted, and on our second evening in Ravinia we played three Brahms sonatas. It was a historic first. The audience loved them.

The concert caused a sensation; it was covered by the *New York Times* and the global news wires picked up the story. International, a music publisher, wanted to republish the sonata and asked me to edit it. It was not under copyright, and appeared within a few months. In the meantime, an international uproar had developed. Hundreds of letters were written, to me and to the *New York Times,* questioning the sonata's authenticity, and some descendants of performers claimed that their fathers, brothers, and grandfathers had played it in a variety of places in the early part of the century. The representatives of the Simrock catalogue quickly issued a version and added the name of Paul Klengel, a violist and brother of the legendary cello teacher Julius Klengel, as the transcriber. Paul Klengel had died in 1935, therefore copyright was claimed on the transcription.

German and English musicologists spent years writing lengthy dissertations on the topic, some even assuming that I was responsible for the transcription. I was amused by this; all I did was put fingerings and bowings in the cello part. I believe that no transcriber would have had the nerve to alter Brahms's writing that much from the violin version. For me the rest is moot. I love the piece, whoever is responsible. These days Laszlo Varga, Yo-Yo Ma, and others play all three violin sonatas in their original key. Bach violin partitas are played on the cello, and cello suites on the viola, bass, marimba, trumpet, tuba, and so on. Why not, if it is well done? I eventually recorded the sonata with Shigeo Neriki.

In '78 my mother passed away. I was on my way to Portugal via Brussels, and stopped in Chicago to have lunch with her. She said, "Go, my son, do your job," and went to bed for her nap while I left for the airport. When the plane landed in Brussels I suddenly got sick and barely made it to the bathroom. After the Lisbon concerts I flew to Essen, where I called my wife, and she told me that Mother was gone. It turned out that it happened just as I got sick in Brussels. As my brothers had died without a trace, my parents and I agreed that no one of us was to be buried, nor ashes kept. But to this day I am in contact with all of them, without believing in an afterlife.

The years from the mid-'70s to the '90s continued in much the same way, though I traveled more and more. Gabrielle changed her name to Gabriela and married for the second time. Gwen married the violinist

William Preucil, who had been a student in my chamber music class. Although I rarely make such remarks, I said to my wife over dinner that I had heard a young man who would one day be a major concertmaster. Gwen, after two years studying in Lausanne and traveling with the chamber orchestra of that city, returned home to finish her studies with Franco Gulli and she and Bill met. Bill's first post was as concertmaster in Nashville, Tennessee, and Gwen was associate concertmaster. They married in 1981. Next year they were in Salt Lake City, then Atlanta, where Gwen was concertmaster of the ballet orchestra. Seven years later, Bill took over the Cleveland Quartet and began a professorship at Eastman School of Music. When the quartet dissolved he became concertmaster of the Cleveland Symphony. I am proud of my predictive powers, which he surpassed as a teacher, performer, and recording artist.

In '78 the little girl into whose hands I put the cello in 1932, Eva Czako Janzer, died. She had come to Bloomington in 1972 with her husband, Georges Janzer, the violist of the Vegh Quartet. Georges joined the faculty at IU, filling the vacancy left by William Primrose's departure. At first Eva assisted me, and soon she became an associate professor. She was an outstanding artist and teacher. To preserve her memory I established the Eva Janzer Memorial Cello Center, which holds an annual celebration to honor cellists for their contributions as performers and teachers, awarding them the title of Chevalier du Violoncelle or Grande Dame du Violoncelle. Its first honoree, in 1979, was Pierre Fournier. Each year the honoree or honorees give classes for our students, are awarded the ceremonial title, hear a cello ensemble play in their honor, and then dine with their assembled colleagues, who have come from all over, even overseas. Friendships are formed and renewed, and a good time is had by all. The list of those honored in twenty-five years reads like the Who's Who of the cello community.

(The title of Chevalier had been invented in 1968, because an honorary doctorate could not be awarded when Gregor Piatigorsky, my friend Grisha, was invited to Bloomington to be honored. The Grande Dame was added in 1981, when the first woman was honored. I drove Piatigorsky from Indianapolis in the company of Bernard Greenhouse and Aldo Parisot, and at one point Grisha said, "Be careful, Janos." I asked, "Why?" "Imagine four famous cellists died. What a celebration

THE WORLD OF MUSIC ACCORDING TO STARKER

With Zuzana Ruzickova and Eva Czako Janzer (1976)

In Bloomington with Bernard Greenhouse and Tsuyoshi Tsutsumi (1980)

the cello world would have." On that occasion eleven of his transcriptions were performed. Listening to them, he marveled, "Did I do that? I don't remember." At the luncheon given by the administration, he was presented with a stack of cables and letters, regrets from cellists who couldn't be present. "I am sad," he said, "that they aren't present. On the other hand, I am pleased. They must be working.")

It is thought-provoking how often cellists have established clubs to promote their instrument and their friendships. The first such clubs were founded in San Francisco and New York. The movement mushroomed to about sixteen clubs, which together formed the American Cello Council. Clubs were formed in Canada, Australia, Japan, Germany, Hungary, France, and Israel. In addition, viola, flute, harp, tuba, bass, and other societies too numerous to mention were also founded. The American Cello Council then sponsored the American Cello Congress, first held in Maryland in 1982, then in Arizona, and in 1986 in Bloomington, attended by performers, teachers, students, and amateurs. The final concert ensemble included close to 200 cellists. Rae and I hosted a dinner party with 415 guests, sitting under tents next to our home. A poster of that event, by the great artist and friend Milton Glazer, adorns my studio. Then the World Cello Congresses began, along with congresses in Manchester, England; Kronberg, Germany; St. Petersburg, Russia; and Towson, Maryland. The latest development is the establishment of the World Cello Society, headquartered in Kronberg. These gatherings focus on future generations of cellists, to help them develop and gain recognition, while educating the greater public in the richness of our art.

In the '60s I began a new activity: writing. At that time there were no in-flight movies, so reading and writing were the best ways to spend the endless hours of travel, especially since I cannot sleep on planes. Some of my writings on musical topics were published; most languished in drawers. Eventually I accumulated enough to make up a book, and at the urging of friends I sent it around to publishers. I received compliments along with rejections; the publishers said it had no mass appeal, which is what I feel while writing now. As I already stated, I am not interested in juicy stories, unless they are funny. I am trying to reflect on the life of a working musician and teacher, who chose the less glamorous, but more beneficent, way to serve his calling.

I also began editing and doing some transcribing. With Peer International and Schirmer I published the Bach suites and gamba sonatas, a Schubert sonatina, sonatas and variations by Beethoven, the Dvořák Concerto, Italian sonatas, encore pieces, and others. My one rather dubious publication was a cartoon book titled *The Roll Call of the Blessed Ones*, published in 1985. In the 1960s I was struck by some of the characteristic traits of the leading musicians of the time, and began to write captions for imaginary cartoons of them. No caption ever tried to cast aspersion on their greatness as musicians. After years of searching I happened upon a very gifted cartoonist, a cellist and member of the Cleveland Symphony, Jorge Sicre. He showed me his drawings of some of the people for whom I had written captions, and we agreed to collaborate. A small D.C. publishing firm, Occidental Press, agreed to publish it. We decided that we would include in the book only musicians who were professionally active, but unfortunately Pierre Fournier and Emil Gilels passed away while it was in press, and it was too late to delete them. A thousand copies were printed and quickly sold, and most of the musical community was amused. However, many of those in the book were not, and neither were some who were not included. As time went on I began to see some negative effects on my bookings. Unfortunately, I had assumed in the foreword that my colleagues at the top of their professions had a sense of humor. I was in many instances dead wrong, and that taught me not to make assumptions based on my own thought processes. Nevertheless, I enjoyed doing the book, and it added some notoriety to my fame.

My family was growing, both numerically and musically. Gwen and I performed the Brahms Double Concerto and the Kodály Duo, giving me immense pleasure, and I performed the same works, plus the Beethoven Triple, with her husband, Bill. In 1984, on my sixtieth birthday, while I was playing and teaching in Varna, Bulgaria, a telegram reached me saying that Gwen and Bill had given me my first grandchild, a girl named Alexandra (Lexi). Gabrielle's second marriage failed and she went to the Philippines. After more than a year she returned, earned

The Preucil family: Alexandra, Nicole, Bill, and Gwen

her master's degree in linguistics, and became one of the directors in the Spanish division of the State Department National Foreign Affairs Training Center for foreign service personnel.

The tours continued, and the recordings as well. More and more often, my concert appearances were combined with master classes. More and more honors, including honorary doctorates and medals, came my way. As traveling became more and more a chore—airports turning into shopping malls, passengers herded like animals into corrals, the endless difficulties of traveling with a cello—I decided to gradually reduce my activities. This meant playing around seventy-five concerts a year instead of a hundred. By combining playing and teaching I could stay longer in one place, avoiding the breakneck rush to catch a flight. Moreover, I could swim more frequently in my indoor pool, which has a sign above it saying, "The pool that Kodály built," recordings of Kodály having done so well for me. It also allows me to observe my annual ritual of a four- or five-day retreat, which I began decades ago with my friend George Lang. "Friend" is an understatement; "brother" is more like it. He had no brothers, and I lost two. We walk, talk, eat, drink, and argue. He is a Renaissance man: a world-famous restaurateur, an author, a former violinist, a historian, an artist, and so on. He keeps me on my toes and I provide him with a sounding board. When the topic of conversation gets sticky we change it, and we laugh a heck of a lot. His autobiography, *Nobody Knows the Truffles I've Seen,* should daunt me in my efforts to compile my own recollections. It is brilliant, amusing, and instructive. As for this book, my primary reason for going down memory lane is to leave a record of myself for my children. All the witnesses are gradually departing. Hundreds of stories have been written about me, hundreds of interviews published. My activities have been documented by others. It is not for me to say whether my life story is worth telling. If these lines have developed into a readable work, then let it be. If not, my descendants will at least have a firsthand source from which to judge. And at least this convoluted story has been edited, eliminating (I hope) the non sequiturs, repetitions, and dangling prepositions.

In any case, I must conclude my story. In the summer of '88 I was booked on an extended tour: to South America in June, and from there to Australia, Japan, and Korea, and in August back to Brazil to teach, play, and record at the festival in João Pessoa. The festival included competitions for violin, viola, and cello, named after Gingold, Giuranna, and Parisot and Starker, respectively. As usual, I refused to judge. In 1956, when the first Casals Competition was held in Mexico, I had been invited to represent Hungary as a juror, and I refused. As the years went by I grew disillusioned by events at various international competitions. In a recent article in *Strad* magazine I expressed my views on the subject and explained why I do not judge competitions, not even those at my own school. The gist of my views is that the first round of a competition should judge instrumental competence, the second round should judge musical competence, and the finals should measure personality and artistry. Winners should not be ranked first, second, and third according to fractional differences in points between them; they should simply be called winners. Above all, the judges of the finals should not be players of the instrument in question. I tested these beliefs in '86 at the cello congress held at Indiana University. The preliminary rounds were held by the nation's cello clubs, and their winners were the finalists at the congress. The jury included no cellists; a violinist, Gingold, presided, and the other members were a violist, a conductor, a journalist, and a pianist. Two winners were selected without a dissenting voice, and both are now principal cellists of major orchestras.

After this grueling tour I was booked to play with the Dallas Symphony to celebrate the fortieth anniversary of my arrival there. The rehearsal went as usual. Afterward I agreed to speak to the ladies of the symphony, and after dinner I retired while my wife was still watching TV and reading. I woke up around 2 A.M. to find that my pillow was covered with blood from a terrible nosebleed. I landed in the hospital, and it took eight hours to stop the bleeding. The doctors did not allow me to play the concerts and the news services reported that I had had a heart attack. It was nothing of the sort. The only reasonable explanation was that the great amount of flying I had done, and the high altitude, caused extreme dryness. I was told not to fly for a while, and had to cancel a performance of Bach cycles in Berlin as well as a few other dates. We had to drive home. It was fortunate my wife was with me, as I had let my driver's license expire and was not able to rent a car. Meanwhile, the principal cellist of the Dallas symphony stepped in to save the concert. I did return to Dallas two years later.

I remember spending a few days in Bonn in '89, at a Beethoven/Bernstein festival. After the concert Leonard Bernstein was asked to sign the guest book in Beethoven's house. He wrote, "L. B. leider kein *von*," meaning "regrettably not *von*"; the particle "von" often indicates noble ancestry. I came next. I said, though I'm not certain I wrote it, "J. S. leider kein Bach."

The year 1990 is particularly memorable because Gabrielle finally met and married the man she loves and has a perfect union with. They have a son, called JP for Jonathan Percy Saxe. In the same year, Rudolf Firkusny and I recorded the three Martinu sonatas for BMG-RCA Records. During the rehearsal period both of us were nominated for Grammys for other CDs, and when the record appeared we were nominated together. I also recorded the Dvořák and Bartók concertos with Leonard Slatkin in St. Louis. I had previously known him as a young

My daughter Gabriella and her family, Robert and JP Saxe

With Eleanor Slatkin, Laszlo Varga, Shirley Trepel, and Raya Garbousova in Bloomington (1990)

lad, watching me play chamber music with his parents in their home in Los Angeles. Felix and Eleanor Slatkin were superb musicians and dear, much admired friends and colleagues.

In '91 I ended my association with the Banff Centre, and began my annual visits to the Orford Arts Centre in Quebec. Performing with the Chamber Players of Toronto, I was conducted by a lady, Agnes Grossmann. I was mightily impressed with her musicianship. When she was appointed to restart the Orford Centre, which had been dormant for years, she asked me to join it. Her husband, the noted conductor Raffi Armenian, codirects the Orford festival and school. They are building the center to prominence among the truly effective educational projects. And there are so many. As the symphony orchestras lengthened their seasons, it was logical to extend into the summers. For the same reason, colleges introduced summer sessions. Enterprising musicians, upon seeing a lovely church, founded a festival in it and soon expanded, with master classes by the hundreds. The trend continues, and summer festivals have proliferated.

I listened to friendly advice and underwent repeat surgery on my hernia, forty-five years after the original operation. I had a five-week recovery period before a tour through Italy that ended in Bonn, Germany. The doctors warned me not to carry heavy suitcases, which is difficult with a cello and considering the lack of porters at airports. Lo and behold, my suitcase was lost in Bologna. I kept buying shirts, and underwear, and eventually a concert suit, complete with shoes and other necessities. Finally, after fourteen days of traveling and performing, I bought a suitcase. That day I was notified that the suitcase was in Germany and would be delivered to me in Bonn, my last stop. When I arrived back in the U.S. with two suitcases I had to pay customs fees on my Italian purchases, but my scar had healed.

In January '95 I again needed hernia surgery. While I was in the hospital Joe Gingold was also brought in, and a few days later he passed away. His death wasn't totally unexpected, as he had been ailing for quite a while, but the shock was immense and never healed. I met Joe in Cleveland in 1950, while on tour with the Met. We were introduced by Jeno Antal, who was later my partner in the Roth Quartet. Around 1954 both Joe and I were invited to Evansville, Indiana, to give classes at the newly formed Symphony League's congress. From 1960 until his death we were colleagues in the School of Music at Indiana University. He did not drive, and after his dear, lovely wife, Gladys, passed away, I would pick him up on my way to school. He taught my daughter Gwen violin. He often spent Christmas and New Year's in my home, and we shared our joys and sorrows. He had a difficult life, but an admirable one. He taught hundreds, and as a mentor he influenced thousands. Orchestras of the world are staffed by his disciples. We made music together often, in public as well as in my home. He was a member of the family, an older brother to me and like a grandfather to my children. His loss is mourned, but with grateful smiles. He was a truly great artist and human being. (Those who are privy to the sad events preceding and following his death should not expect me to provide details. His son, who is a lawyer, is known to spend his retirement in suing people, organizations, instrument dealers, whoever provokes him, and I have no intention of providing him with ammunition. He has to live with himself, and I wish him well.)

I continued doing concerts, tours, and recordings in the '90s, but at a gradually slower pace. I felt that I was becoming less able to produce the kind of virtuoso playing for which I was known. The cello requires greater physical strength than most instruments: not the muscularity that is needed for wrestling or weightlifting, but a strength in the arms, hands, fingers, and back muscles. In order to keep in shape I would have had to practice more, and that did not appeal to me. I practiced mainly by demonstrating while teaching. Swimming, of course, helped, but age slowly took its toll. The hernia operations damaged my stomach muscles, and attacks of lumbago became more frequent. My playing was not affected, but traveling and carrying the cello grew difficult. The only cellist of my vintage who still occasionally performs is Rostropovich. At the same time, more and more exceptionally gifted cellists were appearing on the scene. Instead of jealous, I felt vindicated. The cello standards I set sixty years ago have come to fruition. I don't have to prove anything any more. If I feel like playing and I am wanted, I will perform, but I am done with struggling. Let the younger ones continue the job and keep raising those standards.

I continued making records. The fifth version of the Bach suites received a Grammy. Unfortunately, the BMG-RCA recordings with piano and orchestra were carelessly produced. Although the replays in the studios were satisfactory, when the records were pressed the cello mikes were turned down, resulting in poor balance. The old EMI, Erato, and Mercury recordings were reissued as CDs, as were a slew of old radio broadcasts. The legend of 1956 became the legend of the past.

An interesting aspect of the music business evidenced itself. Orchestras and music societies base their subscription sales on a few artists who are household names, and for whose services they pay enormous fees. Since not much is left in the budget, they pay ridiculously low sums for the others. Since I was considered a second-tier performer but would not accept such low fees, they moved on to the third and fourth tiers, young competition winners who needed the exposure. Gradually I began accepting invitations from third- and fourth-tier orchestras, rather than putting up with low fees from the majors. This made my decision to cut down on travel easier and easier.

Robert Starer, Chou Wen-chung, and Juan Orrego-Salas all wrote concertos for me in the '90s. Starer's was performed and recorded in Boston. The others remained in limbo after their premieres in Carnegie Hall and Bloomington. At that time I decided to consider works written for me only if their composers asked for my help while writing.

The fascination that traveling had held for me in the early years abated, and I needed more and more rest. I did agree to go to Moscow and Beijing for no fee, to help friends, but limited my sightseeing. I went to Mao's tomb to make sure that he was dead, and to Lenin's tomb for the same reason. Both trips were disappointing artistically, though it was heartwarming to be able to help friends. I also refused to use these trips to generate publicity. I went, played, and left. More and more the caption I had written for Erich Leinsdorf in *The Roll Call of the Blessed Ones* became applicable to me: "One who scaled all the heights, but missed many of the sights." It was rehearsal, nap, concert, and room service, next day a flight and the same all over again. When friends and disciples presented themselves, it was at supper after the concert, telling stories, looking at photos of children, and drinking lots of scotch.

In 1999 I found myself at the age of seventy-five. This is generally

With Mstislav Rostropovich in Bloomington (1999)

considered a significant number, and celebrations were held in a variety of places where I performed: Kronberg, Tokyo, Chicago, San Diego, and finally Bloomington. Some were surprise parties, and some were planned by faithful associates, friends, and former students. I appreciated their good wishes, but I had to stifle my long-standing resentment of birthday-year promotional tours. The exception was the celebration in Bloomington in September. Rostropovich graciously came to conduct the Indiana University Philharmonic Orchestra and my son-in-law, Bill Preucil, joined me in the Brahms Double Concerto. Gwen and her daughter, my granddaughter Alexandra, surprised me with a movement from the Bach Double Concerto; Tsuyoshi Tsutsumi, Gary Hoffmann, and Maria Kliegel performed; and then approximately 175 cellists played Popper's Duo, arranged and conducted by Emilio Colón. My daughter Gabrielle gave a tear-provoking speech, as did my buddy George Lang. More speeches, honors, and medals followed, topped by a cake with seventy-five candles. The most poignant memory of the day is the speech given by Gyorgy Sebok. After the celebration I left for Japan and he left for Europe. While there he fell ill, and he passed away in November shortly after his return. He left a void never to be filled.

The end of the millennium was at hand, and a childhood dream was about to materialize. One New Year's Eve when I was something like eleven years old, I thought how exciting it would be to see the clock turn over at midnight into the year 2000. From the time I turned seventy, whenever I felt tired and less than well, I forced myself to swim at night in my indoor pool (that Kodály built), and chanted to myself, as if trying to make a Faustian deal with the devil, "Let me see the clock at midnight turn to 2000 and still be healthy." Well, it worked. I am still here. I beat the odds. I have no unfulfilled dreams except one, that those I care for survive me. Too many are already gone. I watch the world as if it were a movie. I read history and see it all repeating: murder, mayhem, wars, hatred. I see stunning technological advances while remembering oil lamps and outhouses. I see fanatics: crusaders, Nazis, Communists, Fascists, and saintly self-appointed saviors. We are returning to a medieval, even a tribal, system. I watch individual liberties erode as they did when I was in my teens, and I see the hustlers flourishing.

Nevertheless music, the leitmotif of my life, is alive and well, and I take pride in having served it. I still complain about the ills of society, but the turbulence is easing. The rocks I climbed seem smoother on the way down.

13 TWILIGHT AT TIFFANY'S

Young Salo stared at the sky, in which dark clouds were gathering. The flock of sheep he guarded formed a tighter and tighter circle; birds flew back to their nests to protect their young ones. It was the silence before a storm, and then the wind blew up; its sound ascended in pitch and broke open the silence.

Young Salo rose from his resting place and began to climb down the mountainside, the flock slowly following. Not time enough, he thought, to descend to the ranch before the clouds burst. He had been dreaming too much and had let the flock wander farther to graze than usual. He wondered where to find refuge from a storm that looked truly ominous. Distant thunder rumbled, and then lightning struck. He quickened his pace toward a wall of firs that loomed ahead, and when he reached the first trees, he spied a bit of empty space in the midst of a small forest. Young Salo ran back and urged the flock through the bushes.

It was as though night had fallen when he reached the shelter-like clearing, above which trees towered and intertwined. The rain began as he settled down on the ground, hoping for the best. Lightning crackled with regularity now, and the sheep huddled into a huge bundle of wool. A sudden thunderbolt shook Young Salo as lightning lit up the forest.

Off to his right, on an incline, he saw a gaping hole. In darkness again, he groped toward it through torrential rain, stumbling a few times before he reached the opening. The next lightning flash enabled him to enter what seemed a cave. He sighed and sank down on a stone, protected here from the rain.

As the storm reached its height, Young Salo became aware of an echoing reverberation each time the thunder subsided. This cave, he thought, must be quite large. As he lit his pipe, he glimpsed steps ahead, steps that weren't natural but man-made, leading upward. He called out, "Anyone in there?" But his echoing voice provoked no answer. He tried a few more times, without avail, and decided to explore the place. He stumbled toward the steps, counted to seven, then lit his lighter.

Young Salo was not accustomed to surprises. He was twenty-five years old and had been taken by his parents to the preserve when he was ten. He took no time at all to adapt to the new life, which his father told him was really the old life. Preserves were for those who found life in the megalopolis uncomfortable; there, existence was both structured and constricting. No one worked more than five hours a day: sports, meetings, parades, and TV filled the rest of the time year-round. Once a year everyone in a district would pack up and exchange places with those in another, moving into one another's homes and continuing life for a few months as though nothing were different. Only the surroundings, the scenery, changed a little. The food coupons were the same; so were the pills. Parades, TV, and language remained the same.

His father, Old Salo, was a schoolteacher who had often mumbled that he wanted to live like people he had read about—before the big war. Then one day he applied to enter a preserve. He was told, of course, that he'd need to wait for an opening. Preserves, led by elders, were scattered throughout the country. In them families had their own land, tilled it, raised animals, and bartered in the villages. Village shops sold goods made by the families in their homes. Factory-made items came from the outside once a month and were paid for with goods.

After waiting three years, the Salo family received instructions to move to the Eldorado IV preserve. When they arrived, Young Salo couldn't believe his eyes. The ranch assigned to them was like a dream. When he awoke in the morning he ran outdoors to watch the sunrise.

He heard the chatter of birds, or what some called "singing." Animals were everywhere: dogs, cats, horses, chickens, pigs, cows, and sheep. Young Salo thought this must be heaven, the kind old people talked about. He smelled the flowers and feasted his eyes on the beauty of nature.

Years passed. Seasons changed, and each brought new experiences. Young Salo had never seen snow in the megalopolis, or rain, for that matter. Weather stations trained their instruments on the clouds and scattered them at will. Only farm areas received moisture as needed. How different it was here! It was hot in summer and he swam in lakes and streams. It was cold in winter and he donned skis to slide down hills and across the ground. He grew into manhood learning from his father about the world as it had been, according to legend and records in the central library.

Young Salo seldom went to the village, where life seemed dull to him. All he cared for was enjoying nature. He asked to be a shepherd and his father agreed. He was happy alone in the mountains with his flock. He was never afraid of wild animals and even learned to talk to them, to make them his friends. He trained his ears to recognize all the sounds that birds and animals make, which he imitated at will. From time to time he came upon the remnants of a long-abandoned house. Searching for signs of life, he found books and utensils. To amuse himself he imagined how people of long ago might have lived.

Now the thunder was becoming more and more distant, and the rain slackened. Young Salo had the strange feeling of being in someone's home. He looked around and at the top of the stairs he saw a heavy door in the gloom. There was no response to knocking, and he gave up and managed to pry it open. Young Salo found himself in quite a large room. Remembering a flashlight in his rucksack, he got it out and shined the beam around him. For once, Young Salo was thoroughly surprised. He saw rock walls that had been chiseled beautifully smooth, a large table, a desk, and chairs. The walls were almost covered in shelves, and the shelves were stocked with sturdy-looking books. On the walls between the shelf units he saw many pictures. At the far end of the room were two more doors. Uneasily, he opened one of them. Inside was a room with a stove and more shelves that held dishes and

THE WORLD OF MUSIC ACCORDING TO STARKER

cans of assorted sizes. When he opened the other door, he stiffened. Obviously this was a bedroom. Two large beds were in the center, and in one of them two skeletons lay side by side. Young Salo turned away to control his rapid breathing. He walked back to the first door and down the stairs. The storm had ended, a full moon shone, and a myriad of stars glittered in the black sky.

Young Salo was confused. All of the places he'd previously found bore no sign of people in them and none were in the condition of this. Heretofore, the books he had found had tended to fall apart when touched. He decided at length to pass the night on the steps and next morning to explore the abode. He slept restlessly. His dreams were crowded and confused. Most of the time his dreams were eerily empty, like a canvas stretching endlessly with nothing on it; but now he saw huge crowds of people on their knees, wailing, looking skyward, prostrating themselves, and then suddenly struck by incredibly powerful lightning. Flames and dust were followed by floods.

When he awakened, the flock had wandered off to forage. He felt suddenly hungry himself and was grateful to find some bread and a canteen of water in his rucksack. Young Salo walked about in front of the cave and in one sudden moment realized how this place was different from the others he had seen—an enormous rock lay a few yards below the cave's mouth. It must have concealed the entrance for a long time. The top of the stone was covered with vegetation. The turned-up side, however, was bare; it must have fallen recently to reveal the opening.

Young Salo reentered the cavern, determined to discover its secret. To his surprise there was a faint light in the main room. In a far corner he saw a slight opening in the ceiling; underneath was shattered glass from a window that had been broken. The opening was angled, which had prevented the rain from coming through. There was a desk, which appeared as though its owner had been interrupted in the midst of work; pens, pencils, and sheets of paper were scattered on it, and a large book lay open with its left-hand page covered in writing, but its right-hand page empty—totally. Young Salo walked around, touching everything but taking great care, knowing from past experience how easily old paper crumbled. This place, he thought, must have been virtually sealed;

that, or it wasn't as old as the other places he had explored. He studied the pictures—paintings, prints, and photographs. Several were of the same strange-looking man, either standing or sitting, holding in his hand a mysterious object. In some pictures this peculiar object was tucked under his chin and supported by his left shoulder. He gripped its end in his left hand, and in his right he held a long stick which lay across it. Shrugging his shoulders, Young Salo murmured aloud, "What kind of foolish thing is that?"

He continued to poke about. One shelf held no books, but rather a number of large . . . what? They seemed similar to magazines he had seen as a child. Cautiously he opened one to find it filled with marks—black dots, black lines, some small flags, and here and there the letters p and f. But nothing made sense. Other shelves held the same kind of puzzles, some thin, some thick, but inside all of them the same dots and lines. Crazy! And then Young Salo thought, maybe it's some kind of secret language! Every page had five lines, then a space, then five more lines, again a space, over and over from top to bottom. He looked further and saw neat rows of books, but could make neither head nor tail of them. To himself he said, "I must examine these more closely later." As he glanced over the covers, however, he saw that all bore the word "Music."

"Music? Music?" Young Salo asked himself over and over again. The word had no meaning to him, and so he moved on to the next shelf. Immediately a box, oblong in shape, caught his eye. One end was wider than the other, and the whole measured perhaps a meter. He rapped the top to find out what it was made of. It sounded hollow—metal, perhaps, or wood, or both. Then Young Salo realized it could be opened by flipping open small clips around the sides. He lifted up the box carefully, only to find it far lighter than he had imagined. Taking the box to the table, he undid the clips with utmost care and then lifted the lid, gingerly. Inside was that same odd object he had seen in the photographs! As he stared, it suddenly seemed neither funny nor peculiar. He felt instead that he was beholding an odd object, perhaps, but a beautiful one.

He wondered if he could describe it accurately. Its color was yellow, and it was shaped like . . . a body? No, more like two large, stemless

THE WORLD OF MUSIC ACCORDING TO STARKER

tulips, the larger one upside down. Where the tulips joined, he noted openings shaped like one of the letters in those large books, the fancy *f*. Mounted on the body was a thin piece of wood which resembled a long neck but ended in a curve like a snail. The neck had something black on it—a board, perhaps—all the way from the snail to the middle. Upright on the body there was a small piece of wood, like a hurdle used in sports competitions. Again there was a black piece, wood maybe, which ran to the base of the larger upside-down tulip. Four wires came from the snail, followed the black board, crossed the hurdle, and fastened to the second black piece. On both sides of the snail, two earlike objects tapered to, well, tongues within the snail.

Young Salo stared at this object, fascinated. Delicately, he put a finger to one of the wires. As he touched it, a soft sound escaped from the tulips. He jumped back as if he had fingered fire. A quiver traveled down his spine; he felt uncomfortable. Quickly he shut the box and left it on the table. He observed, however, while closing the box that sticks were fastened inside the lid, just like those in the photographs.

Time to start back home, he realized. Young Salo secured the door and descended the stairs. An hour later he had collected all the sheep and begun his long trek back to the preserve. To make certain that he could find his way back he cut marks in the trees along the route and broke off small branches. He knew he would be returning soon.

"Quite a storm last night, son," Old Salo remarked when the young man reached home. "Where were you?"

It was late and Young Salo felt exhausted. "I found a cave." He gulped down supper and fell into bed. The next day he kept close to home, but his thoughts were occupied with his discovery. That evening, cautiously, he asked his father what Music was. Old Salo's forehead wrinkled in surprise.

"Where did you hear that word?"

"I just saw it somewhere and wondered what it was," Young Salo mumbled. His father concentrated, as if trying to remember.

"According to the history books, Music is a form of organized sounds."

"Organized?"

"Yes. People used to sing in the past and also dance."

TWILIGHT AT TIFFANY'S

"Sing? Like birds, father?"

"In a way. The book said, as I recall, 'Sounds of varying pitches and lengths strung into melodies, sung by people and then danced to.' "

A puzzled look crossed Young Salo's face. "Dance?"

"Well, it must have been something like . . . when the competitions begin, and participants march in unison."

"And the drummer hits the gong! Boom, boom, boom," Young Salo added.

"Perhaps so. But this Music must have been more complex than that. I have read that people in those times made what they called 'musical' instruments, and played their music on them, alone or in groups."

"How could they play in groups? Did they know what to play?"

"Some persons, it seems, wrote down what the others were to play."

Young Salo tried to conceal his excitement. "Did you say 'wrote down,' Father? Where?"

"On paper, one supposes. Well! If you are this interested, you can go to a library and read the history books."

Feigning casualness, Young Salo said, "Maybe. Eventually. But what period would I look for?"

"Before the big war."

Young Salo was startled. "But that was more than two hundred years ago!"

"Correct. There's been no such thing as Music since the big war of 2024. I think, in fact, that it stopped even before then. I just remember having seen some objects called 'ancient musical instruments' in the archives of Megalopolis B. They dated from the sixteenth to twenty-first centuries."

Young Salo went outside and stared for hours at the stars. Next morning he rose early, packed a sack full of food, filled extra canteens with water, and took along a storm lamp. He told his parents he would be looking for better grazing land and might not be back for a while; they were not to worry about him. He chased the flock impatiently. By taking short cuts he reached the forest in mid-afternoon. All the time he was smiling to himself. He wouldn't need to go to the library; those books in the cave . . . and then he hesitated. Cave? It wasn't one, really. But what? A house? No, not that. A room? He pondered for a time, then said aloud "music room." Yes! He would call it a music room, his music room! Grinning, he passed through the wall of trees and into the forest. He had decided his first deed would be to bury the skeletons. As his sheep began to scatter, Young Salo realized that they would need water. Then he thought, "These people who lived here once, they must have had water somewhere. I just have to find it."

Before entering the cavern itself, he clambered all over the rocks and finally did discover a cistern full of rainwater from the storm. This problem solved, he moved on into the cave to set about his next task. Searching, he found a shovel, a pail, and buckets. He measured the bed, then dug a large hole outside between two towering firs. Darkness had fallen by the time he carried out the skeletons and bed and covered them with earth. He placed a piece of wood on the grave and scratched the word Music on it. By the time his sheep had been watered, he felt exceedingly tired and ate only a few bites of food before stretching full length on the floor of his "music room." But Young Salo could not sleep. The floor wasn't comfortable. Yet he couldn't quite bring himself to sleep in that other room, from which he had so recently removed the bones of two persons, and so he settled for pushing three chairs together and lying across them. In his dreams this time he saw people marching and jumping up and down aimlessly, and he also saw the man in the photographs standing alone with the yellow object and stick in his hands.

When Young Salo awakened, he was certain that he had heard sounds coming from the yellow object. Surely it was one of those "ancient musical instruments" his father had spoken of! He went directly to the box, still on the table where he'd left it the first time, opened it, and fixed his eyes on the object—the instrument. Finally he lifted it from the box. Carrying it as carefully as if it were a tiny bird, he walked to one of the photographs and tried holding it as the man did—under his chin. It was a form of metal, very light, evidently hollow inside, and felt cold. He took one of the sticks from the lid of the box and tried holding it like the man in the picture. And burst into laughter in spite of himself. The stick had connecting parts, and its length ended in a grip by which the man held it. White strands ran along the stick (which was wooden, he was sure), all bunched together, similar to the hair of an old woman, yet more like the tail of a white horse.

As he touched a string on the instrument with the white hair, Young Salo heard a sound and was even more startled than when he'd touched the string with his finger. Quickly he returned his instrument and stick to their place in the box. At the table, he lit the storm lamp to supplement the faint light from the hole in the ceiling and went to the large open book on the desk. The emptiness of the right section seemed to suggest that someone had planned to go on writing. Only a few pages remained empty. The left portion was thick, however. Lightly, Young Salo turned over dozens of pages of handwriting. Good, he thought! If I read this, I may learn about the people who lived here. Toward the end, the writing suggested that the author had experienced increasing difficulties; the words were almost illegible, with ever greater spaces between them. The last sentence read "I hope that someone will . . ." No more, just that.

Young Salo turned back to the beginning. "The Diary of Clara LeMan" was written there, and the first entry was dated October 15, 2022. Young Salo felt uneasy. It was now the year 2272, two hundred and fifty years since Clara LeMan had written this diary! He felt as he had in childhood, when he searched through his father's drawers and found books hidden. He had been told sternly never to do that again; but now, he was grown up and alone. Here was his "music room." He settled into the chair and began to read.

> I feel foolish starting this. I've never written a diary in my life and have no intention of writing a real one now. Our days are uneventful after so many hectic years, however. If it weren't for Leo, I would not bother, but he insists that I put our memories on paper. I fought with him so long—thinking his predictions stupid and wild—but almost everything he said has come true. Now he insists the world is going to end— that I must keep a record. I hesitate to argue anymore—he may be right again. He says—eventually—the world will renew itself and there should be a trace of all he did—who he was. The years when the world glorified Leo LeMan and his golden fiddle shouldn't be forgotten entirely— Leo was the most important and famous violinist of his time. It isn't his

THE WORLD OF MUSIC ACCORDING TO STARKER

*fault that music and musicians destroyed themselves—and allowed the
world to destroy them. So I promised him I would tell the story as best I
could. Time we have—Leo plays his violin most of the day—taking care
of our "house" requires little effort of me. So let him be happy.*

Young Salo got up and looked again at the box. So that's what it was!
A "violin." And the man was a "violinist." He picked up the instrument,
this "violin," and the stick, as the pictures showed, and wondered what
the man, LeMan, did. Why was he famous because of it? The only
famous people Young Salo knew were winners of athletic competitions,
and they held their fame only for a short time. He ate a small bit of the
food and resumed his reading.

NOVEMBER, 2022

> *I might as well begin by writing something of Leo's early years, al-
> though they are a matter of record in all the textbooks. Leo LeMan was
> born in Brooklyn, New York, in 1948. His father was a schoolteacher and
> his mother played the piano. His father loved the violin—always talked
> about how much he wanted to be a musician—so when Leo was three
> years old they gave him a toy violin—his father showed him how to hold
> it. All day long—every day—his mother played recordings of violin con-
> certos until Leo started humming—then later whistling the melodies—as
> other children sang TV commercials. At age five, Leo started lessons on a
> real violin, by nine he was playing in public and all agreed he would be
> the new Kreisler . . .*
>
> *I met Leo at the Juilliard School—he was fifteen—I was thirteen. We
> loved each other and knew immediately that we could never be separated.
> Of course our parents smiled at us—we could only be together playing in
> string quartets. I played the cello—and because I was a girl and younger—
> and my instrument heavier—we rehearsed most of the time at my home.
> Oh, the great plans we made—how we would travel and play together
> all over the world. When Leo was twenty-one—he had already won all
> the important prizes—we decided not to wait any longer and got mar-
> ried. Everyone said we were crazy—Leo wouldn't be able to make a
> career with the responsibility of a wife, and they were right in a way. We
> both had to play orchestras—taking whatever jobs came along. Leo al-
> ways dreamed of having a fine violin—we lived in a one-room apart-
> ment and had no car—but Leo finally bought his beautiful Stradivarius.
> He was in heaven—practicing all night, every night, until we were
> evicted from the apartment.*

December, 2022

It isn't as easy I thought—writing this diary. When you know you have all the time in the world, you keep thinking about what you are going to write, and then postpone doing it. Where was I? By 1980 Leo was well known—as a potentially great violinist. He played more and more concerts (my cello stayed more and more in the case). My musical existence was narrowed down to criticizing Leo and taking care of him. As years passed Leo became bitter—no one is interested in real music anymore, he used to say. He also felt he couldn't play the music being written in those years—it wasn't for the violin any longer—composers played mathematical games and wrote scratches and noises instead of melodies. Audiences wanted volume instead of finesse or delicacy.

Leo asked, 'How can you play concerts in a hall built for five thousand people? Most of the places have amplification—what's the use of playing a Stradivarius?'

But I was still shocked when Leo came home—it was 1982—with a strange smirk on his face. 'Look what I got,' he said. He opened his case and there was a fiddle made of solid gold! 'What on earth is that,' I asked with a trembling voice. 'You see it, don't you? It is a gold violin—I had Tiffany make it for me!' 'But why,' I asked—'it can't sound!' He laughed and said, 'Listen.' He began to play and it did sound beautiful—a little small, though.

I asked him where he got the money to pay for it. He smiled and said, 'With the price of instruments today, I got one million dollars for the Strad—this gold one only cost two hundred thousand. We have a small fortune!' This turned out to be a stroke of genius on Leo's part . . .

February, 2023

The news is all bad—the fighting all over Africa is spreading. How long can Eurasia stay out of it? America is readying laser arsenals. Leo insists on stockpiling—food, water, batteries—more than ever now.

March, 2023

Leo LeMan and his golden fiddle became the rage of music lovers everywhere—we were constantly on the road. Leo kept saying we had to hurry—it wouldn't last long. Against my wishes, he bought one hundred acres here in Montana—when I saw it, I thought he had gone mad. What would he do with it? Rocks, forests, nothing—nobody around—for miles! He said, 'That's just it!' I asked him, 'You want to build a house?'

'Hell no!' he said. 'Then what?' His answer was, 'I will carve a place out of rock and put everything we'll need inside.' His plan was prophetic.

In 2015, the United Nations finally began to consider outlawing all music—they had to—the situation everywhere had become intolerable. Riots, the police couldn't control them—musicians were killed by the thousands and instruments were chopped to pieces and burned. The American Medical Association and its international affiliates proved beyond doubt that the decibel levels were causing insanity in millions of young people and were also responsible for cancer of the eardrums. The Communists declared music criminally subversive; democratic nations said that the noise infringed on individual human rights. That's when we came here to our rock home—to watch from a safe distance.

May, 2023

Leo says the end is in sight. So what? The U.N. resolution of 2015 outlawed all music. Dancing stopped—perhaps the silence is healthy, as they all say—but what is life without music? A world of animals eating, sleeping, and copulating. Love, what kind of love? There are lasers trained on every city and ships ready to unleash total destruction.

January, 2024

It has finally happened. The last broadcast said, 'Help! Radiation is spreading—flames all around us—those who escape . . . wait, don't move! Learn—build a better world if you can—help! Help!!!' Then total silence. We stayed inside our rock home here for months—the steel doors protected us—the filter system worked. At times the radio carried distant signals, garbled voices, so there were survivors, somewhere—God only knows how many—or where.

December, 2024

Today Leo collapsed while practicing—I am weakening also. We are too old to continue alone in the world; Leo says we must put an end to it all—I begin to agree with him. He asks me to write so that anyone, if they ever find this diary, will know that a world without music is not a world worth living in.

March, 2025

We have decided. Today is the day—the pill is working . . . I hope that someone will . . .

Young Salo sat there, in a daze. He could not understand many of the words, although he knew the alphabet. When he finally went outside, darkness was enveloping the forest. He cared for his flock, then lay across the chairs and slept like a beaten man.

TWILIGHT AT TIFFANY'S

The next two years passed in what seemed only minutes to Young Salo; he spent most of the time in his music room. His father had to tell his brother, Younger Salo, to care for the sheep. Young Salo read all the books in the rock home and taught himself to decipher and interpret the mysterious dots and lines—"notes" and "staves," as they were called by the books. He found out how to tune the strings and to handle the stick, which, by now, he knew to call a bow. He worked for hours every day to master the violin. Then one day his brother followed him secretly and heard beautiful sounds coming from the rock into which Young Salo had stepped. Younger Salo crept to the entrance and saw his brother standing with eyes closed, drawing sounds with a stick out of a yellow box under his chin. He wanted to believe that Young Salo had lost his wits, but his spine tingled in response to the sounds. Never before had Younger Salo experienced such happiness, and he begged a surprised Young Salo to come home and share his discovery with their family. Finally Young Salo agreed, but not without trepidation. His caution proved, however, to be unnecessary.

The villagers quickly gathered round to hear Young Salo and his golden fiddle. Like a grass fire his fame spread, until one day the local cabinetmaker decided that he, too, wanted a fiddle. But there was no gold anywhere to be found. He tried, therefore, to make one from wood. When Young Salo played it, he found its sound to be even lovelier than that of his golden fiddle. And so the cabinetmaker painstakingly constructed more . . . and more . . . and more.

Young Salo stood enraptured, his eyes closed, playing Kreisler's *Liebesfreud* from LeMan's collection of music. At the whine of the sirens, his eyes flew open. And at the first sonic boom from two neutron missiles, he embraced his violin protectively and pleaded in a whisper, "Can't I go on . . . Please?"

EPILOGUE: CODA

After finishing this journey down memory lane I feel an urge to recall the names of those who, through a lifetime, have enriched my existence. Many have appeared on these pages, some have been alluded to, but some have been overlooked. Because of the well-known effects of old age, the names of individuals from the early years are clearer to me than the names of those I met later. Those still alive seem so much a part of the present that I risk taking them for granted. Such are the members of my cello family: Helga Winold and her husband Allen; Tsuyoshi Tsutsumi, his wife Harue, and their children Seizo and Mie; Emilio Colón and his wife Emma; my pianist partners, Reiko and Shigeo Neriki and their son Sho; without them I would not be able to function. Dr. Anya Royce's exemplary dedication to scholarship, teaching, research, writing, and art keeps me from occasional lapses due to the drudgery of academic daily routine. Then there is my adopted "kid" brother Harry Athan, who for decades has looked after our material security, and who has promised to take care of all things necessary after I return to my origin in the galaxy. Beyond that, my eternal friendship

Victor and Eva Aitay, and George Lang

The cello family Tsuyoshi Tsutsumi, Helga Winold, and Emilio Colón

Rae (circa 1962)

With Rae recently

EPILOGUE

My only claim to visual art, New York (1950)

with Victor and Eva Aitay and George Lang matches my love of my children, their husbands, and their offspring, JP, Lexi, and Nikki, and ultimately that of my loving wife of forty-four years, through hell and high water, Rae.

POSTLUDE:
THAT ROOM AT
THE TOP

Not long ago I told a famous musician and his manager a joke that I had recently heard. It was received with a short silence that ended in forced laughter. This is the story: Do you know the history of an international concert star in six brief acts? No? Well, Nemo is a great violinist, and Blunt is a manager. Blunt speaks:

> Act I. Nemo? Who's he?
> Act II. Nemo? Oh, yes. He's good, of course, but you know, there are so many.
> Act III. I must have Nemo. I don't care how much it costs, but I must have him.
> Act IV. You know I must have someone like Nemo.
> Act V. I must have someone like Nemo when he was young.
> Act VI. Nemo? Who's he?

Not a particularly funny joke, perhaps, and especially unfunny to someone who, like my distinguished friend, is in the middle of Act III. But is it uncomfortably true? Nothing is as pat as all that, but this brief history does afford a rough perspective on what artists go through, women as well as men, though few of us ever get beyond Act II. What I myself have to say about the subject can hardly lift the veil of mystery from the face of success; it is mere educated guesswork. But perhaps that is the best anyone can offer.

Before the curtain rises on Act I of a great performer's history, there has been a long, arduous preparation. Nobody ever asks a manager if he has heard of someone named Nemo unless he believes that the young unknown is a potential concert artist, and attaining even the chance of a concert career is a triumph of talent and dedicated hard work.

Young Nemo has this potential because he has put in years of practice, beginning from about the age of six. His father probably loved the fiddle and wanted his son to be the great concert artist he never had a chance to be. Luckily the son had real gifts to begin with. After school he went home for a music lesson or to practice while the other boys played baseball. After high school he entered a conservatory, immersing himself deeper and deeper in the technique and literature of his instrument, practicing six to eight hours a day. He received pedagogical encouragement and played at recitals for young performers. Perhaps he has garnered a medal or two in competitions. But what matters most is something without which all his talent, training, and experience amount to no more than the trappings of a music teacher: an obstinate, obsessive determination to be great.

His next step is a debut. If he has won a competition, there is a good chance that he may have made one already. If not, the first manager he is introduced to will suggest that he do so, and Act I of the history is under way. New York is the best place for this, though to fail there is to have failed at the top. From a New York failure he can go nowhere, except perhaps Europe, from which artists do sometimes return to make the grade at home.

The greatest obstacle to the debut is its cost. When Nemo makes the grade, he will be paid handsomely for the concerts he plays; but in the beginning it is likely to be he who foots the bills—or his friends and relatives.

Nemo tries to work up an interesting program, preferably including something little known and something he has played well before. He goes on stage before an audience of the people who have invested in him, plus a few strangers who have managed to get free tickets, and perhaps even a second-string critic or two, if there are no major musical events scheduled for the same evening.

The aftermath is far less predictable than the concert itself. Even though there may be warm applause and a cheerful party afterward, if his performance hasn't quite measured up to critical standards, this moment of his life may be memorialized by a mere line or two in the newspapers and a small mountain of debts. At this point Nemo, his status as "potential concert artist" seriously endangered, must decide either to get a job with a musical group and try again in a few years, or to give up his precarious hopes of concertizing and go into teaching or some other musical field not involving solo performances, such as managing other musicians or working for a record company. The hard realities of earning a living leave little time or energy for making a second attempt. And so the history often ends with Act I, Scene I. But if the debut has been a fair success in the eyes of managers and critics, Act I will proceed apace.

A contract is the next step, and at this point it seems to Nemo that the way to the top is now smooth and sure. But the manager, Mr. Blunt, makes the offer dryly enough: "Let's hope this will be mutually beneficial. We'll do our best. We want our percentage, after all." (The manager normally receives 20 percent for recitals, and 10 percent for television and radio appearances.) In any case, from now on Blunt is in charge.

The Blunts—of whom a surprising number are women—have a difficult job. They must engage artists and sell them to audiences who may never have known that they wanted to hear a violinist, much less a cellist or an oboist. To do their job well, managers need neither know nor like music. However, managers who care about music do much to raise musical standards by sending first-rate artists into communities where there has never been much demand for excellence. On the other hand, there are managers who care so little about the music itself that they may arrange engagements by checking the ethnic makeup of a community in order to determine whether a Pole or an Italian will go down better.

Not only do the attitudes of managers vary enormously, so do their activities. A manager may have under exclusive contract a small list of

POSTLUDE

artists whom he sells to orchestras, local concert managers (who sponsor a concert series in their city), colleges, and universities. He may be the representative of a particular orchestra and engage artists to play with it. He may be one of a dozen managers in a large agency, each representing several artists, with the resources of a powerful company to help him promote his clients.

Blunt's task with his new client Nemo, then, is to sell him to somebody, and he is going to have quite a job. However, every town has its small but influential group of dedicated music lovers who can exert enough pressure to bring concert series to their local halls and auditoriums. Who are they? Committee women, the board of directors of the local orchestra, conductors, managers. These interested people are constantly listening, reading newspapers, following new recordings, talking shop with friends, making plans for future seasons.

Small as Nemo's chances seem at the outset, all this curiosity and appetite for new talent favors him. He also has on his side the tendency of musicians to be generous about plugging one another. Experienced artists are constantly solicited for their opinions and are glad to suggest promising younger or lesser-known players—even people who play the same instruments—because it all helps the cause of good music, and ultimately their own careers. A colleague's judgment is valued for its objectivity; such praise is probably the strongest factor in making possible the transition from Act I to Act II. Before the world at large can recognize Nemo's quality, his peers must do so.

In planning a season, what a local manager needs above all is three or four stars, for a season can be hung on them, with the rank and file filling the gaps between. A famous name costs far more than an excellent unknown, but without stars it is impossible to secure the steady subscription audience necessary for any concert series.

But how does Nemo get to be a star? While he is still in Act I, simmering with unrecognized promise, the wheels start turning. An out-of-town orchestra is planning its next season and wants as many stars as possible. Perhaps two are in the bag. The third is "unavailable." Someone murmurs the name of Nemo—"a young violinist I heard the other day. Sounds just like so-and-so years ago." Here Blunt may come into the picture, too. He is handling Star No. 1, whom the planning committee has been counting on, and suggests that he *may* present a little difficulty. In the next breath he happens to mention his brilliant young client, Nemo. It is clear to the committee that to include Nemo in the season is a form of insurance. So he is engaged. This kind of thing happens again and again. Nemo is not quite sought out, but he is taken on. And after this has happened a few hundred times, Act II has begun.

In one scene of Act II, the bravos are loud but the reviews bad; in another, Nemo receives good reviews but a tepid reception—though he is convinced that his performance in each scene is basically the same. His colleagues argue over his interpretation of this, criticize his handling of that, but generally agree that he's on his way up. In spite of this, his fees remain low, while his expenses—for his accompanist, manager, publicity, and travel—are tremendous. In Act I he may have been paid from one hundred and fifty to five hundred dollars a concert; in Act II the fees rise to something between five hundred and fifteen hundred dollars, depending on how long he has been around and how seasoned a concert artist he is. After all the expenses of a season are paid, the musician is usually left with about 30 percent of the total take, though pianists, who do without accompanists, end up with twice as much. So although a top star charging high fees can get by on as few as twenty to thirty concerts a year, others must play two or three a week to make ends meet, and they must supplement these earnings by teaching or by playing first chair in a symphony orchestra.

Years pass, and all goes on as before—an exhausting shuttle from city to city, country to country; practicing in hotel rooms; in some places a star, in others a perpetual debutant. Nevertheless, Nemo is good and getting better. His private life is haphazard but as an artist he is now one of the select few, and Act III is at hand ("I must have Nemo. I don't care how much it costs").

How is this? What is he doing that makes him succeed while others who play equally well remain forever in Act II? Every star of the musical scene—the players in Act II—must have certain accomplishments: an exceptional ear, excellent fingers, perfect coordination physically and mentally, a first-rate memory, a studious mind, curiosity, diligence, and the ability and willingness to work with total concentration. He has, of

POSTLUDE

course, spent years and years practicing; he has studied everything of musical importance: other instruments, composition, the history of music.

What more does Nemo have, who finally becomes an international concert star? It's difficult to say. He plays faultlessly, of course, but in addition he has imagination and a sense of color. He strives for construction and balance in a musical work. His tone has warmth and beauty. He sets a high standard for himself and often plays above it, never below. But it isn't this either. Some artists of the first magnitude never quite emerge from Act II; they have these qualities and yet never become true international stars. Still, without them, the world of music would be nothing. They are the carriers of tradition; they create and sustain standards; they provide the climate in which the handful of immortals may have their being.

But what, then, does make the difference? The great star has personality, a charismatic presence, whether or not everyone likes it. He is nervous before concerts, but once on stage he feels completely at ease. The audience believes in him and watches him lovingly, noting his expressions, his gestures.

Not only that: he is absolutely steady. He has definite ideas about the course his career is to follow, step by step; and along this seemingly endless way he moves unhesitatingly. He refuses to be exhausted or worn down by the sheer dreary grind. If he suffers a setback—gets a bad notice, or finds that a conductor doesn't like him, or that his instrument is not popular somewhere—he shakes it off quickly. Bad luck only makes him work harder.

This determination provides him with an air of authority, and perhaps it is in this aura that the ultimate secret of his stardom lies. Opinions of his playing may differ: one critic will say his tempi are too rapid, another the reverse. Some will consider his left hand fabulous, his right so-so. Some say his Bach is superb; others that he is the finest exponent of the romantics. But that he is *it* they agree.

(Qualities of personality occasionally carry an artist into the third act of his musical career even though he lacks a few of the basic prerequisites of technique, musicality, and intelligence. A well-mixed combination of aura, politics, press-pageantry, connections, and showmanship

THE WORLD OF MUSIC ACCORDING TO STARKER

can make a star. But the act will be brief, and it will be the last act. Nobody will ever say afterward, "I must have someone like Nemo.")

Because Nemo is the star of our six-act history of a great musical artist, we can presume he has a happy balance of all qualities essential to true greatness. As time goes on, he receives more offers than he can possibly accept, from all over the world. His trips have to be planned years in advance. Letters from Mr. Blunt have changed their tone and now offer lures: Nemo exercises his prerogative to cancel, alter, choose at will. His consent to play somewhere stirs up excitement.

But time passes, the air mileage rolls into the hundreds of thousands, and Nemo is growing tired. Taxes are so high that he decides to play less and for much higher fees. Fewer budgets can afford him. He spends more time making records and collecting royalties than playing concerts. His name is legend. He and his playing represent a school—the Nemo sound, the Nemo approach. Criticism can no longer hurt him. He is the measure of all things, and, in a sense, only Nemo is qualified to judge Nemo. His fundamental artistic goals and ideals may be incomprehensible to most of his admirers, but it doesn't matter. He is one of half a dozen instrumentalists in the world who can fill any concert hall.

And so Nemo and his peers, a handful out of a whole generation of musicians, pass on into Act IV ("I must have someone like Nemo"). The managers begin to look for artists who can substitute for the great international star, since he can't begin to satisfy the demand for his concerts. A new elite is rising, and new Blunts take charge of them. Nemo's authority is unchallenged, but his physical abilities and musical discipline have begun to show signs of attrition. For a while he is forgiven small falterings and blurrings, since all the magnificence of his artistic concept is still present. But the young have discovered concepts of their own, standards of their own, Nemos of their own. Someone as good as Nemo was when he was young finally appears, and for Nemo himself the penultimate act begins—"I must have someone like Nemo when he was young."

Years later, the last act of all is played. An old conductor and a young Blunt are discussing violinists and their varying interpretations of standard violin repertory. The conductor reflects on the different tempi he

POSTLUDE

has heard used in the scherzo of the Kreutzer Sonata. He sighs and his face lights up: "Nemo—no one ever played that movement as he did." The young Blunt frowns and says, "Nemo? Who's he?"

ORIGINALLY PUBLISHED IN MADEMOISELLE, 1962

APPENDIX: "AN ORGANIZED METHOD OF STRING PLAYING"

Since 1955 I have been giving string seminars regularly on four continents under the title "An Organized Method of String Playing." The following is an attempt to describe what takes place in these public classes.

INTRODUCTION

"An Organized Method of String Playing" (OMSP) is a way of thinking about music and instrumental playing. Its objectives answer professional needs: stability, power, health, maximum use of limited time, increase of confidence and avoidance of stagnation, deterioration, nervousness, and insecurity. Though these needs are based on varying degrees of talent and ability, physical and/or musical, they are aggravated by previous learning processes. The necessary imitative learning of a child is too often continued into adulthood. Changes from concerned to unconcerned teachers, or vice versa, result mostly in the unexplained use of various schools of learning. These schools, often marvelously demonstrated by highly gifted exponents, reflect solutions of the exponents' individual shortcomings or advantages. In order to explain the thinking process behind the approach to OMSP, let me give some background as to its origin.

As a child prodigy from the age of six, I was fortunate in having a great teacher, Adolf Schiffer, a student and successor of David Popper. His forte was in assisting his students to develop their natural abilities. He was a superb cellist and musician, but because of a rather late start as an instrumentalist, he limited his performing activities to string quartet playing. He used no method. He assigned material, corrected musical errors, played fragments to clarify his suggestions, and ridiculed unnatural motions that were contrary to the music. Theatricality was discouraged and dismissed as fitting only for clowns to employ in lieu of talent. Inborn or inbred eccentricities when coupled with talent were considered sufficient to reach recognized stage heights.

Two other exceptional teachers to whose wisdoms I had access were Leo Weiner (piano chamber music) and Imre Waldbauer (string quartets). Weiner, a composer and a mediocre but functional pianist with a powerful musical mind and incredibly disciplined ears, taught his disciples to hear. Waldbauer, a highly respected violinist of the renowned string quartet, had a scientific mind and was preoccupied with the various mechanical ways of producing sounds. He clarified the need for and the possibility of verbal definitions based on experience and on the works of Hugo Riemann and Friedrich Adolph Steinhausen.

After I had reached instrumental maturity and control of a large part of the repertory, World War II caused a year of absence from my instrument. Following this silence I had but two weeks to prepare for my first public appearance. I continued the profession successfully, and shortly thereafter I occupied the solo cellist's post of the Opera and Philharmonic Orchestra of Budapest. A year or so later I found myself listening to a recital in Vienna. One of the most admired instrumentalists of our time was performing, a legendary former child prodigy. His left hand was vibrating indiscriminately and barely managed to arrive at the necessary destinations. A loud irregular breathing penetrated the entire hall. I left in the intermission on the verge of nausea. We are all aware of the pressures of international concertizing and reluctantly accept the fact of human frailty, justifying an occasional "off night." A series of sleepless nights forced on me the realization that the occurrences at that concert involved issues far beyond an "off night." I had nightmarish visions of the legendary peasant eye surgeon who, when told of the dangers involved in his activities, was never able to repeat his feats. The historically low percentage of child prodigies who grow up to be mature artists needed explanation, and it became imperative to have an acceptable reasoning as to what governs the satisfactory mental and physical functions of a performing artist when called on stage.

Through some horror-laden months of ineffective public experimentation, followed by a stretch of self-imposed inactivity, I became aware that only through conscious understanding of the elements that allow music to be produced on an instrument can one become a professional reasonably independent of the constant hazards. Only through conscious understanding can one control the "skill" part of producing art and distinguish the gifted dilettante from the master professional. This realization induced me to search for the "basic" problems involved in playing an instrument; basic problems that are identical for all and inherent in all music irrespective of subjective feelings and judgments. Invariably, when that search reached the point where the problem was defined, solutions presented themselves, explaining and justifying the differing approaches. Invariably, advantages and disadvantages appeared that were humbling to those whose religious fervor for a chosen route deterred all contradictions, while for those with vastly different abilities answers were provided.

The emphases on professionalism are manifold. Regardless of whether a musician performs as a soloist or as a member of a small or a large ensemble, or assists a budding instrumentalist in learning the "trade," the significance of understanding and knowledge of the issues involved is far beyond the value of natural gifts. It would be infantile to discount the lack of democracy in the distribution of talents; however, the goal toward maximum utilization of one's gifts is universal. When talent and fortunate circumstances coincide, there may be no need for theories in order to arrive at great results. Those who are satisfied with their output would never bother about problems, since they do not have them. On the other hand, only those are safe from fear who do not

"AN ORGANIZED METHOD OF STRING PLAYING"

realize the risks involved—risks, not necessarily personal, but artistic. It is one thing to lose a competition or audition because of an inferior showing, and another not to win over someone equally good or better. The risks are that of self-respect, and above all the respect for the music itself. One ought to be nervous before a performance to some degree, not because of fear of the unknown but because of one's respect for the significance of artistic contribution.

ORGANIZATION

After years of investigation I was able to place the various problems in some obvious categories. This categorizing alleviated the universal plague of lack of practice time. I would venture to say that there is no musician who has not said on occasion, "If I'd had more time I could have. . . ." We may deplore the lack of time for all human endeavors that aim toward unreachable goals, but the misuse of time is just as tragic. It is quite usual for a player who practices one hour to spend half that period repeating already well controlled passages and melody lines. Commonplace is the player who endlessly repeats a difficult passage without realizing that the problem is not a left-hand one, but lies in the bowing, string-changing, phrasing, grouping, or holding of the instrument, and so on ad infinitum.

The four categories are: I. Playing Preparation, II. Right Arm—Hand—Fingers, III. Left Arm—Hand—Fingers, IV. Musical Application. The order and titles are clearly arbitrary. The fourth group, musical application, could obviously be first, or should it be? It ought to be taken for granted that all aspects of instrumental playing must be motivated by musical intentions. To play in tune, to produce uninterrupted lines, to eliminate scratchy sounds, to guard against uncontrolled dynamic changes due to changes in bow speed, and to avoid unwritten notes while connecting distant intervals are not technical demands but musical ones. The solutions are technical, nevertheless. So in order to fulfill the inner musical needs, physical conditions must be as close as possible to the ideal so as to allow the musical idea to emerge.

A passage that contains even units should be played evenly. The execution requires technical answers; the motivation remains musical. The element of freedom, the beauty of individual interpretation of black and white notes is taken for granted. However, freedom of interpretation does not justify anarchy due to technical shortcomings. *Rubato* is freedom within the phrase; *agogic* is freedom within the bar. The meaning is clear. Notes lengthened or shortened because of melodic, harmonic, rhythmic, and emotional significance must be balanced so as to preserve the structural unity of phrases and movements. Myriads of individual varieties are within the realm of possibility without destroying the essential balance. Such an approach requires discipline, primarily aural, but in order for the aural senses to function, one needs physical and mental discipline. Well known is the player who hears what he imagines in his inner ear instead of what emanates from his instrument. Well known is the player who thinks that everybody else is too slow, while he races indiscriminately through his passages. Well known is the stage in learning a work when one can only play the difficult passages fast, as the digital learning precedes the musical learning. In other words, discipline must be the basis of one of the classic disciplines, music, and once attained, freedom of expression may spring forth.

The order of learning is significant. Beautiful artistic ideas running rampant without disciplined instrumental control remind one of a ride in a magnificent automobile over unpaved roads. Writing poetry in a language not yet learned seldom succeeds. One must be acquainted with vowels and consonants, so as to form syllables, words, and sentences. Then poetry may eventually emerge. The cold-bloodedness vaguely implied in this approach is a matter to be considered, but only in the light of professionalism versus dilettantism, and some further reference will be made to this when the fourth group is discussed.

Artistic motivation should be understood as the drive toward purity, simplicity, and structure in re-creating masterpieces. Underlying these motivations is what one may call the basic or ideal legato; undisturbed musical sounds that linearly ascend or descend; harmonic successions that continue toward focal points, climactic or anticlimactic; rhythmic consistencies-pulses that are not interfered with by changing rhythms;

dynamic contrasts based on musical content and not on impressive volume effects; and, finally, recognition of the inherent voice examples that are the basis of all musical aspirations.

With these thoughts in mind it may be evident that the attempt to describe OMSP is doomed to partial success at best. Instrumental playing is based on multiple sensations. One may hint at them and induce them on occasion, but ultimately each individual must arrive at these sensations on his own. That is why the maximum results obtained by this thinking process are accomplished in seminars where the participating groups experiment, observe, and, on occasion, discover that some of these "sensations" are either novelties or elements that are known but ignored. None of the problems discussed are original in either their statement or their solution. They are based on previously known principles. The order in which they are proposed is intended to show the interrelations leading to desired musical results.

Category I: Playing Preparation

The problems in the first category involve the use of the muscles and the application of power and weight, as well as motions, balance, breathing, and timing; the last with special consideration of conscious anticipation and delay of all actions.

I have always been preoccupied with the idea that the energy spent to supply the physical needs of playing an instrument should be minimal and thereby allow the mental and emotional faculties to function freely for the sake of communicating the musical message. The visible struggle of a performer may create sympathy, but it has little if anything to do with music. In the field of stagecraft this sympathy can serve us well when the musical message lacks conviction. The adrenaline expended by a perspiring, contorting performer often substitutes for artistic substance. In order to use only the minimum energy required, one must have maximum power available at all times and use only what is necessary.

The power is aimed at the contact points on the strings, via the bow and left fingers. The power of the arm originates in the back muscles. The goal, therefore, is not to hinder the flow of energy from the source. It seems obvious that if the fingers, hands, forearms, upper arms, and

"AN ORGANIZED METHOD OF STRING PLAYING"

shoulders function without the support of the back muscles, the locally used energy will have to increase proportionately.

"Relaxed" playing is in reality the even distribution of muscle tension. Though we are playing an instrument while "making" music, the playing requires power and precludes relaxation. To attain this even distribution of muscle tension we should try to locate the hindrances. Wherever joints meet there is a tendency to disrupt the flow of tension by unequal tensing of the next set of muscles, and forming what we may call angles. The most frequent trouble spots are the shoulder, the forearm (when opening), the thumb, and the muscles beneath the knuckles. We should attempt to avoid angular formations and to create the feeling of curves. At the same time, whenever possible, descending lines should be formed by both arms, as a further means of avoiding the disruption of continuous energy flow. Of course it is impossible for the left arm to create descending lines when playing the violin, the viola, or the first few positions on the cello.

Two simple exercises will help one to recognize the different sensations of this angular versus curved feeling. (1) Raise both shoulders very high, pull the arms back, rotate the arms inward, bring them forward at skull level while bringing the backs of the hands together, then drop both arms to their respective instrumental playing positions, so as to promote the active participation of the back muscles. (2) Tense the upper arm muscles as much as possible but avoid any tension in the hand and fingers. This maximum tension should result in a shaking forearm. Then make a fist. Gradually squeeze the fingers in the fist and slowly open the forearm to allow the upper arm tension to travel into the fist. The natural tendency to tighten the upper arm excessively to produce stronger dynamics and also the crucially wrong tendency of automatically tightening the forearm muscles when accelerating should, by this exercise, be reduced and make one aware of the misuses of tension.

The application of weight can be approached through the suspension of the arms. Again, when lifting the arms, the back muscles, not those of the upper arm, are required for the necessary power. Prior to lifting, total relaxation is experimented with, with the limbs and body devoid of any tension, and only the legs holding the body while standing. The

"AN ORGANIZED METHOD OF STRING PLAYING"

difference in the sensations of weight and pressure in preparation for the eventual needed mixture is advanced in this way.

The ability to apply power to the changing needs of playing high strings, low strings, high positions, and low positions requires the ability to shift the body weight without losing control and, ipso facto, balance. The following simple exercise will aid in achieving controlled body balance: Stand, place the weight of the body on the right side, lift the left leg, bend the right knee. Repeat a few times until reasonably comfortable. Repeat the same exercise on the left side lifting the right leg. Then, while seated on the edge of a chair, place the right foot in the center, lift the left leg, and rise on the right foot. Repeat with the left foot. The difficulties encountered will make one aware of the lack of body control, ill-directed body weight, and the need to feel the changing balance requirements.

Breathing, that is, the use of controlled breathing, can be approached by various means. The general tendency to use excessive speed at the start of all actions is demonstrated by the quick intake of air when inhaling and, similarly, when exhaling. The following exercises divide the amount of air into even groups of 4, 6, 8, 12, 16, 24, etc. Starting with empty lungs, sip air audibly and check the speed of the air intake, with the predetermined group in mind, so as to finish with the lungs completely filled. Do the same while exhaling. Later, when experimenting with control of bow speed, practice synchronizing the division and speed of the bow with exhaling and inhaling.

Lack of controlled breathing results in other noticeable disturbances: Holding the breath while playing difficult passages causes incorrect accents, unplanned groupings of passages, and, most important of all, unprepared starts of phrases and changes. Anticipation of all actions is of the utmost significance in all phases of instrumental playing and music making. The word *anticipation* is used in the sense of preparation, in contrast to delay. The following sentence seems to define the need: Anticipation is part of music itself; therefore it must bear all the characteristics of the music that follows—time, dynamics, melody, and harmony. The start of a phrase requires an anticipatory, preparatory upbeat or cue. This cue must reflect the basic unit of the phrase. A change of character requires a preparatory cue with the change inherent in it. A

"AN ORGANIZED METHOD OF STRING PLAYING"

bow change requires the preparation of directional change. String changes require preparation of the new bow level. Position changes require preparation of the new arm position. Speed changes require preparation of the necessary tension adjustments. If the breathing is not hindered these anticipations can be consciously assisted by the proper intake of air. Naturally, through some training, most of these actions become subconscious, and only in extreme difficulties and in the practicing process does one need the conscious application.

Anticipation is clearly responsible for uninterrupted, continuous, fluent actions, and in a musical sense I like to refer to its result as legato, in contrast to the marcato character resulting from delayed actions.

By now it should be evident that the language employed to describe OMSP deliberately avoids the use of scientific terms. It is the language applied in the classroom during seminars, where the visual and audible aspects are stressed in the form of examples of right and wrong, pleasant and unpleasant, convincing and unconvincing, struggling and effortless, and so on.

In group discussions many of the issues intertwine, as in actual application. For instance, how one holds the instrument belongs to the first category, playing preparation. Nevertheless, it is usually discussed either when the basic legato is explored, or when the guiding principles of the use of the left hand are negotiated. The reason for this is (1) to accommodate the changing requirements of the bow on different strings, and (2) to provide a basis for the left hand so that the fingers can stop the string at an identical angle in all positions.

In the seminars the following elements are experimented with in an effort to find suitable positions for the differing needs of each individual: One must first, as in the balance experiment, secure the ability, seated or standing, to shift the weight of the body left or right at will; second, secure the unhindered function of the arms; and third, confront the issue for cellists of the length of the end pin. This last item evokes intense debates in most seminars. The oversimplified answer as to whether to use the straight, the bent (Tortelier), or the excessively long end pin is that the height and the arm length of the player should be the deciding factors. Holding the instrument more vertically allows the average-sized person to concentrate the power on the contact point on

"AN ORGANIZED METHOD OF STRING PLAYING"

the instrument. It has the disadvantage that the bow tends to slip downward; on the other hand, it makes easier all light, fast bowings and the synchronization of the so-called virtuoso elements. Holding the instrument more horizontally is an advantage for tall players with long arms, as they can use the forearm more comfortably because of the increased distance. The discomfort of holding the arms higher is compensated for by the ready effect of gravity, generally resulting in louder sound production. The ability to *see* the strings is of no consequence, unless it is a psychological advantage.

Therefore, the summation is that whichever end pin is used, it should not hinder the free motion of the arms. All positions should be within reach without the need to alter the body position. The instrument should not interfere with free breathing. The cello should be positioned in such a way that the knees can move it left and right without the upper half of the body moving. The knees should not cover the ribs of the instrument, thus muting the sound. At the same time the knees should be able to apply counterpressure, resistance against the bow, at will.

It is advisable to experiment with various heights of the chair (if it is not adjustable, a pillow or book can serve), until conscious body control is attained. It is of value to experiment with various leg placements and the proper part of the chair to occupy. With a standard end pin the experiments favor the front of the chair. The legs can be positioned either left foot forward on the heel, right foot quite far back on the toes, or the reverse. Both feet planted solidly better serve the users of the curved or long end pins.

Category II: Right Arm–Hand–Fingers

The second and the fourth fingers of the right hand obtain the basic balance: the others transmit power. With the arm suspended, rest the bow flat on the second finger with the little finger counterbalancing on the top of the bow. After a somewhat secure feeling has been obtained, place the first and third fingers, then the thumb, and then grip solidly. Now switch the little finger to the outside into its regular position, without allowing the bow to tilt. A whipping hand motion will test whether the hold is secure enough to prevent the bow from slipping. The power of the arm is transmitted through the thumb and third finger

"AN ORGANIZED METHOD OF STRING PLAYING"

for the down-bow, and through the thumb and first finger for the up-bow. Starting from the middle of the bow, the rotation of the forearm prepares for the next bow direction. Down-bow: pull the entire arm, gradually lift the upper arm, approximately at the middle start opening the forearm and continue to raise the upper arm until the tip of the bow is reached. Through the forearm rotation we arrive at the required position for the up-bow. Up-bow: start with a pushing action, close the forearm in, gradually lower the upper arm, and from approximately the middle of the bow, return the entire arm to its original position. We say "approximately" because of the variations required by the different strings. This entire arm-forearm action defines the basic legato stroke.

The circular function of the arm, as with all limbs, would result in a circular motion on the strings unless the forearm takes over the horizontal line. At the frog the weight of the arm through the bow, combined with the speed of the motion, provides the required friction to set the string in vibration and establish sound. As the arm increases its distance from the string, pressure substitutes for the diminishing weight. The pressure travels through the third finger and thumb, and, as the described arm function continues, in the up-bow the first finger takes over the role of the third finger. The muscles leading to the third finger and thumb are responsible for the power while pulling. The muscles leading to the first finger and thumb are responsible for the power while pushing (supination-pronation). The bow should be at a 90° angle on the second string. On the cello the angle of the bow should increase for the lower strings and decrease for the A-string. On the violin and viola the reverse is true. This basic legato stroke, with the forearm opening and closing without a noticeable change in speed, should provide us with the basis for almost all existing strokes.

I feel the need to remind the reader that this description of the legato action is full of omissions and contradictions. However, the purpose of this summary is not to disprove or replace any of the far more scientifically correct writings on the subject. It is rather to acquaint one with how, in seminars, problems are solved through experiments, and how hoped-for results are obtained.

As the basic legato stroke is practiced slowly, attention should be focused on the position of the arm at all points between the frog and

"AN ORGANIZED METHOD OF STRING PLAYING"

the point. Whatever stroke we use, and whatever part of the bow we use, the arm should be in the position as established in the basic legato stroke. If we play a series of staccato notes up-bow, when we arrive at the middle the entire arm should gradually return to its original position, while continuing the staccato to the frog. If we start a note in the second half of the bow, the forearm should be in "opened" position, and the upper arm accordingly at a higher level. Higher than what? Higher than while playing in the first half of the bow. All strokes that require the bow to leave the string must still follow the same rule. While the bow is in the air the arm motion remains the same as if it were on the string. No change in speed should occur in the air unless the musical notation requires one, and, as such, demands preparation.

Bow changes, as well, must take place in the air if the preceding note has part of its value off the string. The spiccato stroke should be looked upon as a series of fast bow changes. In all bow changes the pressure of the thumb should be reduced immediately prior to the change. In the standard legato stroke the pressure applied through the thumb creates the unity of the forearm and the hand. Any sustained sound requires this unity, and in this sense I prefer to refer to it as sostenuto bowing. When the thumb pressure is reduced, and the forearm tension is reduced accordingly, the hand starts moving independently. As the forearm leads the repeated short notes up and down, with the hands in circular motion (almost no tension in the thumb), it will allow the bow to leave the string and thus spiccato will result. The experimentation is as follows: First, suspend the arm with no tension in any part of the arm or hand. Second, move the forearm horizontally left and right, and let the hand move as a consequence, hanging freely. Third, move the forearm up and down and allow the hand to move accordingly. Fourth, move the forearm clockwise and counterclockwise, allowing the hand to make similar circles. Always remember that it is not the hand that initiates the movements but the arm. Fifth, press the thumb to the index finger very strongly and try the horizontal movement again. As the hand does not move now, continue the arm movement, and gradually reduce the thumb pressure to the point where the hand starts moving again independently. Finally, with bow in hand on the string, try step five, starting at the balance point of the bow.

"AN ORGANIZED METHOD OF STRING PLAYING"

The placement of the thumb is approached with the idea that it should not be placed. When the hand hangs, the thumb is in line with the first finger. When the forearm turns inward, the thumb is in line with the second finger. The significant factor is that when the thumb is "pulled" toward the palm to be in line with the second finger immediate muscle tension results, and that should be avoided. The same is true for the left thumb placement.

In order to preserve the uninterrupted descending line of the arm it is necessary to clarify the role of the elbow and the wrist. Since both are joints, it is preferable to say "raise or lower the upper arm" instead of "raise or lower the elbow." Similarly, "raise or lower the hand," instead of "raise or lower the wrist." The multitude of bowings are discussed in terms of hard and soft consonant attacks, the length of the vowel content on the string, time spent on the string or in the air, stops with consonants or vowels, and notes ending with final consonants as in vocal use—*m* or *n*—so as to avoid dead sound stops.

The self-imposed limitations in the seminars prevent a detailed explanation and clinical description of the known bowings. The emphasis is on recognition, samples, and modes of experimentation. The most common problem, which is quickly recognized, is the lack of sufficient contact with the string toward the tip of the bow. One approach to curing this ailment is to have another person hold the tip of the bow while the player attempts to play an up-bow and a down-bow. If the hold is firm the player must exert considerably more power than usual. Then, in the form of isometric exercises, the player is asked to do the same, imagining that someone is holding the tip of the bow. When the contact is not sufficient, excess bow speed will create whistles instead of sounds; conversely, when too much pressure is applied without commensurate speed, scratching will result.

Category III: Left Arm–Hand–Fingers

When the discussions of the OMSP reach this group a great number of issues are supposed to become self-explanatory. The principles governing the use of the arm, the shoulder, and forearm opening have been discussed in the first and second groups: to distribute muscle tension evenly, to keep from breaking the muscle line, to open the forearm

"AN ORGANIZED METHOD OF STRING PLAYING"

continuously, to avoid all abrupt motions due to sudden changes in speed, to recognize the primary importance of avoiding angular tensing when playing fast passages. After all these questions have been defined and recognized, the placement of the fingers and the three different positions on the cello (versus practically only one on the violin and the viola) have to be explored.

Basically there are three different approaches in placing the fingers on a string: slanted backward; slanted forward, thus having a small finger contact point; and perpendicular, with maximum surface flesh contact. Each of these approaches has advantages and disadvantages, and affects the use and choice of vibrato, the various connections, slides, and the ability to explore all types of musical and virtuoso elements. The obvious suggestion is to master all three ways and apply them according to need.

The perpendicular hold serves well on thicker strings and in the first seven positions (positions counted by half-steps). The large surface contact on the strings gives a feeling of security, and the arm weight is used to more advantage, but when proceeding to higher positions, breaks in the motion and alterations in the sound quality occur. The intonation is considerably less exact than when the contact point is small, but that becomes an issue only on a very high level of music making, where clear overtone responses are aimed for.

The backward slant answers the shortcomings of the perpendicular hold; continuity all through the fingerboard is facilitated, and intonation is far more exact. The backward slant favors the use of the first and second fingers and their extensions. The forward slant favors the use of the third and fourth fingers and their extensions. The disadvantages occur in the lower positions, where the weight and pressure concentrate on a minute part of the fingertip and thus extreme exactness is required. With the perpendicular hold one is more likely to use hand vibrato, moving above and below the center and using the thumb, pressing on the neck, as an axis around which the hand rotates forward and backward. The slanted hold is more suited to arm vibrato, with the thumb only slightly touching the neck and moving with the hand and forearm in an identical direction. The hand-forearm unit is similar to that of the sostenuto sensation of the right arm.

Because of the greater tension used with arm vibrato, the application of indiscriminate vibrato to cover up intonation discrepancies is less likely. The vibrato, an element of decoration, should be applied to enhance the emotional content and to help the notes that are not enriched by natural overtones. Notes such as F, B, A-flat, and E-flat do not have corresponding overtones on a four-stringed instrument, while the notes that parallel the open strings and their harmonics have responding overtones. The vibrato should also be used to correct this tonal discrepancy. I rarely go beyond the rudimentary description of the various elements required in the use of vibrato. In group discussions and experimentations an attempt is made to discover what prevents the individual from functioning at will with a continuous motion. Once the problem is pinpointed, ways to improve are suggested.

In up-and-down glissandi, stop with finger pressure and try to continue the arm motion, as in back-and-forth glissandi. Place a finger on the back of the stretched-out right hand and try to obtain a feeling of continuous motion without the string-stopping pressure. Exchange fingers on the same note and try to maintain a uniform quality in the successive sounds through continuous motion.

Researchers, using complex machinery, have not yet come up with an agreed-upon analysis of the acoustical properties of vibrato. Therefore, we have to rely on our own auditory mechanism, which is developed through individual experiences. At whatever stage that development takes us, we should try to satisfy the inner need, and then strive to expand it. This principle involves all aspects of playing music, and when our concern is the left hand, the inquiry turns to the geography of the fingerboard.

It is generally recognized that the basic, unalterable problem of intonation on a stringed instrument is the diminishing size of the intervals as the pitch rises. Since the frets of yesteryear are preserved only on the guitar, we should aim at developing a mental and physical keyboard on the fingerboard.

The first step is to accept the classification of standard and extended positions. The extended positions require unnatural hand positioning and are therefore dealt with as a deviation from the norm. In my belief they should be used only when they are unavoidable for technical or

"AN ORGANIZED METHOD OF STRING PLAYING"

expressive reasons. On the first half of the cello, when the thumb is not used as a playing finger, we distinguish four-finger positions and three-finger positions. The placement of the first finger defines the position, and therefore it is preferable to name the positions according to the note played by the first finger, instead of the numbering based on the diatonic scale. This helps in visualizing the fingerboard as well as in memorizing. If the chromatic scale is used then we have eight four-finger positions, where the fingers are each placed a half-step apart and enclose a minor third. From the ninth half-step on, the fourth finger is seldom used, though it can be. This area causes immense problems for cellists because of the transition of the thumb into thumb positions. Instead of leaving the thumb in a sort of limbo, if we develop four distinct three-finger positions, the thumb will adjust to a different placement on the side of the neck, as in the fluent preparation for the thumb position. The development of the three-finger position (there are four of them, because if the highest note played is a minor third above the octave, there is no real need for a standard-sized hand to use the thumb on the string) should immediately include the extensions for practicality. The second finger is now a whole-step away from the first finger rather than a half-step, and the enclosed interval remains a minor third, as in the four-finger positions.

The thumb positions are identical with the standard positions on the violin. The interval enclosed between the thumb and third finger is a fourth. The name of the position is defined by the note played by the thumb, and the distance between the first and second fingers can change from a half-step to a whole step. Thus many permutations are possible, and a number of exercises have been devised, based on this system. The exercises, no different from many in traditional exercise books except in their mathematical formulae, are contained in my book *An Organized Method of String Playing–Cello Left Hand Exercises*.[1] The book contains sample exercises to develop the basic four-finger, three-finger, and thumb positions. For various reasons double-stops are used for this development. First, the greater number of fingers that sense a position the greater the security. Second, when playing double-stops, which constitute the major part of a triad, one is more likely to be disturbed by discrepancies in intonation that call for correction. Third, the sense of a

"AN ORGANIZED METHOD OF STRING PLAYING"

note that belongs to changing harmonies readies the player to observe this essential element. When positions are approached with double-stops, the enclosed intervals are considered on two strings. Therefore, in the four-and three-finger positions we speak of a seventh or a major third, and in the thumb positions, octaves or seconds (4-1, 1-4, 3-1, 1-3, Q-3, 3-Q).

Unfortunately the book omits double-stop exercises with open strings. These should be added by each individual. It is not absolutely necessary to practice all the permutative possibilities in a given position once they are recognized. Each player ought to develop a personal formula. To release the excess tension of double-stopping, single-note patterns are used to check the attained results. These single-note patterns are also more usable for less-advanced players with less-developed hands.

The second major step in developing a sense of geography on the fingerboard is the connecting of positions. Because the number of permutations runs into the millions—each note in each position, on each string, connecting to every other one—it will remain the promised land to attain total security forever. Frustrating? Yes, but providing a lifelong chance to progress, as long as the physical conditions are supportive.

The following elements should be observed while connecting positions: Reduce finger tension while traveling on a string. Concentrate on forearm opening and closing to sense the distance. Regardless of which finger goes to which finger, the distance should be based on the first finger's old and new positions, in other words, always connect positions instead of fingers or notes. Preserve the angle of the hand and fingers to the string. Rotate the forearm outward or inward according to the direction and according to the basic approach in finger contact. Anticipate all new positions by preparing the next position of the arm. The same goes for string changes.

Position changes require time just as all travel consumes time. Thus we distinguish two types of position connections, or slides, or shifts—anticipated and delayed. The anticipated "slide" takes its time from the first note. The finger that plays the first note slides. The next finger to play drops in place only on arrival, on the beat. If a bow change occurs between the two notes, the slide takes place on the first bow and the bow changes precisely on arrival with the next finger. The last element is the most frequently neglected. The so-called pure anticipated slides are those of lower fingers connecting to higher ones, and the same fingers connecting. Extreme care should be exercised when the same fingers are connecting, to reduce pressure on the string while traveling. Irrespective of the distances, close or far, these principles are essential. The opposite is true in the case of delayed slides. The time is taken from the second note. The finger to play the next note slides. The slide starts on the next beat. If a bow change is needed, as in most cases, the slide is contained in the next bow.

Combination slides are required when higher fingers change to lower fingers (3 to 1, 4 to 3, 3 to 2, etc.) as anticipated slides. The higher finger still leads the slide, but as close to arrival as possible the next finger pushes out the previous one. On very distant connections the start may be anticipated and the arrival delayed. The decision of which type of slide to use should be based on musical taste. The same goes for how much of the slide should be audible, or even featured. The highly Italianate, crescendoed, backward slides are disturbing to many of us, and seem to be a throwback to the nineteenth century. Russian musicians are fond of featured crescendoed slides, though most of the Western literature seems to negate their use. Reduced pressure of the bow while traveling will cover the slide. Constant or increased pressure will display or feature the slide. A variety of expressions can be attained simply by reapplying pressure before arrival at different points.

To further left-hand security, the hand placement should aim the fingers over two strings, or rather toward the fingerboard under two strings. The feeling of walking a tightrope, when all the fingers hover over one string, is thereby reduced. (This is one more reason for practicing double-stops.) This two-string feeling in thumb positions brings up a problem that is approached differently by the various schools. The usual fifth hold of the thumb on two strings, providing a constant position basis while the other fingers manipulate on the neighboring string, tends to obliterate overtones on the lower string. The thumb hanging in the air, or worse, tensing in the air, vastly reduces security and induces greatly differing vibrato with the changing fingers, but allows for richer overtone response and louder sounds.

For a decade or so a quiet revolution has been in the making to treat this issue, notwithstanding the traditional approaches in playing high positions. It proposes placing the thumb under the fingerboard and moving it there while playing the second half of the fingerboard, thereby continuing the four-finger positions, and, as if playing the violin, gradually including the distance of a fourth between the first and fourth fingers. This approach seems to answer the question of security, the matter of the functioning overtones, and the need for an identical angle between the fingers and the strings in all positions. The disadvantages are caused by the characteristics of the traditional equipment of the cello—the thinness of the fingerboard and the sharp angularity of the block, which hinder the transition of the thumb from under the neck to under the fingerboard. It is my belief that changes will occur to rectify these obstacles and open up new vistas for technical progress on the cello.

Other elements concerning finger actions are: The intensity required to press down the strings should be directed into two fingers, the thumb and the playing finger. This creates a feeling of unity between the two. (A reminder—thumb tension should not be directed toward the neck.) The feeling of unity must constantly change to the finger that takes over. The takeover requires a release of tension in the previous finger and the immediate anticipated increase of tension in the next one. Dramatic harm is caused by retaining tension in one finger while another is called on to serve. The transfer of tension from one finger to another differs only in timing in the various applications. In sostenuto playing the release is delayed, and the next finger anticipates the tension. Therefore, for a short stretch, the two actions frequently intertwine. In the case of the vertical left-hand attack, for stronger impulses and especially for fast passage playing, the release is quicker, allowing the next finger to rise higher. From this height, weight and gravity will provide the needed power to stop the string.

The so-called percussion left-hand pizzicato is discussed in terms of its use when absolutely needed. Connections between fingered notes and open strings require it, primarily to assist the open string to speak. To strengthen the fingers, practice plucking leftward with the fingers. On occasion, a descending run can be clarified by applying this action,

"AN ORGANIZED METHOD OF STRING PLAYING"

but one should not lose sight of the fact that the necessary excess tension will, in the long run, hinder the continuity of motion. The following exercise will focus on the changing tension requirements in the forearm when playing fast runs intermittently with held vibrated notes: a note is vibrated with the first finger, exaggerated tension is applied, then tension is released completely, a fast run of fingers 2-3-4-3-2-1 follows, and renewed vibrato and tension close. The next run is 1-2-3-4-3-2-1, without tension, closing with a vibrated and held second finger. The next finishes on the third finger, and so on; eventually we reach several repeated runs without tension before holding a vibrated note.

Another exercise to avoid cramping of the left hand when playing forte or stronger is practicing fortissimo harmonics. It is just as necessary to avoid the frequent lack of sufficient finger pressure when playing piano, and this should be cured by playing forte in the left hand while using flautato with the bow.

At this stage in the discussion of OMSP, the seminar's attention is turned to such topics as harmonics, extensions, and pizzicato, although it seems logical that they be included in the second group, the right hand. In regard to harmonics, suggestions resort to elements already discussed. The primary reference is to the thumb position, where the enclosed interval of a fourth provides the intonation basis of harmonics, and the rest concerns the tension relationship of the thumb and the unpressed third finger. The significance of the bow speed, contact, and an undisturbed straight line is stressed and experimented with. The undisturbed straight line is required in all phases of string playing, but it is while playing harmonics that the player is likely to realize its significance and what tonal harm the lack of it can cause.

In regard to extensions, with repeated advice to avoid them whenever possible, the suggestion is made to rotate the hand so that the thumb gets closer to the third finger. This results in the feeling that the first finger is stretching back instead of the other fingers stretching forward. The moment when the stretch is not needed the first finger should move a half-step higher to obtain the feeling of the next position.

The two types of pizzicato—horizontal and melodic, or vertical and percussive—are then discussed, starting the experimentation with the hold of the bow. When fast arco-pizzicato exchange is called for the basic bow hold should not change radically. The first finger stretches out and the hand turns downward, allowing the first finger to touch the strings when needed and return for arco. For continuous pizzicato, the bow should be turned so the bottom part of the frog (called the slide) is pressed against the palm. The third and fourth fingers hold the bow, allowing the thumb to lean against the side of the fingerboard, while the first or second finger draws across the string or strings as if bowing toward the end of the fingerboard. This type of pizzicato, resulting in a melodic, ringing sound, is called for in most cases in the literature. Rhythmic percussive sounds are plucked vertically or semivertically. In fast pizzicato the thumb may support the plucking finger. Arpeggiated pizzicato uses the thumb upward and any of the fingers downward. Again this is a rudimentary approach to a complex area in which the demands of the literature bring recognition, experimentation, and decisions based mostly on individual taste.

It should be evident that aside from an occasional reference to the other stringed instruments the OMSP deals primarily with the problems of cello playing. It would be rather pretentious to claim that violinists should adopt cello-playing principles. Rather, I maintain that coinciding principles, and there are many of them, should be observed by all. That is why the thinking process itself can be useful for all instrumentalists, and it has proven itself to be so.

Category IV: Musical Application

Eventually the OMSP turns its attention to the fourth group, musical application, for the sake of which all the previous subjects were explored. At an early phase of this discourse, which I am rather inclined to call a "Short Soundless Summary of the Starker String Seminars" (to practice alliteration), I indicated the implied cold-bloodedness in this approach to making music. May I suggest reading a recent best-seller with the thought-provoking title of *Zen and the Art of Motorcycle Maintenance*, by Robert M. Pirsig, or at least the sixth chapter of that book.[2] The author meditates:

> The romantic mode is primarily inspirations, imaginative, creative, intuitive. Feelings rather than facts predominate. . . . The classic mode, by contrast, proceeds by reason and by laws—which are them-

"AN ORGANIZED METHOD OF STRING PLAYING"

selves underlying forms of thought and behavior. . . . Although surface ugliness is often found in the classic mode of understanding it is not inherent in it. There is a classic esthetic which romantics often miss because of its subtlety. The classic style is straightforward, unadorned, unemotional, economical and carefully proportioned. Its purpose is not to inspire emotionally, but to bring order out of chaos and make the unknown known. It is not an esthetically free and natural style. It is esthetically restrained. Everything is under control. Its value is measured in terms of the skill with which this control is maintained.

To a romantic this classic mode often appears dull, awkward, and ugly, like the mechanical maintenance itself. Everything is in terms of pieces and parts and components and relationships. Nothing is figured out until it's run through the computer a dozen times. Everything's got to be measured and proved. Oppressive. Heavy. Endlessly grey. The death force.

Within the classic mode, however, the romantic has some appearances of his own. Frivolous, irrational, erratic, untrustworthy, interested primarily in pleasure-seeking. Shallow. Of no substance.

These excerpts may explain to the reader that my attempt is to combine the romantic and the classic modes in dealing with the "skill" part of our art.

The "motorcycle," so described, is almost impossible to understand unless you already know how one works.

This sentence may explain the omission of charts, musical examples, and pictures that would be called for in any attempt that deals with mechanical data. I am fully aware that in this chapter I have given only superficial treatment to many complex issues, but I expect the reader to be familiar with these matters and to visualize, when necessary, the proposed solutions or training processes. This same expectation allows me to use only a few perfunctory references to the subjects discussed in the fourth group.

The OMSP, when presented in a seminar group, invariably combines with the standard, stereotyped master classes; master classes where the "master teacher-performer," after having listened to the young inexperienced player, suggests alternate ways of playing a piece, and usually demonstrates his ideas as well. These ideas are the result of a lifelong stage or studio experience, of a lifelong experience of playing and listening to the literature of Bach, Mozart, Beethoven, etc., and of forming musical stylistic preferences based on total exposure to life and music. To my mind the effect of these "end results" is of limited use to a young musician, or to a musician who may or may not ever have similar exposures. What may be of use is learning the means through which his or her individual gifts and experiences will be able to surface, or communicate.

With these principles in mind the fourth group is reserved for aspects of music making such as "sense of rhythm" versus "rhythmic sense" (pulse). As an exercise, beat with alternate feet while playing. Stress the direction of the beat and make the body follow it: a downward motion for the downbeat; an upward motion for the upbeat. Attention must be paid to the significance of constantly changing units. For example, 4/4 bars may have one, two, or four units in them. Several bars may constitute one unit. The importance of every note, short or long, must be stressed. Tempo considerations must be based on audibility and singing quality of the shortest note. Failure to observe this can result in a tempo that is too fast, or one that lacks motion and so produces dullness. Contrasting moods and contrasting dynamics are of maximum importance; so are visual, aural, and digital memorization whether or not one is using music. The use of visual imagery in the style and mood of the music, in order to reproduce the wished-for concepts at will, is also of paramount importance.

EPILOGUE

Just as the length of the discussion of the musical and artistic aspects of string playing is determined by the time available in any given gathering, so must this discourse be terminated by space limitations. To anyone who wishes to find truly scientific data concerning most of the subjects mentioned above, I suggest reading Gerhard Mantel's recent book, *Cello Technique*.[3]

To learn musical truth one has to spend one's life listening and playing as much as is humanly possible. Let us remember that string playing

"AN ORGANIZED METHOD OF STRING PLAYING"

is significant, but it is only a part of music; and music is only a part of man's attempt to satisfy his aesthetic needs after his basic need of survival has been realized. First one has to answer one's own requirements, and then, one hopes, enrich the lives of others. I consider myself fortunate, as my needs have been answered. I hope I have assisted you in finding some answers to yours. This is the basic credo of OMSP.

ORIGINALLY PUBLISHED IN MURRAY GRODNER, ED., CONCEPTS IN STRING PLAYING: REFLECTIONS BY ARTIST-TEACHERS AT THE INDIANA UNIVERSITY SCHOOL OF MUSIC (BLOOMINGTON: INDIANA UNIVERSITY PRESS, 1979)

NOTES

1. New York: Peer International, 1965.
2. New York: William Morrow, 1974.
3. Bloomington: Indiana University Press, 1975.

"AN ORGANIZED METHOD OF STRING PLAYING"

LIST OF RECORDINGS, 1947–1999

ALBÉNIZ, Isaac, 1860–1909

1) *Malagueña, from Rumores de la Coleta* (arr.)
  A) Janos Starker, cello; Leon pommers, piano
      Period 584 (rev. 4/54); Nixa 584; Contrepoint 20054; Everest 3222

BACH, Carl Philipp Emanuel, 1714–1788

2) *Concerto in A major,* H.439/W.172
  A) Janos Starker, cello; Sante Fe Festival Orchestra
      Delos DE 3197 (rec. May 1984; rel. Jan. 1996)

BACH, Johann Sebastian, 1685–1750

3) *Air,* from *Suite no. 3 for orchestra,* S.1068 (arr. Delsart)
  A) Janos Starker, cello; Gerald Moore, piano
      Columbia CX 1700 (rev. 6/60); Japanese EMI TOCE-8235 titled "The Best of Janos Starker" (rec. Oct. 4, 1957; reissued on CD 1994)

4) *Arioso,* from *Harpsichord concerto* no. 5, S.1056 (arr. Franko)
  A) Janos Starker, cello; Gerald Moore, piano
      Columbia CX 1700 (rev. 6/60); Japanese EMI TOCE-8235

titled "The Best of Janos Starker" (rec. Oct. 4, 1957; reissued on CD 1994)

B) Janos Starker, cello; Shuku Iwasaki, piano
Columbia OX 7041 (rec. May 1975); Denon OX 7041-ND; Denon C37-7302 (CD); Star XO 5

5) *Largo,* from *Organ concerto,* S.596 (arr.)

A) Janos Starker, cello; Shuku Iwasaki, piano
Columbia OX 7041 (rec. May 1975); Denon OX 7041-ND; Denon C37-7302 (CD); Star XO 5

6) *Sonata no. 1 in G major for viola da gamba,* S.1027 (ed. Starker)

A) Janos Starker, cello; György Sebök, piano
Mercury SR 90480 (Schwann 8/77); Mercury SRI 75104

B) Janos Starker, cello; Zuzana Ruzickova, harpsichord
Supraphon 1111 2485 (rev. 10/80)

7) *Sonata no. 2 in D major for viola da gamba,* S.1028 (ed. Starker)

A) Janos Starker, cello; György Sebök, piano
Mercury SR 90480 (Schwann 8/77); Mercury SRI 75104

B) Janos Starker, cello; Zuzana Ruzickova, harpsichord
Supraphon 1111 2485 (rev. 10/80)

8) *Sonata no. 3 in E minor for viola da gamba,* S.1029 (ed. Starker)

A) Janos Starker, cello; György Sebök, piano
Mercury SR 90480 (Schwann 8/77); Mercury SRI 75104; Mercury Living Presence CD 434-344-2 (set rec. April 1963; CD remastered 1991)

B) Janos Starker, cello; Zuzana Ruzickova, harpsichord
Supraphon 1111 2485 (rev. 10/80)

9) *Suite no. 1 in G major for unaccompanied cello,* S.1007

A) Janos Starker, cello
Period 582 (rec. 1951); Nixa 582; Contrepoint 20047

B) Janos Starker, cello
Columbia CX 1656 (rev. 9/59); Columbia C91028; EMI/Angel TOCE-8233-34 (rec. June 9, 1959, except no. 2, rec. 1957; reissued 1994, 2 CDs)

C) Janos Starker, cello
Mercury set 3-9016 (rev. 4/66); Mercury set OL3-116; Mercury set SRI 3-77002; Philips 820008; Philips set 6755.004;

Philips set 6768.224; Mercury Living Presence CD 432-756-2 (set rec. 1963–65; remastered for CD in 1991)

D) Janos Starker, cello
Sefel set 300 (rec. 1984); Sefel CD 300A (CD)

E) *Sarabande in D minor* from *Suite,* S. 1007
Janos Starker, cello
Ermitage, ERM 147 ADD (rec. live in Italy; Orchestra Radiotelevisione della Svizzera; CD rel. 1994)

F) Janos Starker, cello
(rec. June 1992 in New York City) BMG Classics/RCA Victor Red Seal CD set 61436-1 & 2 (Japan rel. Fall 1995; Europe and N. America rel. 3/11/97)

10) *Suite no. 2 in D minor for unaccompanied cello,* S.1008

A) Janos Starker, cello
Columbia CX 1515 (rev. 4/58); Columbia C90911; EMI/Angel TOCE-233-34 (rec. June 9, 1959, except no. 2, rec. 1957; reissued 1994, 2 CDs)

B) Janos Starker, cello
Mercury MG 50370 (rev. 4/64); Mercury SR 90370; Mercury set OL3-116; Mercury set SRI 3-77002; Mercury set 3-9016; Philips 820008; Philipsset 6755.004; Mercury Living Presence CD 432-756-2 (set rec. 1963–65; remastered for CD in 1991)

C) Janos Starker, cello
Sefel set 300 (rec. 1984); Sefel CD 300A (CD)

D) Janos Starker, cello
(rec. June 1992 in New York City) BMG Classics/RCA Victor Red Seal CD set 61436-1 & 2 (Japan rel. Fall 1995; Europe and N. America rel. 3/11/97)

11) *Suite no. 3 in C major for unaccompanied cello,* S.1009

A) Janos Starker, cello
Period 582 (rec. 1951); Nixa 582; Contrepoint 20047

B) Janos Starker, cello
Columbia CX 1656 (rev. 9/59); Columbia C91028; EMI/Angel TOCE-8233-34 (rec. June 9, 1959, except no. 2, rec. 1957; reissued 1994, 2 CDs)

C) Janos Starker, cello
Mercury set 3-9016 (rev. 4/66); Mercury set OL3-116; Mercury set SRI 3-77002; Philips 820008; Philips set 6755.004; Mercury Living Presence CD 432-756-2 (set rec. 1963–65; CD remastered 1991)

D) Janos Starker, cello
Sefel set 300 (rec. 1984); Sefel CD 300A (CD)

E) (rec. June 1992 in New York City) BMG Classics/RCA Victor Red Seal CD set 61436-1 & 2 (Japan rel. Fall 1995; Europe and N. America rel. 3/11/97)

12) *Suite no. 4 in E-flat major for unaccompanied cello,* S.1010

A) Janos Starker, cello
Period 582 (rec. 1951); Nixa 582; Contrepoint 20047

B) Janos Starker, cello
Columbia CX 1745 (rev. 6/61); EMI/Angel TOCE-8233-34 (rec. June 9, 1959, except no. 2, rec. 1957; reissued 1994, 2 CDs)

C) Janos Starker, cello
Mercury set 3-9016 (rev. 4/66); Mercury set OL3-116; Mercury set SRI 3-77002; Philips 820009; Philips set 6755.004; Mercury Living Presence CD 432-756-2 (set rec. 1963–65; CD remastered 1991)

D) Janos Starker, cello
Sefel set 300 (rec. 1984); Sefel CD 300B (CD)

E) (rec. June 1992 in New York City) BMG Classics/RCA Victor Red Seal CD set 61436-1 & 2 (Japan rel. Fall 1995; Europe and N. America rel. 3/11/97)

13) *Suite no. 5 in C minor for unaccompanied cello,* S.1011

A) Janos Starker, cello
Columbia CX 1515 (rev. 4/58); Columbia C90911; EMI/ Angel TOCE-8233-34 (rec. June 9, 1959, except no. 2, rec. 1957; reissued 1994, 2 CDs)

B) Janos Starker, cello
Mercury MG 50370 (rev. 4/64); Mercury SR 90280; Mercury set OL3-116; Mercury set SR3-9016; Mercury set SRI 3-

77002; Philips 820009; Philips set 6755.004; Mercury Living Presence CD 432-756-2 (set rec. 1963–65; CD remastered 1991)

C) Janos Starker, cello
Sefel set 300 (rec. 1984); Sefel CD 300B (CD)

D) (rec. June 1992 in New York City) BMG Classics/RCA Victor Red Seal CD set 61436-1 & 2 (Japan rel. Fall 1995; Europe and N. America rel. 3/11/97)

14) *Suite no. 6 in D major for unaccompanied cello,* S.1012

A) Janos Starker, cello
Period 582 (rec. 1951); Nixa 582; Classic 6164

B) Janos Starker, cello
Columbia CX 1745 (rev. 6/61); Columbia MPS-8; EMI/Angel TOCE-8233-34 (rec. June 9, 1959, except no. 2, rec. 1957; reissued 1994, 2 CDs)

C) Janos Starker, cello
Mercury set SR3-9016 (rev. 4/66); Mercury set OL3-116; Mercury set SRI 3-77002; Philips 820009; Philips set 6755.004; Mercury Living Presence CD 432-756-2 (set rec. 1963–65; CD remastered 1991)

D) Janos Starker, cello
Sefel set 300 (rec. 1984); Sefel CD 300B (CD)

E) (rec. June 1992 in New York City) BMG Classics/RCA Victor Red Seal CD set 61436-1 & 2 (Japan rel. Fall 1995; Europe and N. America rel. 3/11/97)

BACH, Wilhelm Friedemann, 1710–1784

15) *Grave* for cello and piano

A) (See Bach, J. S.; *Largo,* from *Organ concerto,* S.596)

BAKER, David, b. 1931

16) *Singers of Songs/Weavers of Dreams, for cello & 17 percussion instruments*

A) Janos Starker, cello; George Gaber, percussion
"Starker plays Baker," Laurel Records LP 117 (rec. July 1980 at Indiana Univ.; re-released: LR-817CD, Fall 1994)

17) *Sonata for cello and piano*

A) Janos Starker, cello; Alain Planès, piano
"Starker plays Baker," Laurel Records LP 117 (rec. July 1980
at Indiana Univ.; re-released: LR-817CD, Fall 1994)

BARTÓK, Béla, 1881–1945

18) *Cello Concerto* (*Viola concerto* realized for cello by Tibor Serly)

A) Janos Starker, cello; Saint Louis Symphony Orchestra,
Leonard Slatkin, cond.
BMG Classics/RCA Victor Red Seal 60717-2-RC CD
(rec. St. Louis, Sept. 1990; rel. May 15, 1991)

19) *Rhapsody no. 1 for violin and orchestra* (arr.)

A) Janos Starker, cello; Otto Herz, piano
Program 702 (rev. 5/51); Period 602; Period set 715; Period
set 1093; Nixa 16019; Contrepoint MC 20031; Nixa EXLP
702

B) Janos Starker, cello; György Sebők, piano
Mercury MG 50405; Mercury SR 90405; Mercury Living
Presence CD 434 358-2 (rec. Oct. 1963; re-released Fall
1995)

20) *Rumanian Folk Dances* (arr.)

A) Janos Starker, cello; Shuku Iwasaki, piano
Columbia OX 7041 (rec. May 1975); Denon OX 7041-ND;
Denon C37-7302 (CD); Star XO 5

B) Janos Starker, cello; Reiko Shigeoka-Neriki, piano
(recorded in live perf. May 15, 1992 by Concerts Under the
Dome, Evanston, Ill., NAIM Audio CD; limited edition)

BEETHOVEN, Ludwig van, 1770–1827

21) *Concerto in C major,* op. 56, for piano, violin, cello, and orchestra

A) Claudio Arrau, piano; Henryk Szeryng, violin; Janos Starker,
cello; New Philharmonia Orchestra, Eliahu Inbal, cond.
Philips 6500.129 (rev. 12/71); Philips 6500.070; Philips
6527.121; Philips 6747.352; Philips set 6768.350

22) *Sonata no. 1 in F major,* op. 5, no. 1, for piano and cello

A) Janos Starker, cello; Abba Bogin, piano
Period 561 (rev. 1/53); Period set 562; Period set 1002;
Contrepoint MC 20050; Saga 5176

B) Janos Starker, cello; György Sebők, piano

Musical Heritage Society set 596-597 (rev. 3/65); Erato EJA 6; Christophorus CGLP 75785; Erato 4509-97237-2 (rec. 11/59; 2 CD set rel. Fall 1994)

    C) Janos Starker, cello; Rudolf Buchbinder, piano
Telefunken set 6.35430 (rev. 10/79); Telefunken 4.35430 (cassette); Teldec set 3635450; Teldec 3435450 (cassette)

23) *Sonata no. 21 in G minor,* op. 5, no. 2, for piano and cello

    A) Janos Starker, cello; Abba Bogin, piano
Period 560 (rev. 1/53); Period set 562; Period set 1002; Contrepoint MC 20050; Saga 5177

    B) Janos Starker, cello; György Sebök, piano
Musical Heritage Society set 596-597 (rev. 3/65); Erato EJA 7; Christophorus CGLP 75786; Erato 4509-97237-2 (rec. 11/59; 2 CD set rel. Fall 1994)

    C) Janos Starker, cello; Rudolf Buchbinder, piano
Telefunken set 6.35430 (rev. 10/79); Telefunken 4.35430 (cassette); Teldec set 3635450; Teldec 3435450 (cassette)

24) *Sonata no. 3 in A major,* op. 5, no. 3, for piano and cello

    A) Janos Starker, cello; Abba Bogin, piano
Period 561 (rev. 1/53); Period set 562; Period set 1002; Contrepoint MC 20051; Saga 5177

    B) Janos Starker, cello; György Sebök, piano
Musical Heritage Society set 596-597 (rev. 3/65); Erato EJA 7; Christophorus CGLP 75786; Erato 4509-97237-2 (rec. 11/59; 2 CD set rel. Fall 1994)

    C) Janos Starker, cello; Rudolf Buchbinder, piano
Telefunken set 6.35430 (rev. 10/79); Telefunken 4.35430 (cassette); Teldec set 3635450; Teldec 3435450 (cassette)

    D) Janos Starker, cello; Shuku Iwasaki, piano
Trio 1017

    E) Janos Starker, cello; Alain Planès, piano
Institut National de L'Audiovisual; INA mémorie vive 262012 (rec. in live perf. by Radio France, April 1978; CD issued 1993)

25) *Sonata no. 4 in C major,* op. 102, no. 1, for piano and cello

    A) Janos Starker, cello; Abba Bogin, piano

Period 561 (rev. 1/53); Period set 562; Period set 1002; Contrepoint MC 20051; Saga 5176

B) Janos Starker, cello; György Sebök, piano
Musical Heritage Society set 596-597 (rev. 3/65); Erato EJA 6; Christophorus CGLP 75785; Erato 4509-97237-2 (rec. 11/59; 2 CD set rel. Fall 1994)

C) Janos Starker, cello; Rudolf Buchbinder, piano
Telefunken set 6.35430 (rev. 10/79); Telefunken 4.35430 (cassette); Teldec set 3635450; Teldec 3435450 (cassette)

D) Janos Starker, cello; Shuku Iwasaki, piano
Trio 1017

26) *Sonata no. 5 in D major*, op. 102, no. 2, for piano and cello
A) Janos Starker, cello; Abba Bogin, piano
Period 561 (rev. 1/53); Period set 562; Period set 1002; Contrepoint MC 20051; Saga 5176

B) Janos Starker, cello; György Sebök, piano
Musical Heritage Society set 596-597 (rev. 3/65); Erato EJA 6; Christophorus CGLP 75785; Erato 4509-97237-2 (rec. 11/59; 2 CD set rel. Fall 1994)

C) Janos Starker, cello; Rudolf Buchbinder, piano
Telefunken set 6.35430 (rev. 10/79); Telefunken 4.35430 (cassette); Teldec set 3635450; Teldec 3435450 (cassette)

27) *Trio no. 7 in B-flat* ("Archduke"), op. 97, for violin, cello, and piano
A) Victor Aitay, violin; Janos Starker, cello; Agi Jambor, piano
Program 707 (rev. 8/52); Contrepoint MC 20080

28) *Variations on "Ein Mädchen oder Weibchen," op. 66, for cello and piano*
A) Janos Starker, cello; Rudolf Buchbinder, piano
Telefunken set 6.35430 (rev. 10/79); Telefunken 4.35430 (cassette); Teldec set 3635450; Teldec 3435450 (cassette)

B) Janos Starker, cello; Shuku Iwasaki, piano
Trio 1017

29) *Variations on a theme from Handel's "Judas Maccabeus," WoO45, for cello and piano*
A) Janos Starker, cello; Rudolf Buchbinder, piano
Telefunken set 6.35430 (rev. 10/79); Telefunken 4.35430 (cassette); Teldec set 3635450; Teldec 3435450 (cassette)

30) *Variations on "Bei Männern welche Liebe Fühlen," WoO 46, for cello and piano*
   A)   Janos Starker, cello; Rudolf Buchbinder, piano
        Telefunken set 6.35430 (rev. 10/79); Telefunken 4.35430 (cassette); Teldec set 3635450; Teldec 3435450 (cassette)

BLOCH, Ernest, 1880–1959

31) *Prayer, from "From a Jewish Life" (arr.)*
   A)   Janos Starker, cello; Shuku Iwasaki, piano
        Columbia OX 7041 (rec. May 1975); Denon OX 7041-ND; Denon C37-7302 (CD); Star XO 5

32) *Quartet no. 1 in B minor*
   A)   Roth String Quartet (Roth, Antal, Harsanyi, Starker)
        Mercury 11156 (rev. 8/56); Mercury MG 50110

33) *Schelomo, Hebraic rhapsody for cello and orchestra*
   A)   Janos Starker, cello; Israel Philharmonic Orchestra, Zubin Mehta, cond.
        Decca SXL 6440 (rev. 7/70); London CS 6661; London 414166 (cassette)

34) *Voice in the wilderness,* for orchestra with cello obbligato
   A)   Janos Starker, cello; Israel Philharmonic Orchestra, Zubin Mehta, cond.
        Decca SXL 6440 (rev. 7/70); London CS 6661; London 414166 (cassette)

BOCCHERINI, Luigi, 1743–1805

35) *Concerto in B-flat major for cello and orchestra*
   A)   Janos Starker, cello; Castle Hill Festival Orchestra, Maximilian Pilzer, cond.
        Period 579 (rev. 12/53); Period set 1093; Period SHO 301; Contrepoint MC 20057; Everest 3257; Sina Qua Non 112
   B)   Janos Starker, cello; Philharmonia Orchestra, Carlo Maria Giulini, cond.
        Angel 35715 (rev. 10/59); Angel S35735; Angel FL 32070; Columbia CX 1665; Columbia C 91046; Seraphim EAC 30115

36) *Concerto in G major, G. 480*
   A)   Janos Starker, cello; Santa Fe Festival Orchestra

Delos DE 3197 (rec. May 1984; rel. Jan. 1996)

37) *Adagio and allegro,* from *Sonata in A major* (ed. Piatti)

   A) Janos Starker, cello; Stephen Swedish, piano
       Mercury MG 50460 (rev. 9/67); Mercury SR 90460; Mercury Living Presence CD 434-344-2 (set rec. March 1966, CD remastered 1991)

   B) Janos Starker, cello; Reiko Shigeoka-Neriki, piano
       (rec. in live perf. May 15, 1992, by Concerts Under the Dome, Oak Park, Ill., NAIM Audio CD; limited edition)

BOTTERMUND, Hans, 1892–1949

[and] STARKER, Janos, b. 1924

38) *Variations on a Theme of Paganini*

   A) Janos Starker, cello
       Victor 3085 (Japan); Delos CD 1015 (rec. Japan 1978; CD reissue)

BRAHMS, Johannes, 1833–1897

39) *Concerto in A minor, Op. 102, for violin, cello, and orchestra*

   A) Wolfgana Schneiderhan, violin; Janos Starker, cello; Radio Symphony Orchestra of Berlin, Ferenc Fricsay, cond.
       DGG 18753 (rev. 8/62); DGG 138753; DGG 17237; DGG 2535.140; DGG 2726.008; DGG 138126; DGG 3335.140 (cassette); Book of the Month Club 90-3733

   B) Henryk Szeryng, violin; Janos Starker, cello; Concertgebouw Orchestra, Bernard Haitink, cond.
       Philips 6500.137 (rev. 2/72); Philips set 6747.270

   C) Emmy Verhey, violin; Janos Starker, cello; Amsterdam Philharmonic Orch., Arpad Joó, cond.
       Sefel 5023 (rec. 5/83); Sefel SECD 5023 (CD)

40) *Sonata no. 1 in E minor, op. 38, for cello and piano*

   A) Janos Starker, cello; Abba Bogin, piano
       Period 593 (rev. 4/54); Nixa 593; Contrepoint MC 20070; Everest 3235

   B) Janos Starker, cello; György Sebök, piano
       Mercury MG 50293 (rev. 2/66); Mercury SR 90392; Philips 838432; Philips 412396; Philips set 6768146; Erato CD 4509-97237-2 (rec. Dec. 1959; reissued Fall 1994)

C) Janos Starker, cello; Rudolf Buchbinder, piano
BMG Classics/RCA Victor Red Seal 09026-61562-2
(rec. Nov. 29 & 30, 1992; rel. June 1994)

41) *Sonata no. 2 in F major, op. 99, for cello and piano*
   A) Janos Starker, cello; Abba Bogin, piano
   Period 593 (rev. 4/54); Nixa 593; Contrepoint MC 20070;
   Everest 3235
   B) Janos Starker, cello; György Sebök, piano
   Mercury MG 50293 (rev. 2/66); Mercury SR 90392;
   Philips 838432; Philips 412396; Philips set 6768146;
   Erato CD 4509-97237-2 (rec. Dec. 1959; reissued Fall
   1994)
   C) Janos Starker, cello; Juilius Katchen, piano
   Decca SXL 6589 (rev. 6/72); London CS 6814; Decca Ace
   of Diamonds SDD 541; Decca set 592.163
   D) Janos Starker, cello; Rudolf Buchbinder, piano
   BMG Classics/RCA Victor Red Seal 09026-61562-2
   (rec. Nov. 29 & 30, 1992; rel. June 1994)

42) *Sonata in D major, op. 78, for cello and piano*
   A) Janos Starker, cello; Shigeo Neriki, piano
   BMG Classics/RCA Victor Red Seal 09026-60598-2-CD-
   DD (rec. New York, July 1990; rel. 11/10/91)

43) *Trio no. 1 in B major, op. 8, for violin, cello, and piano*
   A) Josef Suk, violin; Janos Starker, cello; Julius Katchen, piano
   London CS 6611 (rec. 7/68); Decca SXL 6387; Decca Ace of
   Diamonds SDD 540; Decca set 592.163; Decca Ace of Dia-
   monds KSDC 540 (cassette); Decca SAD 22053; London
   421 152-2 (remastered CD 1988)

44) *Trio no. 2 in C major, op. 87, for violin, cello, and piano*
   A) Josef Suk, violin; Janos Starker, cello; Julius Katchen, piano
   London CS 6814 (rec. 6/68); Decca Ace of Diamonds SDD
   541; Decca set 592.163; Decca SXL 6589; London 421 152-
   2 (remastered CD 1988)

45) *Trio no. 3 in C minor, op. 101, for violin, cello, and piano*
   A) Josef Suk, violin; Janos Starker, cello; Julius Katchen, piano
   London CS 6611 (rec. 5/69); Decca SXL 6387; Decca

Ace of Diamonds SDD 540; Decca set 592.163; Decca
Ace of Diamonds KSDC 540 (cassette); Decca SAD
22053

BREVAL, Jean Baptiste, 1753–1823

46) *Sonata in G major for cello and piano* (arr. Moffat)
   A) Janos Starker, cello; Leon Pommers, piano
      Period 708 (rev. 4/55); Period 741; Nixa 708

BRUCH, Max, 1838–1920

47) *Kol nidrei, op. 47, for cello and orchestra*
   A) Janos Starker, cello; London Symphony Orchestra, Antal
      Dorati, cond.
      Mercury MG 50303 (rec. 1962, rev. 1/63); Mercury SR
      90303; Mercury 75045; Mercury 120531; Mercury 130531;
      Mercury MMA 11183; Mercury AMS 16133; Philips 6531
      013; Philips FG 216; Mercury Living Presence CD 432001-
      2 (remastered 1990)

CASSADO, Gaspar, 1897–1966

48) *Dance of the green devil*
   A) Janos Starker, cello; Leon Pommers, piano
      Period 584 (rev. 4/54); Nixa 7584; Contrepoint MC 20054;
      Everest 3222

49) *Requiebros*
   A) Janos Starker, cello; Leon Pommers, piano
      Period 584 (rev. 4/54); Nixa 7584; Contrepoint MC 20054;
      Everest 3222

50) *Suite for solo violoncello* (1926)
   A) Janos Starker, cello
      Columbia OX 7171 (rec. June 1978); Denon OX 7171-ND;
      Star XO 3
   B) Janos Starker, cello
      Institut National de L'Audiovisual; INA mémorie vive
      262012 (rec. in live perf. by Radio France, April 1978; CD
      issued 1993)
   C) Janos Starker, cello
      Broadcast performance (date unknown); first public issue:
      Parnassas Records CD PACD 97-008 (1997)

CHOPIN, Frédéric, 1810–1849

51) *Nocurne in E-flat, op. 9, no. 2* (arr. Popper)
    A) Janos Starker, cello; Gerald Moore; piano
           Columbia CX 1700 (rev. 6/60); Japanese EMI TOCE-8235
           "The Best of Janos Starker" (rec. Oct. 4, 1957; reissued 1994)

52) *Polonaise brilliante in C major, op. 3* (1830) (arr.)
    A) Janos Starker, cello; György Sebök, piano
           Mercury MG 50405 (rev. 9/65); Mercury SR 90405; Mercury
           Living Presence CD 434 358-2 (rec. Oct. 1963; re-released
           on CD Fall 1995)

53) *Sonata in G minor, op. 65, for cello and piano*
    A) Janos Starker, cello; György Sebök, piano
           Mercury MG 50320 (rev. 5/63); Mercury SR 90320; Philips
           AL 3460; Philips SAL 3460; Philips 838401; Mercury Living
           Presence CD 434 358-2 (rec. July 1962; re-released on CD
           Fall 1995)
    B) Janos Starker, cello; Shigeo Neriki, piano
           Columbia OX 7171 (rec. June 1978); Denon OX 7171-ND

CORELLI, Arcangelo, 1653–1713

54) *Sonata in D major, op. 5, no. 7* (arr. Lindner)
    A) Janos Starker, cello; Marilyn Meyers, piano
           Paradox PL 10003 (rev. 2/51); Period 540; Concerteum CP
           317; Musidisc RC 870; Delta 8002 (45 rpm)
    B) Janos Starker, cello; Stephen Swedish, piano
           Mercury MG 50460 (rev. 9/67); Mercury SR 90460; Mercury
           Living Presence CD 434-344-2 (set rec. March 1966, CD
           remastered 1991)

COUPERIN, François, 1668–1733

55) *Pastorale* (arr. Cassadó)
    A) Janos Starker, cello; Leon Pommers, piano
           Period 708 (rev. 4/55); Period SPL 741

56) *Pièces en concert for cello and strings*
    A) Janos Starker, cello; Festival Strings Lucerne, Rudolf Baum-
           gartner, cond.
           Ermitage, ERM 147 ADD (rec. in live perf. in Italy; CD rel.
           1994)

B) Janos Starker, cello; Santa Fe Festival Orch.
Delos DE 3197 (rec. May 1984; rel. Jan. 1996)

DEBUSSY, Claude, 1862–1918

57) *La Fille aux cheveux de lin* (arr. from *Préludes, Book 1*)
    A) Janos Starker, cello; Gerald Moore, piano
       Columbia CX 1700 (rev. 6/60); Japanese EMI TOCE-8235
       titled "The Best of Janos Starker" (rec. Oct. 4, 1957; reissued
       1994)
    B) Janos Starker, cello; Shigeo Neriki, piano
       Columbia OX 7140; Denon OX 7140-ND; Star XO 6;
       Denon C37-7812 (rec. 6/20/78, CD issued 1978)

58) *Menuet* (arr. from *Petite suite*)
    A) Janos Starker, cello; Gerald Moore, piano
       Columbia CX 1700 (rev. 6/60)

59) *Sonata No. 1 in D minor for cello and piano*
    A) Janos Starker, cello; Leon Pommers, piano
       Period 708 (rev. 4/55); Period SPL 741; Nixa 708
    B) Janos Starker, cello; György Sebök, piano
       Mercury MG 50405; Mercury MG 50405; Mercury SR
       90405; Mercury Living Presence CD 434 358-2 (rec. Oct.
       1963; re-released on CD Fall 1995)

DIAMOND, David, b. 1915

60) *Kaddish for Violoncello and Orchestra*
    A) Janos Starker, cello; Seattle Symphony, Gerard Schwarz, cond.
       Delos DE 3103 (rec. Sep. 1990; rel. June 1991)

DORATI, Antal, 1906–1988

61) *Concerto for cello and orchestra*
    A) Janos Starker, cello; Louisville Orchestra, Jorge Mester, cond.
       Louisville LS 759 (rev. 3/78)

DOTZAUER, Friedrich, 1783–1860

62) *Op. 120: Etudes nos. 2 & 8, & Exercise no. 32*
    A) Janos Starker, cello
       Virtuoso 3296 (rec. in Bloomington, Ind., 1967); Star XO1;
       Parnassus Records 1997 CD reissue PACD 97-008

DUPORT, Jean-Louis, 1749–1819

63) *Etudes nos. 7, 8, 9, 10, 11, & 13*

A) Janos Starker, cello

Virtuoso 3296 (rec. in Bloomington, Ind., 1967); Star XO1; Nos. 7, 8, & 13 on Parnassus Records, CD reissue, PACD 97-008 (1997)

DVOŘÁK, Antonín, 1841–1904

64) *Concerto in B minor, op. 104, for cello and orchestra*

A) Janos Starker, cello; Philharmonia Orchestra, Walter Süsskind, cond.

Angel 34517 (rev. 6/57); Columbia CX 1477; Columbia STAC 91018; Columbia SAX 2263; Classics for Pleasure 40070

B) Janos Starker, cello; London Symphony Orchestra, Antal Dorati, cond.

Mercury MG 50303 (rec. 1962, rev. 1/63); Mercury SR 90303; Mercury 75045; Mercury 130581; Mercury MMA 11183; Mercury AMS 16133; Philips FH-16; Philips 6531 013; Philips FG 216; Mercury Living Presence MLP CD 432-0102 (remaster 1990)

C) Janos Starker, cello; Saint Louis Symphony Orchestra, Leonard Slatkin, cond.

BMG Classics/RCA Victor Red Seal 60717-2-RC (rec. St. Louis, Sept. 1990; rel. May 15, 1991)

ELGAR, Sir Edward, 1857–1934

65) *Concerto in E minor, op. 85, for cello and orchestra* (1919)

A) Janos Starker, cello; Philharmonia of London, Leonard Slatkin, cond.

BMG Classics/RCA Victor Red Seal (rec. London, May 1992)

FALLA, Manuel de, 1876–1946

66) *Canciones populares españolas* (arr. Marechal)

A) Janos Starker, cello; G. Solchani, piano

Pacific PIZ 6170/6171 (78-rpm discs; rec. 1948)

B) Janos Starker, cello; Leon Pommers, piano

Period 584 (rev. 4/54); Nixa 584; Contrepoint 20054; Everest 3222

67) *Ritual fire dance, from "El Amor Brujo"* (arr.)

A) Janos Starker, cello; Leon Pommers, piano

Period 584 (rev. 4/54); Nixa 584; Contrepoint 20054; Everest
3222

B)   Janos Starker, cello; Shigeo Neriki, piano
Columbia OX 7140; Star XO 6; Denon OX 7140-ND;
Denon C37-7812 (rec. 6/20/78, CD issued 1978)

FAURÉ, Gabriel, 1845–1924

68) *"Après un rêve"* (arr.)

A)   Janos Starker, cello; Leon Pommers, piano
Period 708 (rev. 4/55); Period 741

B)   Janos Starker, cello; Shigeo Neriki, piano
Columbia OX 7140; Denon OX 7140-ND; Denon C37-
7812 (CD); Star XO 6

69) *Elégie, op. 24, for cello and orchestra*

A)   Janos Starker, cello; Philharmonia Orchestra,
Walter Süsskind, cond.
Angel 34517 (rev. 6/57); Columbia CX 1477; Columbia CAS
2263; Columbia STC 91018

70) *"Papillon," op. 77* (arr.)

A)   Janos Starker, cello; Leon Pommers, piano
Period 708 (rev. 4/55); Period 741

FRANCK, César, 1822–1890

71) *Sonata in A major for violin and piano* (arr.)

A)   Janos Starker, cello; György Sebök, piano
Victor 3086 (Japan)

FRANCOEUR, François, 1698–1787

72) *Sonata in E major for violin and harpsichord* (arr. Trowell)

A)   Janos Starker, cello; Leon Pommers, piano
Period 708 (rev. 4/55); Period 741

FRESCOBALDI, Girolamo, 1583–1643

73) *Tocatta* (arr. Cassadó)

A)   Janos Starker, cello; Shuku Iwasaki, piano
Columbia OX 7041 (rec. May 1975); Denon OX 7041-ND;
Denon C37-7302 (CD); Star XO 5

GRANADOS, Enrique, 1867–1916

74) *"Andaluza,"* from *Spanish dances* (arr.)

A)   Janos Starker, cello; Leon Pommers, piano

Period 584 (rev. 4/54); Nixa 584; Contrepoint 20054; Everest 3222

75) *Intermezzo,* from *"Goyescas"* (arr. Cassadó)

    A)   Janos Starker, cello; Leon Pommers, piano
         Period 584 (rev. 4/54); Nixa 584); Contrepoint 20054; Everest 3222

    B)   Janos Starker, cello; Shigeo Neriki, piano
         Columbia OX 7140; Star XO 6; Denon OX 7140-ND; Denon C37-7812 (rec. 6/20/78, CD issued 1978)

GRÜTZMACHER, Friedrich, 1832–1903

76) *Etude in D major, op. 38, no. 21*

    A)   Janos Starker, cello
         Virtuoso 3296 (rec. in Bloomington, Ind., 1967); Star XO1; Parnassus Records CD reissue, PACD 97-008 (1997)

HANDEL, George Frideric, 1685–1759

77) *Siciliene,* from *Il Pensieroso* (arr. Weiner)

    A)   Janos Starker, cello; Shigeo Neriki, piano
         Columbia OX 7140; Denon OX 7140-ND; Denon C37-7812 (CD); Star XO 6

HAYDN, Franz Joseph, 1732–1809

78) *Concerto in C major, H.VIIb, 1, for cello and orchestra* (cadenzas Starker)

    A)   Janos Starker, cello; Scottish Chamber Orchestra, Gerard Schwarz, cond.
         Delos D/CD 3062 (rec. Jan. 1987, rel. Dec. 1991)

    B)   Janos Starker, cello; Festival Strings Lucerne, Rudolf Baumgartner, cond.
         Ermitage, ERM 147 ADD (historic live performance rec. in Italy; CD issued 1994)

79) *Concerto in D major, H.VIIb, 2, for cello and orchestra* (cadenzas Starker)

    A)   Janos Starker, cello; Philharmonia Orchestra, Carlo Maria Giulini, cond.
         Angel 35725 (rev. 10/59); Angel S35725; Angel RL 32070; Columbia CX 1665; Columbia C 91046; His Master's Voice CLP 1840; Seraphim EAC 30115

B)   Janos Starker, cello; Scottish Chamber Orchestra,
Gerard Schwarz, cond.
Delos D/CD 3063 (rec. Jan. 1987, rel. Dec. 1991)

80) *Divertimento* (arr. Piatigorsky)

    A)   Janos Starker, cello; Shuku Iwasaki, piano
Columbia OX 7041 (rec. May 1975); Denon OX 7041-ND;
Denon C37-7302 (CD); Star XO 5

HEIDEN, Bernhard, 1910–2000

81) *Sonata no. 2 for cello and piano*

    A)   Janos Starker, cello; Menahem Pressler, piano
Fidelio 003; Star XO 2

82) *Variations on "Liliburlero"*

    A)   Janos Starker, cello
Broadcast performance (date unknown); first public issue;
Parnassas Records CD PACD 97-008 (1997)

HINDEMITH, Paul, 1895–1963

83) *Sonata for cello and piano, op. 11, no. 3*

    A)   Janos Starker, cello; pianist unknown
Pacific Records, 1948

    B)   Janos Starker, cello; Leon Pommers, piano
Period 715 (rev. 3/55); Period 741; Nixa 16019

    C)   Janos Starker, cello; Alain Planès, piano
Institut National de L'Audiovisual: INA mémorie vive
262012 (rec. in live perf. by Radio France April 1978; issued
1993)

84) *Sonata for solo cello, op. 25, no. 3*

    A)   Broadcast performance (date unknown); first public issue:
Parnassas Records CD PACD 97-008 (1997)

85) *Concerto for Cello and Orchestra* (1940)

    A)   Janos Starker, cello; Bamberger Symphoniker,
Dennis Russell Davies, cond.
BMG Classics/RCA Victor Red Seal (rec. Bamberg, July 19–
21, 1994; rel. 1995)

    B)   Janos Starker, cello; Chicago Symphony Orchestra,
Fritz Reiner, cond.
Broadcast performance over WFMT, 1955

HOVHANESS, Alan, 1911–2000

86) *Concerto for cello and orchestra, Op. 17*
- A) Janos Starker, cello; Seattle Symphony,
  Dennis Russell Davies, cond.
  Naxos 8.559187; Naxos 8.559158

JANSON, Jean-Baptiste-Aimé, c. 1742–1803

87) *Concerto in D major*
- A) Janos Starker, cello; Santa Fe Festival Orchestra
  Delos DE 3197 (rec. May 1984; rel. Jan. 1996)

KODÁLY, Zoltán, 1882–1967

88) *Duo for violin and cello, op. 7*
- A) Arnold Eidus, violin; Janos Starker, cello
  Period 720 (rev. 12/55); Period 510; Period set 1093; Nixa 510; Saga 5386
- B) Emmy Verhey, violin; Janos Starker, cello
  CBS 71096 LP (rec. 1/1/1980)
- C) Josef Gingold, violin; Janos Starker, cello
  Fidelio 003; Delos CD 1015 (CD)

89) *Quartet no. 1, op. 2*
- A) Roth String Quartet (Roth, Antal, Harsanyi, Starker)
  Mercury MG 50094; Mercury MG 80004; Philips World Series PHC 9093

90) *Sonata, op. 4, for cello and piano*
- A) Janos Starker, cello; Otto Herz, piano
  Program 702 (rev. 5/51); Period 702; Period set 1093; Period 602; Nixa EXLP 702; Contrepoint MC 20031
- B) Janos Starker, cello; György Sebök, piano
  Vogue (France) VG 671 672011 (rec. Aug. 12, 1959; CD issued 1989)

91) *Sonata, op. 8, for unaccompanied cello*
- A) Janos Starker, cello
  Pacific PIZ 1561/1564 (78-rpm discs, rev. 4/48); Pacific 6160/6163 (78-rpm discs); Pacific LDP F-29; Pacific N-29
- B) Janos Starker, cello
  Period 510 (rec. 1951); Period set 1093; Nixa 510; Saga 5386
- C) Janos Starker, cello

Columbia CX 1595 (rec. 1956); Angel 35627; Sina Qua Non 112

D) Janos Starker, cello
Victor 3085; Star XO 3

E) Janos Starker, cello
Delos CD 1015 (CD)

F) Janos Starker, cello
Japanese EMI TOCE-8235 titled "The Best of Janos Starker" (rec. Oct. 4, 1947 in France; received the *Grand prix du disque,* reissued 1994 in Japan)

KREISLER, Fritz, 1875–1962

92) *Allegretto in the style of Boccherini* (arr.)

A) Janos Starker, cello; Gerald Moore, piano
Columbia CX 1700 (rec. Oct. 4, 1957; rev. 6/60); Japanese EMI TOCE-8235 titled "The Best of Janos Starker" (reissued 1994)

LALO, Édouard, 1823–1892

93) *Concerto in D minor for cello and orchestra*

A) Janos Starker, cello; London Symphony Orchestra, Stanislaw Skrowaczewski, cond.
Mercury MG 50347 (rec. 1962, rev. 11/63); Mercury SR 90347; Philips AL 3482; Philips SAL 3482; Philips 6538.023; Mercury Living Presence MLP CD 432-0102 (remastered 1990)

LAMBERT, Constant, 1905–1951

94) *Concerto for piano and nine instruments*

A) Menahem Pressler, piano; Janos Starker, cello; and eight others; Theodore Bloomfield, cond.
M-G-M 3081 (Schwann 3/54)

LEE, Sebastian, 1805–1887

95) *Etudes, Op. 70, nos. 4, 11, 20, & 24*

A) Janos Starker, cello
Virtuoso 3296 (rec. in Bloomington, Ind., 1967); Star XO1; Parnassus Records CD reissue, PACD 97-008 (1997)

LOCATELLI, Pietro, 1695–1764

96) *Sonata in D major* (arr. Piatti)
    A) Janos Starker, cello; Stephen Swedish, piano
        Mercury MG 50460 (rev. 9/67); Mercury SR 90460; Mercury Living Presence CD 434-344-2 (set rec. March 1966, CD remaster 1991)

MARTINŮ, Bohuslav, 1890–1959

97) *Sonata no. 1, for cello and piano*
    A) Janos Starker, cello; Rudolf Firkusny, piano
        BMG/RCA Victor Red Seal 09026-61220-2 (rec. New York, Oct. 1990; rel. Nov. 1992; three-sonata album nominated for Grammy Award)

98) *Sonata no. 2, for cello and piano*
    A) Janos Starker, cello; György Sebök, piano
        Vogue VG 671 672011 (rec. 8/12/59; CD rel. 1989)
    B) Janos Starker, cello; Rudolf Firkusny, piano
        BMG/RCA Victor Red Seal 09026-61229-2 (rec. New York, Oct. 1990; rel. Nov. 1992; three-sonata album nominated for Grammy Award)

99) *Sonata no. 3, for cello and piano*
    A) Janos Starker, cello; Rudolf Firkusny, piano
        BMG/RCA Victor Red Seal 09026-61220-2 (rec. New York, Oct. 1990; rel. Nov. 1992; three-sonata album nominated for Grammy Award)

100) Variations on a Theme of Rossini
    A) Janos Starker, cello; György Sebök, piano
        Mercury MG 50405 (rec. 10/63; rev. 9/65); Mercury SR 90405; Mercury Living Presence CD 434 358-2 (re-released on CD in Fall 1995)

MENDELSSOHN-BARTHOLDY, Felix, 1809–1847

101) *Sonata no. 2 in D major, op. 58, for cello and piano*
    A) Janos Starker, cello; György Sebök, piano
        Mercury MG 50320 (rev. 5/63); Mercury SR 90320; Philips AL 3460; Philips SAL 3460; Philips 838401

102) *Variations concertantes, op. 17*
    A) Janos Starker, cello; György Sebök, piano

Mercury MG 50405 (rec. Oct. 1963); Mercury SR 90405;
Mercury Living Presence CD 434 358-2 (re-released on CD
Fall 1995)

MENIN, Peter, 1923–1983

103) *Concerto for cello and orchestra*
   A) Janos Starker, cello; Louisville Orchestra, Jorge Mester,
       cond.
       Louisville LS 693 (Schwann 7/69)

MESSIAËN, Olivier, 1908–1992

104) *La Transfiguration de Notre Seigneur Jésus-Christ,* for vocal and
    instrumental soloists, chorus, and orchestra
   A) Janos Starker, cello; other soloists; Westminster Symphonic
       Choir, National Symphony Orchestra, Antal Dorati, cond.
       Decca HEAD 1-2 (rev. 5/74); Decca 593-025; London
       HEAD 1-2; London OSA 1298

MILHAUD, Darius, 1892–1974

105) *Concerto no. 1 for cello and orchestra*
   A) Janos Starker, cello; Philharmonia Orchestra,
       Walter Süsskind, cond.
       Angel 35418 (rev. 7/57); Columbia CX 1525

MORENO-TORROBA, Frederico, b. 1891

106) *Fandanguillo* (arr.)
   A) Janos Starker, cello; G. Solchani, piano
       Pacific PIZ 1565 (78-rpm disc, rec. 1948)
   B) Janos Starker, cello; Leon Pommers, piano
       Period 584 (rev. 4/54); Nixa 584; Contrepoint MC 20056;
       Everest 3222

MOZART, Wolfgang Amadeus, 1756–1791

107) *Concerto in E-flat, K.447, for horn and orchestra* (arr. Fischer)
   A) Janos Starker, cello; Castle Hill Festival Orchestra;
       Maximilian Pilzer, cond.
       Period 579 (rev. 12/53); Period set 1093; Everest 3257
108) *Quartet in G major, K.387*
   A) Roth String Quartet (Roth, Antal, Harsanyi, Starker)
       Mercury MG 10108 (rev. 2/52); Mercury set MGL 8
109) *Quartet in D minor, K.421*

A) Roth String Quartet (Roth, Antal, Harsanyi, Starker)
Mercury MG 10108 (rev. 2/52); Mercury set MGL 8

110) *Quartet in E-flat major, K.428*
A) Roth String Quartet (Roth, Antal, Harsanyi, Starker)
Mercury MG 10109 (rev. 2/52); Mercury set MGL 8

111) *Quartet in B-flat major, K.458*
A) Roth String Quartet (Roth, Antal, Harsanyi, Starker)
Mercury MG 10109 (rev. 2/52); Mercury set MGL 8

112) *Quartet in A major, K.464*
A) Roth String Quartet (Roth, Antal, Harsanyi, Starker)
Mercury MG 10110 (rev. 2/52); Mercury set MGL 8

113) *Quartet in C major, K.465*
A) Roth String Quartet (Roth, Antal, Harsanyi, Starker)
Mercury MG 10110 (rev. 2/52); Mercury set MGL 8

114) *Quartet in D major, K.499*
A) Roth String Quartet (Roth, Antal, Harsanyi, Starker)
Mercury MG 10133

115) *Quartet in D major, K.575*
A) Roth String Quartet (Roth, Antal, Harsanyi, Starker)
Mercury MG 10133

116) *Quartet in B-flat major, K.589*
A) Roth String Quartet (Roth, Antal, Harsanyi, Starker)
Mercury MG 10134

117) *Quartet in F major, K.590*
A) Roth String Quartet (Roth, Antal, Harsanyi, Starker)
Mercury MG 10134

118) *Trio no. 1 in G major, K.496, for violin, cello, and piano*
A) Victor Aitay, violin; Janos Starker, cello; Agi Jambor, piano
Period 523 (rev. 8/51); Period set 524; Period set 1013; Nixa 523; Classic 6072

119) *Trio no. 2 in B-flat major, K.502, for violin, cello, and piano*
A) Victor Aitay, violin; Janos Starker, cello; Agi Jambor, piano
Period 522 (rev. 8/51); Period set 524; Period set 1013; Nixa 522; Classic 6072; Concerteum SPR 323

120) *Trio no. 3 in B-flat major, K.542, for violin, cello, and piano*
A) Victor Aitay, violin; Janos Starker, cello; Agi Jambor, piano

Period 521 (rev. 8/51); Period set 524; Period set 1013; Nixa 521; Classic 6135

121) *Trio no. 4 in C major, K.548, for violin, cello, and piano*
   A) Victor Aitay, violin; Janos Starker, cello; Agi Jambor, piano
   Period 522 (rev. 8/51); Period set 524; Period set 1013; Nixa 522; Classic 6066; Saga 5235; Concerteum SPR 323

122) *Trio no. 5 in G major, K.564, for violin, cello, and piano*
   A) Victor Aitay, violin; Janos Starker, cello; Agi Jambor, piano
   Period 521 (rev. 8/51); Period set 524; Period set 1013; Nixa 521; Classic 6135; Saga 5235

123) *Trio no. 6 in B-flat major, K.254, for violin, cello, and piano*
   A) Victor Aitay, violin; Janos Starker, cello; Agi Jambor, piano
   Period 523 (rev. 8/51); Period set 524; Period set 1013; Nixa 523; Classic 6066

MUSSORGSKY, Modest, 1839–1881

124) *Hopak, from The Fair at Sorochinsk* (arr.)
   A) Janos Starker, cello; Gerald Moore, piano
   Columbia CX 1700 (rec. Oct. 4, 1957; rev. 6/60); Japanese EMI TOCE-8235 titled "The Best of Janos Starker" (reissued on CD 1994)

PAGANINI, Niccolò, 1782–1840

125) *Caprice in B-flat, op. 1, no. 13* (arr. Kreisler)
   A) Janos Starker, cello; Gerald Moore, piano
   Columbia CX 1700 (rec. Oct. 4, 1957; rev. 6/60); Star XO 1; Japanese EMI TOCE-8235 titled "The Best of Janos Starker" (reissued on CD 1994); Parnassus Records CD reissue, PACD 97-008 (1997)

126) *Variations on one string on a theme from Rossini's "Mosé in Efitto"* (arr.)
   A) Janos Starker, cello; Shigeo Neriki, piano
   Columbia OX 7140; Denon OX 7140-ND; Denon C37-7812 (CD); Star XO 6

PIATTI, Alfredo, 1822–1901

127) *Four Etudes, op. 25, nos. 7, 8, 9, and 11*
   A) Janos Starker, cello

Virtuoso 3296 (rec. in Bloomington, Ind., 1967); Star XO1;
Parnassus Records CD reissue, PACD 97-008 (1997)

POPPER, David, 1843–1913

128) *Ten Etudes, op. 73, nos. 2, 6, 7, 13, 15, 22, 28, 34, 36, and 40*

    A)   Janos Starker, cello
        Virtuoso 3296; Star XO 1; Parnassus Records CD issued
        1997 titled "The Road to Cello Playing"

129) *Hungarian rhapsody, op. 68*

    A)   Janos Starker, cello; Gerald Moore, piano
        Columbia CX 1700 (rec. Oct. 4, 1957; rev. 6/60); Japanese
        EMI TOCE-8235 titled "The Best of Janos Starker"
        (reissued on CD 1994)

    B)   Janos Starker, cello; Shigeo Neriki, piano
        Columbia OX 7140; Star XO 6; Denon OX 7140-ND;
        Denon C37-7812 (rec. 6/68; CD issued 1986)

130) *Once Upon More Beautiful Days (In Memory of My Parents)*

    A)   Janos Starker, cello; Shigeo Neriki, piano
        Delos DE 3065, titled *Romantic Cello Favorites, a Tribute to
        David Popper* (rec. Bloomington, Ind., May 1988, rel. 1989;
        Grammy Award Nomination)

131) *Gavotte in D minor*

    A)   Janos Starker, cello; Shigeo Neriki, piano
        Delos DE 3065, titled *Romantic Cello Favorites, a Tribute to
        David Popper* (rec. Bloomington, Ind., May 1988, rel. 1989;
        Grammy Award Nomination)

132) *Mazurka*

    A)   Janos Starker, cello; Shigeo Neriki, piano
        Delos DE 3065, titled *Romantic Cello Favorites, a Tribute to
        David Popper* (rec. Bloomington, Ind., May 1988, rel. 1989;
        Grammy Award Nomination)

133) *Vito*

    A)   Janos Starker, cello; Shigeo Neriki, piano
        Delos DE 3065, titled *Romantic Cello Favorites, a Tribute to
        David Popper* (rec. Bloomington, Ind., May 1988, rel. 1989;
        Grammy Award Nomination)

134) *Fantasie über Klein-russische Theme*
   A)   Janos Starker, cello; Shigeo Neriki, piano
        Delos DE 3065, titled *Romantic Cello Favorites, a Tribute to David Popper* (rec. Bloomington, Ind., May 1988, rel. 1989; Grammy Award Nomination)

135) *Begegnung*
   A)   Janos Starker, cello; Shigeo Neriki, piano
        Delos DE 3065, titled *Romantic Cello Favorites, a Tribute to David Popper* (rec. Bloomington, Ind., May 1988, rel. 1989; Grammy Award Nomination)

136) *Papillon*
   A)   Janos Starker, cello; Shigeo Neriki, piano
        Delos DE 3065, titled *Romantic Cello Favorites, a Tribute to David Popper* (rec. Bloomington, Ind., May 1988, rel. 1989; Grammy Award Nomination)

137) *Herbstblume*
   A)   Janos Starker, cello; Shigeo Neriki, piano
        Delos DE 3065, titled *Romantic Cello Favorites, a Tribute to David Popper* (rec. Bloomington, Ind., May 1988, rel. 1989; Grammy Award Nomination)

138) *Gnomentanz*
   A)   Janos Starker, cello; Shigeo Neriki, piano
        Delos DE 3065, titled *Romantic Cello Favorites, a Tribute to David Popper* (rec. Bloomington, Ind., May 1988, rel. 1989; Grammy Award Nomination)

139) *Spanischer Carneval*
   A)   Janos Starker, cello; Shigeo Neriki, piano
        Delos DE 3065, titled *Romantic Cello Favorites, a Tribute to David Popper* (rec. Bloomington, Ind., May 1988, rel. 1989; Grammy Award Nomination)

140) *Nocturne*
   A)   Janos Starker, cello; Shigeo Neriki, piano
        Delos DE 3065, titled *Romantic Cello Favorites, a Tribute to David Popper* (rec. Bloomington, Ind., May 1988, rel. 1989; Grammy Award Nomination)

141) *Gavotte in D major*

A) Janos Starker, cello; Shigeo Neriki, piano
Delos DE 3065, titled *Romantic Cello Favorites, a Tribute to David Popper* (rec. Bloomington, Ind., May 1988, rel. 1989; Grammy Award Nomination)

142) *Chanson Villageoise*

A) Janos Starker, cello; Shigeo Neriki, piano
Delos DE 3065, titled *Romantic Cello Favorites, a Tribute to David Popper* (rec. Bloomington, Ind., May 1988, rel. 1989; Grammy Award Nomination)

143) *Wiegenlied*

A) Janos Starker, cello; Shigeo Neriki, piano
Delos DE 3065, titled *Romantic Cello Favorites, a Tribute to David Popper* (rec. Bloomington, Ind., May 1988, rel. 1989; Grammy Award Nomination)

144) *Elfentanz*

A) Janos Starker, cello; Shigeo Neriki, piano
Delos DE 3065, titled *Romantic Cello Favorites, a Tribute to David Popper* (rec. Bloomington, Ind., May 1988, rel. 1989; Grammy Award Nomination)

145) *Serenade*

A) Janos Starker, cello; Shigeo Neriki, piano
Delos DE 3065, titled *Romantic Cello Favorites, a Tribute to David Popper* (rec. Bloomington, Ind., May 1988, rel. 1989; Grammy Award Nomination)

146) *Spinning Song*

A) Janos Starker, cello; Shigeo Neriki, piano
Delos DE 3065, titled *Romantic Cello Favorites, a Tribute to David Popper* (rec. Bloomington, Ind., May 1988, rel. 1989; Grammy Award Nomination)

147) *Feuillet d'album*

A) Janos Starker, cello; Shigeo Neriki, piano
Delos DE 3065, titled *Romantic Cello Favorites, a Tribute to David Popper* (rec. Bloomington, Ind., May 1988, rel. 1989; Grammy Award Nomination)

148) *Menuetto*

A) Janos Starker, cello; Shigeo Neriki, piano

Delos DE 3065, titled *Romantic Cello Favorites, a Tribute to David Popper* (rec. Bloomington, Ind., May 1988, rel. 1989; Grammy Award Nomination)

149) *Tarantelle, op. 33*

    A) Janos Starker, cello; Shigeo Neriki, piano
Delos DE 3065, titled *Romantic Cello Favorites, a Tribute to David Popper* (rec. Bloomington, Ind., May 1988, rel. 1989; Grammy Award Nomination)

    B) Janos Starker, cello; Shuku Iwasaki, piano
Columbia OX 7041 (rec. May 1975); Denon OX 7041-ND; Denon C37-3812 (CD); Star XO 5

POULENC, Francis, 1899–1963

150) *Serenade from Chansons gaillardes* (arr. Gendson)

    A) Janos Starker, cello; Leon Pommers, piano
Period 708 (rev. 4/55); Period 741; Nixa 708

PROKOFIEV, Sergei, 1891–1953

151) *Concerto no. 1, op. 58, for cello and orchestra*

    A) Janos Starker, cello; Philharmonia Orchestra, Walter Süsskind, cond.
Angel 35418 (rev. 7/57); Columbia CS 1525

152) *Sonata for cello and piano, in C major, op. 119*

    A) Janos Starker, cello; Alain Planès, piano
Institut National de L'Audiovisual; INA mémorie vive 262012 (Radio France perf. rec. 4/78; rel. 1993)

    B) Janos Starker, cello; György Sebök, piano
Vogue (France) VG 671 672011 (rec. August 12, 1959; CD issued 1989)

RACHMANINOFF, Sergei, 1873–1943

153) *Sonata in G minor, op. 19*

    A) Janos Starker, cello; Shigeo Neriki, piano
BMG Classics/RCA Victor Red Seal 09020-60598-2 (rec. New York, July 1990; rel. Nov. 10, 1991)

RAVEL, Maurice, 1875–1937

154) *Pièce en forme de Habanera* (arr.)

    A) Janos Starker, cello; Leon Pommers, piano
Period 708 (rev. 4/55); Period 741; Nixa 708

B) Janos Starker, cello; Shigeo Neriki, piano
Columbia OX 7140; Denon OX 7140-ND; Star XO 6;
Denon C37-7812 (rec. 6/20/78, CD issued 1978)

ROSSINI, Giochino, 1792–1868

155) *Largo al factotum,* from *The Barber of Seville* (arr. Castelnuovo-Tedesco)

A) Janos Starker, cello; Shigeo Neriki, piano
Columbia OX 7140; Denon OX 7140-ND; Denon C37-7812 (CD); Star XO 6

RÓZSA, Miklós, 1907–1995

156) *Concerto for cello and orchestra*

A) Janos Starker, cello; Munich Philharmonic Orchestra, Moshe Atzmon, cond.
Pantheon FSM 53901 (rev. 2/85)

SAINT-SAËNS, Camille, 1835–1921

157) *Allegro appassionato, op. 43*

A) Janos Starker, cello; Gerald Moore, piano
Columbia CX 1700 (rev. 6/60); Japanese EMI TOCE-8235 titled "The Best of Janos Starker" (reissued on CD 1994)

158) *Concerto no. 1 in A minor, op. 33, for cello and orchestra*

A) Janos Starker, cello; London Symphony Orchestra, Antal Dorati, cond.
Mercury MG 50409 (rec. 1962; rev. 7/65); Mercury SR 90409; Philips 6702.015; Philips 838423; Mercury Living Presence MLP CD 432-0102 (remastered 1990)

159) *The Swan,* from *Carnival of the Animals*

A) Janos Starker, cello; Shuku Iwasaki, piano
Columbia OX 7041 (rec. May 1975); Denon OX 7041-ND; Denon C37-7302 (CD); Star XO 5

SCHRÖDER, Karl, 1848–1935

160) *Two Etudes, op. 31, nos. 12 and 24*

A) Janos Starker, cello
Virtuso 3296 (rec. in Bloomington, Ind., 1967); Star XO1; No. 12 only reissued on Parnassus Records CD, PACD 97-008 (1997)

SCHUBERT, Franz, 1797–1828

161) *Allegretto gracioso*
    A)   Janos Starker, cello
          Columbia CX 1700 (rec. Oct. 4, 1957; rev. 6/60); Japanese
          EMI TOCE-8235 titled "The Best of Janos Starker"
          (reissued on CD 1994)

162) *Moment musical, op. 92, op. 3, in F minor, D.780* (arr.)
    A)   Janos Starker, cello; Gerald Moore, piano
          Columbia CX 1700 (rec. Oct. 4, 1957; rev. 6/60); Japanese
          EMI TOCE-8235 titled "The Best of Janos Starker"
          (reissued on CD 1994)
    B)   Janos Starker, cello; Shuku Iwasaki, piano
          Columbia OX 7041 (rec. May 1975); Denon OX 7041-ND;
          Denon C37-7302 (CD); Star XO 5

163) *Sonata for arpeggione and piano, D.821*
    A)   Janos Starker, cello; Shuku Iwasaki, piano
          Victor 3086; Star XO 4

164) *Sonatina for violin and piano, D.384* (arr. Starker)
    A)   Janos Starker, cello; Shigeo Neriki, piano
          Columbia OX 7171; Denon OX 7171-ND

SCHUMANN, Robert, 1810–1856

165) *Abenlied, from Klavierstücke für kleine und grosse Kinder, op. 85, no. 12* (arr.)
    A)   Janos Starker, cello; Shuku Iwasaki, piano
          Columbia OX 7041 (rec. May 1975); Denon OX 7041-ND;
          Denon C37-7302 (CD); Star XO 5

166) *Adagio & Allegro, op. 70*
    A)   Janos Starker, cello; Rudolf Buchbinder, piano
          BMG Classics/RCA Victor Red Seal 09026-61562-2
          (rec. Nov. 29 & 30, 1992; rel. June 1994)

167) *Concerto in A minor, op. 129, for cello and orchestra*
    A)   Janos Starker, cello; Philharmonia Orchestra,
          Carlo Maria Giulini, cond.
          Angel 35598 (rev. 8/58); Columbia CX 1579; Seraphim S-
          60266; Seraphim EAC 30163
    B)   Janos Starker, cello; Stanislaw Skrowaczewski, cond.
          Mercury MG 50347 (rec. 1962, rev. 11/63); Mercury SR

90347; Philips AL 3482; Philips SAL 3482; Mercury Living
Presence MLP CD 432-0102 (remastered 1990)

C) Janos Starker, cello; Bamberger Symphoniker,
    Dennis Russell Davies, cond.
    BMG Classics/RCA Victor Red Seal (rec. Bamberg, July
    19–21, 1994; rel. 1995)

168) *Träumerei,* from *Kinderscenen,* op. 15 (arr.)

A) Janos Starker, cello; Gerald Moore, piano
    Columbia CX 1700 (rec. Oct. 4, 1957; rev. 6/60); Japanese
    EMI TOCE-8235 titled "The Best of Janos Starker"
    (reissued on CD 1994)

B) Janos Starker, cello; Shuku Iwasaki, piano
    Columbia OX 7041 (rec. May 1975); Denon OX 7041-ND;
    Denon C37-7302 (CD); Star XO 5

169) *Fantasiestücke, op. 73*

A) Janos Starker, cello; Shigeo Neriki, piano
    BMG Classics/RCA Victor Red Seal 09026-60598-2 CD-
    DD (rec. New York, July 1990; rel. 11/10/91)

SHOSTAKOVICH, Dmitri, 1906–1975

170) *Concerto no. 1 for cello and orchestra, op. 107* (1959)

A) Janos Starker, cello; Orchestra della Radiotelevisione della
    Svizzera Italiana, Marc Andreae, cond.
    Ermitage ERM 147 ADD (rec. in Italy during a live perf.;
    CD rel. 1994)

STARER, Robert, b. 1924

171) *Cello Concerto* (1988)

A) Janos Starker, cello; Pro Arte Chamber Orchestra of Boston,
    Leon Botstein, cond.
    Composers Recordings Inc., CRI CD 618 (rec. Feb. 1990)

STARKER, Janos (see Bottermund)
STRAUSS, Richard, 1864–1949

172) *Don Quixote, op. 35, variations,* based on Cervantes

A) Janos Starker, cello; French Radio Orchestra,
    Jascha Horenstein, cond.
    Disques Montaigne TCE 8862 (2 CDs), dist. by Harmonia
    Mundi (live radio perf. rec. 2/24/71)

B)   Andrés Rohn, violin; Oskar Lysy, viola; Janos Starker, cello;
Symphony Orchestra of the Bavarian Radio,
Leonard Slatkin, cond.
BMG Classics/RCA Victor Red Seal 09026-60561-2 CD-
DD (rec. June 1990)

TCHAIKOVSKY, Peter I., 1840–1893

173) *Variations on a rococo theme, op. 33, for cello and orchestra*
A)   Janos Starker, cello; London Symphony Orchestra,
Antal Dorati, cond.
Mercury MG 50409 (rec. 1964; rev. 1/65); Mercury SR
90409; Philips 6511.026; Philips 838423; Mercury Living
Presence MLP CD 432-0102 (remastered 1990)

TCHEREPNIN, Alexander, 1899–1977

174) *Ode*
A)   Janos Starker, cello; G. Solchani, piano
Pacific PZ 1565 (78-rpm disc, rec. 1948)
B)   Janos Starker, cello; Gerald Moore, piano
Columbia CX 1700 (rec. Oct. 4, 1957; rev. 6/60); Japanese
EMI TOCE-8235 titled "The Best of Janos Starker"
(reissued on CD 1994)

VALENTINI, Giuseppe, c. 1680–1759

175) *Sonata in E major* (arr. Piatti)
A)   Janos Starker, cello; Stephen Swedish, piano
Mercury MG 50460 (rev. 9/67); Mercury SR 90460;
Mercury Living Presence CD 434-344-2 (set rec. March
1966, CD remaster 1991)

VILLA-LOBOS, Heitor, 1887–1959

176) *Fantasia for cello and orchestra*
A)   Janos Starker, cello; Orquestra Sinfônica da Paraíba,
Eleazar de Carvalho, cond.
Delos CD 1017 titled "A Brazilian Extravaganza"
(rec. João Pessoa, Paraíba, Brazil, Aug. 1988)

VIVALDI, Antonio, 1678–1741

177) *Concerto in D major, op. 3, no. 8* (arr. Marechal)
A)   Janos Starker, cello; Marilyn Meyers, piano
Paradox PL 10003 (rev. 2/51); Period 540; Delta

8002 (45-rpm disc); Concerteum CR 317; Musicdisc RE 870

B) Janos Starker, cello; Sante Fe Festival Orchestra
Delos DE 3197 (rec. May 1984; rel. Jan. 1996)

178) *Concerto for Two Cellos*

A) Janos Starker, cello; Aldo Parisot, cello; Orquestra Sinfônica da Paraíba, Eleazar de Carvalho, cond.
Delos CD 1018 (rec. João Pessoa, Paraíba, Brazil, Aug. 1988; see also Delos "DEMO II" DE 3504)

179) *Sonata in E minor for cello and piano* (arr.)

A) Janos Starker, cello; Stephen Swedish, piano
Mercury MG 50460 (rev. 9/67); Mercury SR 90460; Mercury Living Presence CD 434-344-2 (set rec. March 1966, CD remastered 1991)

VON DOHNÁNYI, Ernst, 1877–1960

180) *Konzertstück, op. 12, for cello and orchestra*

A) Janos Starker, cello; Philharmonia Orchestra, Walter Süsskind, cond.
Angel 35627 (rev. 11/58); Columbia CX 1595

B) Janos Starker, cello; Seattle Symphony, Gerard Schwarz, cond.
Delos CD, DE 3095 (rec. Seattle, June 1990)

C) Janos Starker, cello; Kroenberg Festival Orchestra, Raimund Trenkler, cond.
Unreleased recording, 1999

WALTON, Sir William, 1902–1983

181) *Concerto for cello and orchestra* (1957)

A) Janos Starker, cello; Philharmonia of London, Leonard Slatkin, cond.
BMG Classics/RCA Victor Red Seal (rec. London, May 1992)

WEBER, Carl Maria von, 1786–1826

182) *Adagio and rondo, from Sonata in G major for violin and piano* (arr.)

A) Janos Starker, cello; Shuku Iwasaki, piano
Columbia OX 7041 (rec. May 1975); Denon OX 7041-ND; Denon C37-7302; Star XO 5

WEINER, Léo, 1885–1960

183) *Lakodalmas, op. 21b (Hungarian Wedding Dance)*

A) Janos Starker, cello; Otto Herz, piano
Program 702 (rev. 5/51); Period 702; Period 715; Period set 1093; Nixa 16019; Contrepoint MC 20031

B) Janos Starker, cello; György Sebök, piano
Mercury MG 50405 (rec. Oct. 1963); Mercury SR 90405; Mercury Living Presence CD 434 358-2 (re-released on CD Fall 1995)

LIST OF MUSIC PUBLICATIONS

Bach, Johann Sebastian. Six Suites for unaccompanied violoncello. Edited by Janos Starker. New York: Peer International, 1971

Bach, Johann Sebastian. Three sonatas for violoncello and piano: Originally composed for viola da gamba. Edited by Janos Starker and György Sebök. New York: Peer International, 1979

Beethoven, Ludwig van. Triple Concerto in C, Op. 56. Boca Raton, Fla.: Masters Music, forthcoming

Beethoven, Ludwig van. Five Sonatas for cello and piano. New York: G. Schirmer, 1981

Beethoven, Ludwig van. The Complete Variations for cello and piano. Edited by Janos Starker. New York: G. Schirmer, 1980

Bloch, Ernest. *Schelomo: Rhapsodie hébraïque.* For violoncello and piano. Edited by Janos Starker in collaboration with Emilio Colón. Boca Raton, Fla.: Masters Music, 2003

Bottermund, Hans. *Variations on a theme of Paganini: For unaccompanied violoncello.* Edited by Janos Starker. Hamburg: Peer Musikverlag: New York: Peer International, 1979

Brahms, Johannes. Double Concerto in A minor, Op. 102. Boca Raton, Fla.: Masters Music, forthcoming

Brahms, Johannes. Sonata in D major, opus 78: For cello and piano. Edited by Janos Starker. New York: International Music Co., 1975

Debussy, Claude. Sonata in D minor. Boca Raton, Fla.: Masters Music, forthcoming

Dvořák, Antonín. Concerto in B minor for cello and piano. Edited by Janos Starker. New York: G. Schirmer, 1981

Elgar, Edward. Concerto in E minor, Op. 85. Edited by Janos Starker. Boca Raton, Fla.: Masters Music, 2003

Encores for Cello. Arranged and edited by Janos Starker. New York: G. Schirmer, 1985. Includes the following: Franz Schubert, Moment musical, op. 94, no. 3; Robert Schumann, Abendlied, op. 85, no. 12; Gabriel Fauré, Sicilienne, op. 78; Camille Saint-Saëns, The swan; Hungarian rhapsody, op. 68; David Popper, Tarantelle, op. 33

Five Italian Sonatas: For Cello and Piano. Edited by Janos Starker. New York: G. Schirmer; Winona, Minn.: Distributed by Hal Leonard Publishing Corp., 1987. Includes the following: Arcangelo Corelli, Sonata in D minor op. 5, no. 8; Giuseppe Valentini, Sonata in E major; Pietro Locatelli, Sonata in D major; Giovanni Battista Sammartini, Sonata in G major; Luigi Boccherini, Sonata in A major

Grodner, Murray. *An Organized Method of String Playing: Double bass exercises for the left hand.* Derived from *An Organized Method of String Playing: Violoncello exercises for the left hand,* by Janos Starker, assisted by George Bekefi. New York: Peer International, 1977

Haydn, Joseph. Adagio from Symphony No. 13 (Hob. I, No. 13). Edited by Janos Starker. New York: International Music, n.d.

Kodály, Zoltán. Sonata for Cello Solo, Op. 8. Boca Raton, Fla.: Masters Music, forthcoming

Kodály, Zoltán. Sonata for Cello and Piano, Op. 4. Boca Raton, Fla.: Masters Music, forthcoming

Kodály, Zoltán. Duo for Violin and Cello, Op. 7. Boca Raton, Fla.: Masters Music, forthcoming

Lalo, Edouard. Concerto in D minor. Boca Raton, Fla.: Masters Music, forthcoming

Marcello, Benedetto. Two Sonatas in C major and in G major for cello and piano. Edited by Janos Starker. New York: International Music, 1966

Saint-Saëns, Camille. Concerto in A minor, Op. 33. Boca Raton, Fla.: Masters Music, forthcoming

Schubert, Franz. Sonatina, Op. 137, no. 1. Transcribed for violoncello and piano by Janos Starker. New York: Peer International, 1978

Schumann, Robert. Concerto in A minor, Op. 129. Boca Raton, Fla.: Masters Music, forthcoming

Starker, Janos, assisted by George Bekefi. *An Organized Method of String Playing: Violoncello exercises for the left hand.* New York: Peer International, 1965

Starker, Janos. *Cadenzas for Violoncello.* New York: Peer International, 1976. Includes the following: Robert Schumann, Concerto in A-minor; Joseph Haydn, Concerto in D major (Altmann version); Joseph Haydn, Concerto in C major; Luigi Boccherini, Concerto in B-flat; Peter Illich Tchaikovsky, Variations on a rococo theme

Strauss, Richard. *Don Quixote,* Op. 35. Boca Raton, Fla.: Masters Music, forthcoming

Strauss, Richard. Sonata in F, Op. 6. Boca Raton, Fla.: Masters Music, forthcoming

Telemann, Georg Philipp. Six Canonic Sonatas: For two cellos. Edited by Janos Starker. New York: International Music, 1977

Veracini, Francesco Maria. *Largo.* Edited by Janos Starker. New York: International Music, n.d.

Vivaldi, Antonio. Concerto in G minor, F. III n. 2, P. 411, for two cellos and piano. Piano reduction by Giorgio Federico Ghedini. Edited by Janos Starker. New York: International Music, 1975

von Dohnányi, Ernst. Sonata in B flat, Op. 8. Boca Raton, Fla.: Masters Music, forthcoming

von Dohnányi, Ernst. *Konzertstück,* Op. 12. Boca Raton, Fla.: Masters Music, forthcoming

LIST OF CHEVALIER DU VIOLONCELLE AND GRANDE DAME DU VIOLONCELLE CERTIFICATE AWARDS

Since the founding of the Eva Janzer Memorial Cello Center, the following cellists-teachers, luthiers, composers, and important members of the cello community have been honored in Bloomington, Ind., with the Chevalier du Violoncelle or Grande Dame du Violoncelle Certificate Awards.

Pierre Fournier	1979–80
Bernard Greenhouse	1980–81
Raya Garbousova	1981–82
Margaret Rowell	1982–83
Fritz Magg	1983–84
Aldo Parisot	1985–86
Zara Nelsova	1986–87
Gabor Rejto	1987–88 (posth.)
Samuel Mayes	1987–88
Eleanor Slatkin	1988–89
Harvey Shapiro	1988–89
Paul Tortelier	1989–90

Janos Scholz	1990–91
Shirley Trepel	1990–91
Lev Aronson	1990–91 (posth.)
Jacques Français	1990–91
Eva Heinitz	1991–92
Richard Kapuscinski	1991–92 (posth.)
Laszlo Varga	1991–92
Daniel Saidenberg	1992–93
David Soyer	1992–93
Etienne Batelot	1992–93
Erling Blöndel-Bengtsson	1993–94
Eleonore Schoenfeld	1993–94
Takayori Atsumi	1994–95
Jules Eskin	1994–95
Martin Ormandy	1994–95
David N. Baker	1995–96
Lawrence Block	1995–96
Robert LaMarchina	1995–96
Louis Potter	1995–96
George Neikrug	1996–97
Uzi Wiesel	1996–97
Guy Fallot	1997–98
Alan Shulman	1997–98
Mihaly Virizlay	1997–98
Amadeo Baldovino	1998–99 (posth.)
Siegfried Palm	1998–99
George Sopkin	1998–99
Rene A. Morel	1998–99
Janos Starker	1999–2000
Phyllis Young	2000–1
Ronald Leonard	2000–1
Gabriel Magyar	2000–1 (in absentia)
Orlando Cole	2001–2
Carlos Prieto	2001–2
Allen Winold	2001–2
Paul Katz	2002–3

Angelica May	2002–3
Dimitry Markevitch	2002–3 (posth.)
Milos Sádlo	2002–3 (in absentia)
Joel Krosnick	2003–4
Tsuyoshi Tsutsumi	2003–4
Helga Winold	2003–4

INDEX

Note: Page references in *italics* refer to illustrations.

INDEX

Szekely, Mihaly, 44
Szell, George, 130–31
Szeryng, Henryk, 191, 199–200
Szigeti, Joseph, 114–15
Szulner, Laszlo, 28

talents, 14
tardiness for rehearsals, 106
Tauszig, Emil, 85, 87, 119
Taverniti, Helen, 190
teaching career: Banff Centre, 227; be-
    ginning, 14; Dallas, 99; in Europe, 217;
    honors, 224, 234; Indiana University,
    33, 154, 177–80, 184–85, 187–88;
    master classes, 2, 146, 234; Mishkenot
    Sha'ananim in Jerusalem, 227; ongoing
    opportunities, 119, 200, 234; sabbati-
    cal, 218; in South America, 227, 235;
    Volkwang Hochschule in Essen, 217–
    18
Teichert, Hans, 134–35
Teller, Fritz, 12
Teraspulsky, Leopold, 180
Texas, 96–100, 150
theatricality, 8, 113–14, 270
Thompson, Virgil, 133–34
Tortelier, Paul, 88, 136, 218
Toszeghi, Anton, 40
touring: Africa, 159–76, 178, 181, 185;
    Asia, 179, 181–84, 203, 217, 218, 220–
    22, 235, 240; Australia, 223–24, 235;
    Berlin Philharmonic, 181, 185–86;
    Concertgebouw Orchestra, 199; de-
    creasing, 240; Europe, 139–40, 141,
    156, 185, 188, 192–94, 195–96, 199–
    200, 221–23, 238, 240; Metropolitan
    Opera, 105; Middle East, 187, 227–28;
    North America, 103, 146, 188, 217;
    ongoing opportunities, 218, 234, 239;
    Paquet Voyages, 224, 227; policy on,
    217; South America, 196–98, 227, 235
transcription of music, 233
travels, 32, 218, 228, 234, 240. *See also*
    touring
Trepel, Shirley, 110, *237*
Tsutsumi, Tsuyoshi, *231*, 242, 257, *258*

Ungar, Imre, 19
unions, 97, 100, 104, 120
United States, 8, 93–95, 96, 138, 149–50
Universal Publishing Company, 50–51
Uranyi, Eva. *See* Starker, Eva

Vajda, Julius, *226*, 227
Van Praag, Maurice, 118
Van Wyck, Wilfrid, 138, 139, 141, 179
Varga, Laszlo, 110, 111, 229, *237*
Vargas, Domingo, 177–78
Vegh, Sandor, 52
Vegh Quartet, 54, 224
Verberne, Marijke, 43
Verrandeau, Raymonde, 55
Vienna, Austria, 48–52
Vienna Hungarian Institute, 50
Virizlay, Mihaly, 146, *147*, 155–56
Vronsky, Vitya, 156

W. E. Hill & Sons, 41
Waldbauer, Imre, 15, 52, 270
Wallenberg, Raoul, 27
Walter, Bruno, 104, 130
Warren, Kenneth, Sr., 41, 43
Webb, Charles, 188, 219
Weicher, John, 129
Weiner, Leo, 15, 19, 83, *139*, 270
Wells, Herman B, 33, 93
Werro, Henry, 40
Wilke, Lawrence, 41
William Moennig & Son, 41
Winold, Allen, 154, 257
Winold, Helga, 257, *258*
wives. *See* Starker, Eva; Starker, Rae
women in orchestras, 104, 128
World Cello Congresses, 232
World Cello Society, 232
World War II, 15–31, 35–39, 132
writing, 32, 86, 232–33, 235

Yamaguchi, Shirley, 190
youth, 10–31, *11*, *13*, *17*

Zathureczky, Ede, 179